GARY SNYDER AND THE AMERICAN UNCONSCIOUS

Gary Snyder and the American Unconscious

Inhabiting the Ground

TIM DEAN

The Johns Hopkins University

St. Martin's Press   New York

First published in the United States of America in 1991

Printed in Hong Kong

ISBN 0–312–04762–2

Library of Congress Cataloging-in-Publication Data
Dean, Tim, 1964–
    Gary Snyder and the American unconscious: inhabiting
    the ground / Tim Dean.
       p.   cm.
    Includes bibliographical references.
    ISBN 0–312–04762–2
    1. Snyder, Gary—Criticism and interpretation.
2. Subconsciousness in literature.   I. Title.
PS3569.N88Z63   1990
811'.54—dc20   90–32685
                                        CIP

Contents

List of Plates

The author and publishers have made every effort to contact all copyright holders, but if any have been inadvertently overlooked, they will be pleased to make the necessary arrangements at the first opportunity.

List of Abbreviations

The following abbreviations are used throughout to refer to sources of quotations from Snyder's work:

AH   *Axe Handles* (San Francisco: North Point Press, 1983).

BC   *The Back Country* (New York: New Directions, 1968).

EHH   *Earth House Hold: Technical Notes & Queries to Fellow Dharma Revolutionaries* (New York: New Directions, 1969).

LR   *Left Out in the Rain: New Poems 1947–1985* (San Francisco: North Point Press, 1986).

MT   *Myths & Texts* (New York: New Directions, 1960).

OW   *The Old Ways* (San Francisco: City Lights Books, 1977).

RR   *Riprap & Cold Mountain Poems* (San Francisco: Grey Fox Press, 1965).

RWave *Regarding Wave* (New York: New Directions, 1970).

RWork *The Real Work: Interviews & Talks, 1964–1979*, ed. William Scott McLean (New York: New Directions, 1980).

TI   *Turtle Island* (New York: New Directions, 1974).

Acknowledgements

As a theory of American culture by an English student of that culture, this book has been a long time in the making and is, in a sense, the record of my own discovery of the meanings of a culture which still seems 'foreign', but which I inhabit as best I can. My education in the field of American Studies has incurred many intellectual and practical debts along the way which I begin to note here.

At the University of East Anglia in the summer of 1986, Helen McNeil suggested a study of Gary Snyder's poetry, and when a first draft of that study had been completed over one year later she offered her generous commentary. More broadly, Dr McNeil taught me how to begin to think about American poetry and culture during my years at East Anglia; this book has been inspired in every sense by her example, for which reason it is dedicated to her with gratitude.

East Anglia's Eric Homberger was the one with sufficient commitment to my project that he sent it to the publisher. Without his effort on my behalf there would quite simply still be no book on Snyder by somebody English. He recognised what I had discovered in my research, which is that the extant critical discourse on Snyder is wholly inadequate. This intervention, facilitated by Dr Homberger's experience, enabled the designation of a place from which proper appreciation of Snyder's poetry might begin. What I have learned from other teachers at East Anglia – Chris Bigsby, Robert Clark, Ellman Crasnow, Jacqueline Fear, Susanne Kappeler, Roger Thompson – is inscribed in this book in various and subtle ways, whether or not they will ever read or recognise it.

The first version of the text was written in the summer of 1987 in Waltham, Massachusetts, where I had spent a year studying at Brandeis University. The Inter-Library Loan staff of Brandeis libraries were extremely helpful when I began my research by making numerous requests of their assistance, and a small grant from the Undergraduate Research Program at Brandeis helped me survive that summer. Most thanks are due, however, to Brandeis's Allen Grossman, whom I was fortunate enough to have supervising my work. His enormous experience as a poet, critic and teacher, his awesome reserves of knowledge, patience and kindness with both intellectual and financial assistance, together with his wise judgement (which allowed him to laugh uninhibitedly at my more preposterous claims) have been of inestimable value in encouraging the project.

Work continued in the summer of 1988 in Norwich, where V. J. Rayward-Smith of the School of Information Sciences at East Anglia allowed me use of a computer when the going looked bleak. That year Chris Lane and Julia Long were the models of support and encouragement; Chris Lane's suggestions helped make the text more readable than it might otherwise have been. My editor at Macmillan, Sarah Roberts-West, has been patient with delays and supportive of my aim.

At the Johns Hopkins University, my thinking about American poetry has been challenged and refined by Sharon Cameron and Hugh Kenner. Professor Cameron, in particular, made many helpful suggestions about the project and many more about American poetry in general. The dialogues in which we have engaged, both actual and imaginary, have sharpened the critical faculty brought to this book at its completion and in its final revision. My thinking about theoretical matters, particularly poetics and aesthetics, has also been stimulated and assisted by discussions with Frances Ferguson. I am grateful to the chairman of the Hopkins English Department, Ronald Paulson, and to the Ballman Fund of that Department, for a grant which helped me survive another American summer, this one in Baltimore. My colleague and friend, Cathy Jurca, made that summer a more pleasant one.

Thanks are also due to Patrick Murphy of the Indiana University of Pennsylvania, who is editing a collection of essays on Snyder for publication and who has been willing to share the results of some of his own research with me.

Finally, my gratitude goes to Gary Snyder himself, who has engaged me in written correspondence and telephone conversation, thereby helping me remember the existence of something significant and lively behind the signature affixed to the texts on which I was working. Mr Snyder commented usefully on the first draft of the book when it was still an essay; he sent me unpublished poems and answered my questions, prompting the conclusion that I could hardly have picked a more generous and open subject of study.

And, at the very end, for help with proof-reading, and much

more, my thanks to Jason Friedman.

The author and publishers wish to thank the following for permission to reproduce copyright material:

Henry Holt and Co. Inc., for the extracts from *The Poetry of Robert Frost*, edited by Edward Connery Lathem, copyright 1942, © 1961, 1962 by Robert Frost; copyright 1969 by Holt, Rinehart and Winston; copyright 1970 by Lesley Frost Ballantine.

New Directions Publishing Corporation, for the extracts from Gary Snyder, *Myths & Texts*, copyright © 1960–78 by Gary Snyder.

North Point Press, for the extracts from 'For/From Lew', 'Look Back', '24:IV:40075, 3:30pm', 'For All' and 'Axe Handles', all from *Axe Handles*, copyright © 1983 by Gary Snyder.

Gary Snyder and Grey Fox Press, for the extracts from *Riprap & Cold Mountain Poems*, copyright © 1958–1965 by Gary Snyder.

Baltimore   T. J. DEAN

Chronology

1929	24 Oct.: Stock market crashes.
1930	8 May: Gary Snyder born in San Francisco; Hart Crane, *The Bridge*; Ezra Pound, *A Draft of XXX Cantos*.
1932	Snyder's family moves to Washington State; family is extremely poor during Depression years; Hart Crane commits suicide; Sylvia Plath born.
1939	William Butler Yeats dies.
1941	7 Dec.: Japanese attack on Pearl Harbor; US enters Second World War.
1942	Snyder's family moves to Portland, Oregon.
1945	President Truman authorises dropping of atomic bombs on Hiroshima and Nagasaki; end of Second World War.
1946	William Carlos Williams, *Paterson, Book One*; Robert Lowell, *Lord Weary's Castle*.
1947	Autumn: Snyder begins undergraduate study at Reed College, Portland, Oregon, on scholarship.
1948	Summer: Snyder ships out for New York as seaman; John Berryman, *The Dispossessed*; Theodore Roethke, *The Lost Son*.
1950	Charles Olson, 'Projective Verse'; US population officially reaches 151 million; Snyder marries Alison Gass; Snyder publishes first poems in Reed College student publication; Summer: Snyder works for Park Service excavating the archaeological site of Fort Vancouver.
1950–1	Snyder writes senior thesis at Reed: *The Dimensions of a Haida Myth*.
1951	Spring: Snyder graduates from Reed with BA in anthropology and literature; Summer: Snyder works as timber scaler on Warm Springs Indian Reservation, Oregon; Autumn: Snyder begins graduate programme in anthropology at Indiana University, Bloomington, Indiana, but stays only one semester.
1952	Spring: Snyder returns to San Francisco, does odd jobs, lives with Philip Whalen, also a Zen Buddhist; Summer: Snyder works as mountain forest lookout in Baker National Forest; divorces Alison Gass.

1953–6	Snyder studies Oriental culture and languages at University of California at Berkeley.
1953	Summer: Snyder works as lookout in Baker National Forest on Sourdough Mountain; Autumn: Snyder meets Kenneth Rexroth.
1954	Summer: Snyder works at lumber camp; Wallace Stevens, *Collected Poems*.
1955	Summer: Snyder works on trail crew at Yosemite National Park – experiential source of *Riprap*; translates *Cold Mountain Poems*; Autumn: the retrospectively named San Francisco Renaissance is inaugurated as Allen Ginsberg reads *Howl* at the Six Gallery, San Francisco; Snyder meets Ginsberg and Kerouac in San Francisco; lives with Kerouac in cabin in Mill Valley – source of Kerouac's *The Dharma Bums*; Wallace Stevens dies.
1956	May: Snyder goes to Japan for first time on scholarship from First Zen Institute of America; lives in Zen Temple; October: Ginsberg, *Howl and Other Poems*.
1957	August: Snyder boards *Sappa Creek* in Yokohama, works as wiper in engine room; visits: Persian Gulf five times, Italy, Turkey, Okinawa, Wake, Guam, Ceylon, Pago Pago, Samoa; Jack Kerouac, *On the Road*.
1958	April: Snyder gets off ship, returns to San Francisco; Jack Kerouac, *The Dharma Bums*.
1959–65	Snyder lives in Kyoto, Japan; studies under Zen master Oda Sesso Roshi.
1959	Snyder, *Riprap*; Robert Lowell, *Life Studies*; Robert Duncan, *Selected Poems*.
1960	Snyder, *Myths & Texts*; Donald Allen (ed.), *The New American Poetry*; Charles Olson, first volume of *The Maximus Poems*; Snyder marries Joanne Kyger.
1961	20 Jan.: Inauguration of J. F. Kennedy as US President; Allen Ginsberg, *Kaddish*.
1962	John Ashberry, *The Tennis Court Oath*.
1963	November: assassination of President Kennedy; William Carlos Williams dies; 11 Feb.: Sylvia Plath commits suicide.
1964–5	Snyder is lecturer in English at University of California at Berkeley.

1964 Snyder receives Bess Hoskin Prize; separates from Joanne Kyger.

1965–8 Snyder studies Zen Buddhism in Japan; race riots shake US.

1965 Snyder, *Riprap, and Cold Mountain Poems; Six Sections from Mountains and Rivers Without End*; Sylvia Plath, *Ariel*; T. S. Eliot dies; Autumn: Snyder returns to Japan; divorces Joanne Kyger.

1966 Snyder awarded prize by National Institute of Arts and Letters; returns to US; *A Range of Poems* published in England.

1967 March: Snyder returns to Japan, lives on Banyan Ashram, marries Masa Uehara on rim of active volcano.

1968–72 Student protests on US campuses across nation.

1968 Snyder publishes *The Back Country*; returns to US; receives Levinson Prize from *Poetry* (Chicago), and is awarded Guggenheim Fellowship; son Kai born; Charles Olson, *Maximus Poems: IV, V, VI*; assassination of Robert Kennedy and Martin Luther King.

1969 Snyder, *Earth House Hold*; Vine Deloria, Jr, *Custer Died For Your Sins*; Snyder's son Gen born.

1970 Snyder, *Regarding Wave*; Charles Olson dies; National Guard fires on students at Kent State University, Ohio.

1971 Snyder builds his own house, 'Kitkitdizze', in foothills of Sierra Nevada.

1972 Ezra Pound dies; *boundary 2: a journal of postmodern culture* founded by William Spanos and Robert Kroetsch; Snyder attends United Nations Conference on Human Environment, Stockholm, Sweden.

1973 Snyder, *The Fudo Trilogy*; war in Vietnam officially over.

1974 Snyder, *Turtle Island*; Anne Sexton commits suicide.

1975 Snyder awarded Pulitzer Prize for Poetry for *Turtle Island*; Olson, *The Maximus Poems: Volume Three*; 27 Dec.: first MLA panel on Snyder's poetry held in San Francisco.

1976 First critical book-length study of Snyder published: Bob Steuding, *Gary Snyder*.

1977 Snyder, *The Old Ways*; Robert Lowell dies.

1978 Snyder publishes his Reed thesis: *He Who Hunted Birds in His Father's Village: The Dimensions of a Haida Myth*.

1980   Snyder, *The Real Work.*
1983   Snyder, *Axe Handles*; second critical study of Snyder appears: Charles Molesworth, *Gary Snyder's Vision.*
1986   Snyder, *Left Out in the Rain* (previously unpublished poems written between 1947 and 1985).
1987   20 May: Snyder inducted into American Academy and Institute of Arts and Letters.
1990   December: MLA panel in Chicago: 'Gary Snyder at 60'.

Introduction: For All

I pledge allegiance to the soil
of Turtle Island,
and to the beings who thereon dwell
one ecosystem
in diversity
under the sun
With joyful interpenetration for all.

Freud concludes one of his last works, *Civilization and its Discontents* – which was published in 1930, the year of Gary Snyder's birth – by announcing the prospect that 'we may expect that one day someone will venture to embark upon a pathology of cultural communities'. Although Freud explicitly articulates earlier in the text that he will resist the urge to take the United States as his example – will avoid, that is, 'the temptation of entering upon a critique of American civilization' – what is undertaken here represents the venture Freud proposed sixty years ago.[1]

This book presents my theory of American culture – how it is constituted as a culture, and what makes it specifically American. The theory has been developed as a consequence of my reading the poetry of Gary Snyder, a contemporary American poet. Snyder is thus the focus of this book not because his work represents a convenient canon to which the theory can be applied, nor yet even because his work exemplifies the theory, but rather because Snyder's work has itself *produced* the theory in the sense that his poetry articulates most cogently what it means to speak to and for American culture today. Such a poetic stance is necessarily historical and political in that it implies an understanding of the origins and trajectory of American culture. Thus despite his Zen Buddhist practice, his decade of living in Japan and his extensive travels in India and the Pacific, Gary Snyder is quintessentially a poet of America. However, the stereotyping of Snyder's work at the hands of the critics – as Beat, Orientalist, ecological and 'merely' political (that is, political at the expense of poetical) – has produced a situation in which students of American culture are apt to consider Snyder – if they consider his work at all – as marginal to what is

1

central and most important to the study of American literature and culture. This is a mistake whose effects my book attempts to redress. To refuse to recognise the importance of Snyder's work is to participate in the maintenance of those American ideologies which Snyder more than any other writer can help us identify and assess.

My claim for Snyder's importance extends beyond the question of American Studies/Cultural Studies, however, to claims for Snyder's *literary* achievement. By this I mean that it would be possible to produce an account of why a certain cultural practice (such as poetry) might be important for an understanding of that culture without necessarily claiming any aesthetic value for the practice – indeed, some versions of cultural studies see cultural significance and aesthetic privilege as mutually exclusive. In other words, one could make the argument for Snyder as a *culturally interesting* writer without having to say that he was any good. This is not my claim. Instead, I shall also be demonstrating the achievement of Snyder's poetic technique, the propensity of his work to exemplify aesthetically excellent craft as well as obtaining a significant bearing on the larger question of American culture in general.

What is often forgotten about the United States of America – although it is Snyder's persistent concern, and anyone who has travelled around the States by means other than the air will be less apt to forget – is the fundamental importance of its land. The 'land of opportunity' is before anything else a *land.* America's discovery in the fifteenth century (1492) posed a problem which it is difficult to overestimate, simply because 'America' was not supposed to be there. The shock was double, for not only was the giant continent in existence, but it was peopled too. What we know as the United States, therefore, came into being based on its destruction of the native inhabitants – the American Indians – and its expropriation of their home, the land. Because the European settlement of America began as a political and religious experiment intended to represent the pinnacle of civilisation and the morally best form of social organisation (the sense of self-conscious exemplarity expressed by John Winthrop's description of it as 'a city upon a hill'), the destruction upon which it was founded constitutes not just a paradox or a national embarrassment; rather, it constitutes something absolutely inadmissible to American consciousness. To be American, truly American, means not to know in a profound way the meaning of the United States's origins. This 'not-knowing' is not a function of ignorance; it is rather a function of the unconscious. The fantasy of America – to 'make it new' – depends upon the transformation of a cultural text inscribed with the marks of an earlier (Indian) civilisation into a *tabula rasa*, a blank slate. The rubbing clean of an always already inscribed upon slate is indeed one metaphor Freud develops to describe the process of repression, in which what is erased persists palimpsestically as the traces of the unconscious.[2] 'The American unconscious' to which my book's title refers therefore consists of nothing other than a relation to the American ground itself. Part 1 elaborates this argument and explains the methodological deployment of psychoanalytic theory – the precise significance, that is, of what I intend by the term 'unconscious'.

I have said that Snyder is a quintessential American poet, and I have asserted that to be truly American is not to know the meaning of American land: these two fundamental propositions are legible as consistent when we read Snyder speaking of and to America about its ground which he desires to inhabit and indeed make habitable. Although Snyder is not immune to the ideological representations by which the American ground has historically been apprehended, he is conscious as few other cultural representatives are of what is at stake in the effort to 'inhabit the ground'. His work articulates the desire for an unmediated relation to the land – a relation whose impossibility it refuses to recognise, which thus makes of poetic effects another representational matrix mediating between American subject and American ground. However, the desire to inhabit the ground obtains different formations, some of which are closer to commensurability with the land than others. In this regard, the poetry of Gary Snyder is exemplary. Although the unconscious cannot be spoken by anybody (poet or critic), certain features of the American unconscious are made accessible via Snyder, and there is an extent to which Snyder as poet functions analogously to the psychoanalyst in terms of bringing to consciousness elements which would otherwise remain unknown. This, then, is the meaning of Snyder as the poet of America.

Beyond the fact that one function of the unconscious consists of the disallowance of wholeness, we may see that there is an integrity to Snyder's poetry which is dependent upon his wholehearted commitment to the American land. The effort to

rehabilitate the ground has been more or less implicit throughout
Snyder's work, but it appears most clearly in one of his poems of
the past decade, 'For All', which I read here as an appropriate
introduction to both Snyder and what I shall have to say about
him:

For All

Ah to be alive
        on a mid-September morn
        fording a stream
        barefoot, pants rolled up,
        holding boots, pack on,
        sunshine, ice in the shallows,
        northern rockies.

Rustle and shimmer of icy creek waters
stones turn underfoot, small and hard as toes
        cold nose dripping
        singing inside
        creek music, heart music,
        smell of sun on gravel.

I pledge allegiance

I pledge allegiance to the soil
        of Turtle Island,
and to the beings who thereon dwell
        one ecosystem
        in diversity
        under the sun
With joyful interpenetration for all.
                    (*AH*, pp. 113–14)

The syntax and uncharacteristically abstract diction reveal this
poem as a formal articulation of the Snyderian creed. The syntactical repetition of 'I pledge allegiance' recalls the discourse of
Protestant religion, drawing as it does from the lexical register
structured by versicle and response which the priest employs to
introduce the 'Apostles' Creed' in the Protestant church service.
The echo of this dialogic religious structure, together with the

archaic coinage of 'who thereon dwell' (which sounds faintly biblical) and the allusion to the ritual formula by which the Trinity is known – 'One God, in three' – 'one ecosystem / in diversity', designates the text as an article of faith, an expression of commitment. In this case, the 'ecosystem' of the earth substitutes for the god in heaven, and thus the apostrophe with which the poem begins is addressed outwards to the land and – inevitably – to the reader, rather than being addressed upward to a single interlocutor, the deity.

The breathless metonymic detailing of life's pleasures in the opening stanza sets the speaker in a natural wilderness *topos* and a stance of action and attention, thereby indicating that 'to be alive' depends upon one's awareness of location, the consciousness of one's specific topographical context. The participial verbs – 'fording', 'holding', 'dripping', 'singing' – and the cataloguing of the constitutive features of the self and the surrounding landscape are reminiscent of Whitman's poetic technique, to which Snyder is indeed indebted. And although the speaker 'is' Snyder in the way that the speaker of Whitman's lyrics generally 'is' Whitman (both poets tend to deem inappropriately mediate any overtly mythic personae), we can register Snyder's difference from Whitman by noting the absence of the first-person pronoun 'I' from the first half of the poem. There is a sense in which that 'I' does not exist except in its function of commitment to 'the soil' – is only an 'I', that is, in so far as it is related to the ground as the constitutive source of its existence. Thus the second stanza's utilisation of conventionally poetic features, such as sibilant alliteration and sensual description, draws an analogy between human poetry ('heart music') and natural poetry ('creek music'), which leads to the constitutive relation between land and 'I'.

The poetic revelation of this relation between inner and outer has as its precondition the speaker's attention and commitment to the otherness of the ground which he traverses, an attention which apprehends the riverbed pebbles beneath the feet as other toes, but which resists reliance on the hierarchical structure of metaphor which would privilege the subjecthood of the poet over the otherness of the land. That is, although the simile 'hard as toes' assimilates the land to the economy of the human (and is thereby tropologically consonant with the dominant poetic technique of imaginative projection by which the landscape is anthropomorphised), the metaphor 'cold nose dripping' assimilates by its context

the human to the economy of the land – the poet's nose (and his
poetry) is like a stream in the northern Rockies. The reversal of
structural priority in these unobtrusive poetic figures thereby
achieves a non-hierarchical equivalence between interior expression and the voice of the wilderness, which in turn produces an 'I'
characterised by consciousness of dependence upon the land for
its dwelling.

'Turtle Island' is an old Indian name for the North American
continent which Snyder substitutes for 'the United States'. In thus
'making it new', Snyder makes it much older: the historically
derived metonym stakes a claim to originality not by the substitutive positing of an absolute newness but by the return to an
occluded origin, one Snyder considers a more appropriate place
from which to begin making a home in the land. The appeal is thus
to (Indian) myth as a greater source of authenticity and immediacy
than more recent, empirically verifiable, history. Snyder's poetic
effort is to produce a grounded mythology which will eventuate as
more 'real' and immediate than the dominant myth of the United
States which has naturalised itself as American reality. In thus
proposing re-nominalisation as a primary means of access to a less
mediate relation to the land, the poem gestures toward a central
paradox of Snyder's poetic project: that the recognition of the way
in which a certain system of representation perverts the culture's
inhabitation simultaneously advocates as its (paradoxical) corollary
the substitution of a new representational order – that of Snyder's
poetry – as the means to establishing a more intimate relation with
the land.

The intimacy and naturalness of the new, desired relation is
hinted at by the image of toes touching toes, as if inhabiting the
ground were as easy as bodily contact. One thinks of the sense
adduced by Whitman's lyrics, that 'Who touches this book touches
a man'; the difference here being that where Whitman desires
erotic contact with his reader, including his future reader, Snyder
desires the comfortable contact of homeliness with the land. The
poetic commitment is to the impossible immediacy of this relation
– impossible as a consequence of representation's dependence on
figuration (even the intimately immediate has to be figured by the
metaphor of sensual touch).

The individually specified instance of this relation in the form of
lyric speaker and riverbed is generalised at the poem's conclusion
to include the complete continent: this relation is precisely 'for all'.

The intimacy of the relation is such that its discrete elements can be sublated to a single entity, 'one ecosystem'; yet the fulfilment of relationship entails no mystical fusion since the 'one' is balanced by the 'di' (two) of 'diversity'. The concern at the poem's close is precisely with the structuring of the relation between man and land, the arrangement of habitation. Thus the article of faith and commitment which substitutes 'one ecosystem' for one God (the embodiment of Oneness) depends upon the etymological implication of 'ecosystem' as having to do with ordering the house ('eco' from *oikos*, the Greek for house). Pledging oneself to the American continent's ecosystem therefore implies a commitment to the work of inhabitation, and if the pledge is one of *allegiance* then the inhabitation is specifically devoted to the ground, since 'allegiance' originally implied one's tie of obligation to the liege lord, a tie based on land. The avowal of commitment to the work of inhabiting the ground thereby acknowledges the groundedness of words as well as the necessary groundness of life.

The desire for the origin which characterises Snyder's poetics of inhabitation obtains at the level of poetic form as well as poetic content, which accounts for the tendency of his poetic diction to favour 'the hard, precise, steady, monosyllables of our earlier vocabulary'.[3] That is, his diction is predominantly Anglo-Saxon in origin (evidencing a preference for concrete nouns and participles) as opposed to Latinate and polysyllabic. The appearance of such abstract, non-Anglo-Saxon words as 'allegiance', 'diversity' and 'interpenetration' is therefore explicable by reference to the way in which they are grounded as words – that is, by reference to their etymological implications, their linguistic origins (Snyder is a trained linguist). Thus we find in 'allegiance' the sense of a commitment to the land; in 'ecosystem' the sense of structuring a habitation; in 'diversity' the resistance to unicity which would make of the structural relation a mere absorption; and in 'interpenetration' we find a further specification of the structural relation. The implication of 'interpenetration' as a mutual penetration, one that operates in both directions, echoes the structural reversal of metaphoric organisation which I have described with respect to the mutual assimilation of the economies of human and land to each other: it is never a question of dominance or priority but of a joining of each to the other ('one ecosystem') which yet resists fusion ('in diversity'). Structurally, therefore, interpenetration seems to operate horizontally rather than vertically, and hence democratically rather than hierarchically.

The word 'interpenetration' first appears in the literary discourse of the early nineteenth century: its origins are Romantic, according to the *Oxford English Dictionary*, which cites as the first instance of its appearance lines from Shelley's 1818 poem, 'Lines Written Among the Euganean Hills' (the word also occurs in Shelley's 'A Defence of Poetry', 1821). Reminiscent of Wordsworth's more famous pantheistic outburst –

> a sense sublime
> Of something far more deeply interfused,
> Whose dwelling is the light of setting suns,
> And the round ocean, and the living air,
> And the blue sky, and in the mind of man –
> A motion and a spirit that impels
> All thinking things, all objects of all thoughts,
> And rolls through all things.
> > 'Tintern Abbey' (1798) (ll. 96–103)

– Shelley writes in 'The Euganean Hills', substituting 'interpenetrated' for Wordsworth's 'interfused':

> And of living things each one;
> And my spirit, which so long
> Darkened this swift stream of song,
> Interpenetrated lie
> By the glory of the sky:
> Be it love, light, harmony,
> Odour, or the soul of all
> Which from heaven like dew doth fall,
> Or the mind which feeds this verse
> Peopling this lone universe.
> > 'Lines Written Among the
> > Euganean Hills' (ll. 310–19)

There are differences both between Wordsworth and Shelley here as well as between the English Romantics and Snyder; and in this instance both differences and similarities are telling. What fills and sustains the universe in each case is not the deity one might expect; and although Shelley seems the most uncertain of what name or features to attribute to Wordsworth's universally animating 'motion and . . . spirit', our biographical knowledge of Shelley's atheism prevents the interpretation of the interpenetrating 'glory of the sky' as a trope for God. In thus resisting conventional categories of transcendence, 'the glory of the sky' thereby allows a provisional alignment of Shelley's couplet 'Interpenetrated lie / By the glory of the sky' and Wordsworth's 'something far more deeply interfused, / Whose dwelling is the light of setting suns', with Snyder's 'under the sun / With joyful interpenetration for all' – the alignment depending upon the shared sense that the relation between earth and sun is reciprocal rather than hierarchical.

A striking difference here between the Romantics and Snyder consists of the prominence given the subjectivity of the lyric speaker. Thus in Shelley, although one possible tenor for the vehicle of 'the glory of the sky' is 'the soul of all' (proleptic of American Romanticism's non-Christian Transcendentalist embodiment of the Emersonian 'Oversoul'), the final possibility offered by the speaker is the more subjectively specific 'mind which feeds this verse', just as in Wordsworth the allusion to a generalised 'mind of man' gives way to the specifically individualised response of 'Therefore am I still . . .'. By contrast, in the Snyder poem, poetic subjectivity is subordinated to the 'all' which partakes of the ecosystem, thereby indicating that *relation* takes priority over – if it is not predicative of – the 'I'.

There exists a further interpretive possibility for the etymologically based significance of structure in Snyder's poem, which has to do with the Old French (as well as Latinate) roots of words like 'allegiance' and 'diversity'. A certain school of highly self-conscious theoretical literary criticism – which is associated with the institutionalisation of deconstruction in the United States via Yale University, and which privileges Romantic poets like Wordsworth and Shelley as exemplars of the nature of poetic language and poetic authority while completely ignoring a poet such as Snyder[4] – might read an echo of the link between inner 'heart music' and outer 'creek music' at the centre of the poem in the climatic 'one ecosystem / in diversity' by emphasising – and punning on – the *vers* of 'diversity' as a reflexive indicator of the means by which heart music and creek music are made homologous. The verse encoded within 'diversity', such an interpretation would run, represents the inscription of that organising principle – the poem-maker – which orders the land into an ecosystem of which man is a part in order to sing of its harmonious relation.

Such an interpretive possibility suggests the aesthetic sophistication of Snyder's poem (which has been entirely lost on such
hegemonic American poetry critics as Bloom); yet this linguistically
encoded index of relation's predicate is ultimately secondary to the
business of Snyder's poem. For the poem is about ground-
inhabiting rather than verse-making, and its emphasis is on
precisely the land and one's relationship with it rather than on – as
is the case with Wordsworth and Shelley – the poet's capacity for
apprehension.

Thus it is that Snyder's poem begins with 'For All' (as its title)
and ends with 'for all', having delineated in between the structural
relations which make the 'all' possible. The echo of the poem's title
at its close draws a circle which encloses the system of relationships in the same way that any ecosystem provides for a
complete, coherent and balanced arrangement of relations. 'Interpenetration' is the proper name for such relational reciprocity, and
if the poetic elements of 'For All' have not been seen to exactly
penetrate each other, there yet has been an insistence on contact –
the speaker fording the stream, then the reversal by the image of
stones as toes, which gives the impression of the riverbed above
(and touching) the speaker – and an insistence on relation by the
prepositional repetition of 'on': the poet has on his pack, he is alive
on a September morning, he is 'on' the stream, then the stream is
'on' him; which structural relation is then repeated at the macrocosmic level by reference to the people living 'on' 'Turtle Island',
who have 'on' them the sun. The boundaries of the universe are
thus inscribed within the structure of inhabitation ('one ecosystem') analogously to the structural relation of intimate contiguity
– somewhere between penetration and touch – which obtains for
man and land, and which is figured by the minute synecdochial
detail of toes touching pebbles.

The rhetorical means by which contiguity is conveyed consists in
the trope of metonymy (substitution by name or word rather than
by resemblance), of which synecdoche (substitution of part for
whole) is a variant, and together metonymy and synecdoche
comprise two prominent elements of the Snyderian poetic (as later
readings will demonstrate in greater detail). Meanwhile, we can
conclude by registering the poetic instance of 'For All' as delineative of a structure by which a desired relation of inhabitation might
be achieved. It is in this sense that the poem is itself synechdochial,
the salient part standing not only for the whole Snyderian canon

(via its formal articulation of ethical-poetic commitment), but standing also for the significance of that canon for our larger understanding of American culture. Snyder is indeed 'For All'.

1
The American Unconscious

S(Ø) (Lacan)

This section elaborates in two stages what I mean by 'the American Unconscious': first, by concentrating on the *unconscious* dimension with an explanation of my psychoanalytic methodology; and secondly, by specifying more historically the constitutive features of the *American* unconscious – what, that is, American culture has to repress in order to constitute itself as such. Having established the theoretical and historical groundwork, the second section then focuses on the manifest relation of Snyder's poetry to the American unconscious so delineated.

THEORISING THE UNCONSCIOUS

The theory I bring to bear upon Snyder's poetry in order to produce a new theory of American culture is derived from the work of the French psychoanalyst, Jacques Lacan (1901–81). As Freud's most prominent disciple and *reader*, one of the consequences of Lacan's revision of psychoanalysis has been the provision of a critical discourse more amenable to the study of culture and literary texts. This has to do with Lacan's unprecedented attention to language – language not as something that has to be interpreted but as something that is itself always already engaged in an interpretive process. However, various factors – the general American resistance to psychoanalysis (although not to various forms of psychotherapy), the tendency to refute Lacan as incomprehensible, irrelevant or overbearingly arrogant, the claim that Lacanian theory is insufficiently grounded in clinical practice, and a general failure to understand Lacan or to misunderstand his teaching – have produced a condition in which any sustained critical engagement with his theories demands explanation. What follows is thus my necessary justification for using – and limited explication of – Lacanian theory. Since Lacan is virtually unknown in the field of

American Studies, my explanation begins with those initial resistances to the psychoanalytic most often encountered.

A general objection to the use of psychoanalysis in literary and cultural criticism consists of the claim that psychoanalysis focuses on the individual at the expense of the social and that it reduces everything to sexual phenomena. Psychoanalysis, it is adduced, sets itself up as a master discourse authorised to translate everything into symptoms of sexual pathology, including objections to its own procedures, which are interpreted by the psychoanalyst (or psychoanalytically oriented critic) as 'resistance'. Several discrete critiques are operative here: there is objection to the totalising impulse, to the reduction of all phenomena to the question of sexuality, and to the elision of the socio-political dimension.[1]

Although such objections are indeed appropriate critiques of unsophisticated psychoanalytic criticism, Lacanian theory provides critical possibilities well in excess of all these objections. To begin with, Lacan's 'return to Freud' after the Second World War was characterised by a consequential shift of emphasis from the dominance accorded by Freud to the sexual configuration of the Oedipus complex to a new stress on the signifying relation of the transference,[2] an alteration of emphasis which persists throughout Lacan's work and which constitutes nothing less than a paradigm shift for psychoanalysis. One pertinent consequence of Lacan's analysis of transference and its effects is the precipitation of an insistence that the sexual is indeed not directly translatable into language. It is therefore less a question of some latent sexual content lurking beneath the surface of utterance – literary or otherwise – which then requires translation by more or less vulgar 'Freudian' literary criticism, than it is a question of the way in which meaning is produced as an effect of the *impossibility* of sexuality's direct translation into language. The Lacanian literary critic thus indicates the meaning of and processes by which significance substitutes for sexuality, rather than simply substituting 'sexual meaning' for literary significance. This is not just the Lacanian method; according to Lacan, it is also properly Freudian.

An early, exemplary text by Lacan to which I shall have recourse is 'Intervention on Transference', first presented in 1951.[3] It is possible to read in that title a metaphor for Lacan's whole canon, since his work consists of a massive and sustained intervention on the previously marginalised topic of transference. By focusing on the transference – that language-based relationship between analyst and analysand – Lacan assured the remembrance that psychoanalysis is indeed a clinically derived theory of practice; and Lacan was himself above all a clinician (in contradistinction to those other Continental theorists who are known under the rubric of structuralism and post-structuralism).[4] Yet despite the fact that the application of a therapeutically derived discourse to the study of literature and culture might seem inappropriate or perverse, Lacan's emphasis on the transference provides an account of the subject's relation to language as the proper object of psychoanalytic inquiry. And as soon as one focuses on a relationship to language as the foundational aspect of all intersubjective relationships (including sexual ones), then the domain of literary criticism, which also focuses on the use and importance of language, becomes disciplinarily congruent. Thus Lacan says at the beginning of 'Intervention on Transference':

> What happens in an analysis is that the subject is, strictly speaking, constituted through a discourse, to which the mere presence of the analyst brings, before any intervention, the dimension of dialogue. (p. 62)

Psychoanalysis counsels the direction of attention not so much to the content of utterance – *what* is said – than to its form – *how* it is said; and so here the psychoanalytically oriented critic's attention might fasten on the apparently superfluous phrase, 'strictly speaking'. Jacqueline Rose has translated the content of the sentence accurately, but something has been lost at the level of form which is perceptible in the French original:

> *Dans une psychanalyse en effet, le sujet, à proprement parler, se constitue par un discours où la seule présence du psychanalyste apporte, avant toute intervention, la dimension du dialogue.*[5]

What is striking is that in the original the subject (*le sujet*) has no verb of being – does not, that is, *exist* – until it has spoken properly (*à proprement parler*). Attention to the initially insignificant phrase thereby gives a new sense to the possible translation, namely, 'What happens in an analysis is that the subject, speaking properly, constitutes itself . . .'. There is no subject before speech: that is what Lacan's discourse conveys; and beyond this, there is the additional notion that it is not any old speech which enables the constitution of the subject, but rather speech in dialogue, addressed somewhere in expectation of a response.[6]

The insistence on the transference – and hence on psychoanalysis itself – as irreducibly intersubjective as a consequence of utterance – as comprising, that is, two subjects in relation rather than one subject (the analyst) operating on an object (the patient) – also means that psychoanalysis is always already socially oriented rather than individually oriented. Lacan's diatribes against American ego-psychology (which he viewed as a corruption of Freud) gain their significance from precisely this point. Rather than see the function of psychoanalysis as the strengthening of an individual ego (the impetus of ego-psychology), Lacan sees the function of psychoanalysis as precisely the dissolution of this debilitating fantasy of egoistic self-sufficiency – and hence his expressed contempt for the individualism of 'the American way of life' (a term that recurs in English in his French discourse). The sociality of the irreducibly dialogic dimension of the subject means that the notion of the individual is nothing other than a fantasy, a peculiarly American ideology which, as we shall see, is ideologically requisite for the formation of American nationalism.

The emphasis on the ego has historically tended to obtain as its corollary a proportional decrease in emphasis on the concept of the unconscious, which Lacan correctly assesses as Freud's most important and radical discovery. Against the ideological notion of the autonomous individual, Lacan therefore develops an account of the human subject as dialectically constituted in an interlocutory relationship. And inseparable from his theory of the subject – indeed its predicate – is the Other, which pertains to both the dimension of the unconscious and to the domain of language[7] (hence the famous Lacanian motifs, 'the unconscious is the discourse of the Other' and 'the unconscious is structured like a language'). Thus as preliminary to elucidating the history and meaning of these concepts, we may summarise the innovation of Lacanian psychoanalysis by iterating the terms whose conceptual significance is crucial to my analysis: *subject, Other, unconscious,* a theoretically specific notion of *language* (and the key concept of the *phallus* together with a revision of the notion of *feminine sexuality*).[8] We do not attempt to minimise the importance of other elements of Lacan's conceptual framework, but rather to assert that the terms enumerated here, together with their conceptual referents, constitute those fundamental notions without cognizance of which the analysis I wish to undertake would be impossible.

As I have indicated, and as the American ideology of individualism with its concomitant Americanist tendency to substitute versions of ego-psychology for Freudian psychoanalysis would imply, the discipline of American Studies has hitherto been virtually immune to the influence Lacanian theory has obtained in other disciplines of the Humanities. With an audience primarily composed of Americanists in mind, I therefore find my discursive positioning very much one of having to *introduce* Lacan to the reader. In Britain, Lacan entered intellectual life in the late 1960s and early 1970s via the work of Louis Althusser – the principal French revisionist of Marx – and, institutionally, via the left-wing film theory journal *Screen*.[9] Althusser developed Lacan's theories of the subject and the Imaginary (the dimension of images and subjective identification) to provide Marxism with a much-needed account of subjectivity. Via his central notion of *interpellation*, in which ideology addresses a subject it constitutes by the very process of address and identification, Althusser worked towards both a more sophisticated account of ideology than that provided by classical Marxism, and a partial realisation of the political potential of Lacanian theory (the latter task of which has since fallen to feminism, both in Britain and the United States). Thus my point is that Lacan enters British intellectual life already politicised, a politicisation in which the commitment of *Screen* is a central factor.

In the United States, on the other hand, Lacan enters intellectual life at a more precise moment – the year 1966 – and in a more academically institutionalised mode; specifically, via university departments of French and Comparative literature. The conditions of such an entry therefore partially account for the misunderstandings of Lacan's work which arise when one conceives of his project as merely another strand of structuralism (or poststructuralism), and as having to do with blanket statements about language – hence the misguided but none the less oft-repeated charge that Lacan reduces everything to language (*Lacanianism* reduces all phenomena to language, not Lacan).[10] Three things occur in 1966: first, Lacan's massive 900-page *Écrits* is published in France; secondly, the first text from the *Écrits* is translated into English and published in a special issue of *Yale French Studies* devoted to structuralism as 'The insistence of the letter in the unconscious'; and thirdly, Lacan attends an international conference on structuralism at the Johns Hopkins University and presents a paper entitled 'Of Structure as an Inmixing of an Otherness Prerequisite to Any Subject Whatever', which is received in chaos.[11] Hence the American tendency to index Lacan under the academic rubric of structuralism.[12]

The subsequent institutional assimilation of Lacanian theory has proceeded similarly in England and the United States, with feminists in French departments and film theorists leading the way.[13] However, the Anglo-American reception of Lacan, which has been considered relatively enthusiastic by many (indeed, too enthusiastic by some), pales by comparison with the acclaim accorded his work in South American countries (one notes with delighted disbelief the degree requirement for all students at the University of Buenos Aires, regardless of major, of one year's credit in Lacanian theory).[14] American Studies starts to look positively retarded. I mention such historical and anecdotal instances in order to contextualise that dimension of my argument which will claim that what Lacanian theory is able to expose of the ideological foundations of American culture represents an urgent incentive to the American resistance to Lacan. What Lacan counsels of attention to the Other, together with his deconstruction of the possibility of the individual (and hence the dominant American ideology of individualism), threatens to undermine those very stakes by which American culture is constituted.

Thus to proceed from historical introduction to conceptual elaboration, we can begin by asserting that the *subject* is inseparable from the *Other*. 'Subject' here means the occupation of a place in language which enables the articulation of the first-person pronoun, 'I'. The subject is neither a person, an individual, nor the reification into a *thing* of a momentary and shifting linguistically determined enunciative condition. The category of the subject was imported into psychoanalysis from philosophy by Lacan; but the Lacanian subject – similarly but not identically to the subject of deconstruction, which is decentred and disseminated by language[15] – is radically anti-Cartesian. That which undoes the subject in Lacan – undoes it at the very moment of its constitution as such – is the divisive operation of the unconscious as an effect of language. It could be argued (Mikkel Borch-Jacobsen has done so) that the Freudian subject merely consists of an inversion of the Cartesian subject of consciousness so that its attributes fall wholesale to the subject of the unconscious.[16] And although

Borch-Jacobsen's subsequent development of his own account of the subject in Freud has posited that the Lacanian subject is the same as – and in fact *is* – the Other, this identification seems to me unconvincing.[17]

Lacan's return to Freud allows revision of Freudian theory as a consequence of one main factor: Lacan's access to structural linguistics – principally, the work of Saussure, but also the related work of Jakobson and the structural anthropology of Lévi-Strauss.[18] Most of what now counts as literary theory (as opposed to social or cultural theory) derives from Saussure's analysis of the sign. Since confusion still exists – even among those critics who write theoretically informed criticism[19] – about the sign and Lacan's modification of the emphasis placed on its components, some clarification is necessary here.

Conceptually, the sign and its referent correspond to the word for a thing and the thing itself. Thus the sign 'dog' has as its referent the animal barking outside my window. Since a French person would call that same animal by a different name, there is no necessary correspondence between the sign and its referent. Saussure thus posits language as a system of differences without positive terms. However, there is much more to the problematic of the arbitrariness of the sign than this, since the sign itself is composed of two elements, the signifier and the signified (confusion typically arises when words are referred to as signifiers and things as signifieds). The signifier is that material part of language, the part one hears or sees written on a page or a wall without necessarily knowing what it means – or, more importantly for psychoanalysis, *mistaking* its meaning. The signified is the idea that is associated with the signifier; thus when I write the letters d-o-g in sequence, the signified conjured up is a mental picture of a domestic animal. If I spell d-o-g to some native of China, that person will hear the signifiers but will not necessarily get the mental picture that accompanies d-o-g for English speakers. There is thus also no essential correspondence between signifier and signified; their relationship is both arbitrary and conventionally fixed. This disjunction between signifier and signified is crucial to the Lacanian accounts of language and the unconscious since it designates the disjunction at the heart of subjectivity itself.

Lacan refers to the emergence of linguistic science in the first decades of the twentieth century via the work of Saussure as 'a revolution in knowledge', one which he claims is founded on the algorithm for the sign which Saussure invented without ever quite writing it as such.[20] The algorithm for the sign looks like a mathematical fraction (S/s) and is formed by placing the signifier, S, over a line beneath which is the signified, s. Lacan makes the relationship hierarchical in order to indicate the predominance of the signifier, the material dimension of language, for his theory of the subject of psychoanalysis (S/s) (ibid.). The signifier becomes most overtly dominant in instances such as ones where I say 'peanuts' and you hear 'penis': the signified of the sign I have uttered slips, but the signifier produces an excess of meaning, which for psychoanalysis is always interpretable (and not just because my example reveals something sexual in something apparently non-sexual). The signified of the utterance ('peanuts') vanishes, slips away, but the signifier persists with the production of meaning ('penis'). Thus Lacan in 1958 in 'The signification of the phallus':

> This passion of the signifier now becomes a new dimension of the human condition in that it is not only man who speaks, but that in man and through man *it* speaks (*ça parle*), that his nature is woven by effects in which is to be found the structure of language, of which he becomes the material, and that therefore there resounds in him, beyond what could be conceived of by a psychology of ideas, the relation of speech.[21]

Lacan calls the significatory excess of language the unconscious, which is why he can say that the unconscious is structured like a language. Since the subject is always an effect of language, brought into being by enunciation of the 'I', the subject is also subject of the signifier and thence of the unconscious. This is what Lacan means by saying that the subject is subject *to* the signifier, which then enables him to define the signifier as 'that which represents a subject for another signifier'.[22] Commonsensically, one would expect a signifier to represent a signifier for another subject, because commonsense (the ideology of the rational) tells us that language is an instrument of communication between people who are in command of language – people who know, that is, what they are saying and what they mean (even if they do not mean what they say). Lacan – the whole direction of whose work is antithetical to anything one might care to designate as 'commonsense' – reverses this priority, however, by showing how the signifier is in command of the subject. No one (including Lacan) can control language:

> The discovery of the unconscious, such as it appears at the moment of its historical emergence, with its own dimension, is that the full significance of meaning far surpasses the signs manipulated by the individual. Man is always manipulating a great many more signs than he thinks. That's what the Freudian discovery is about – a new attitude to man. That's what man after Freud is.[23]

There is no going back on the unconscious, since as an effect of language the unconscious itself speaks: when I say 'peanuts' and you hear 'penis' who – or what – *says* 'penis'? The Lacanian answer is that the unconscious has spoken it: 'It speaks, does the unconscious, so that it depends on language.'[24] The unconscious thus represents that difference between what is spoken and what is said, and the difference is intelligible precisely as a consequence of the Freudian discovery that such slips are neither mechanical nor 'accidental' (such, indeed, is the whole import of the early, foundational texts of psychoanalysis in which the discovery of the unconscious is articulated – *The Interpretation of Dreams*, 1900; *The Psychopathology of Everyday Life*, 1901; *Jokes and Their Relation to the Unconscious*, 1905).[25]

It is precisely as a consequence of being subject of the signifier – subject, that is, to the way in which signification always refers to further signification rather than directly referring to things themselves – that the subject can never become reified ('you' can take the place of the 'I' as easily as 'I' can). Thus 'the speaking subject' (a tautological formulation) can be designated as 'the subject in process' – as it is by a Lacanian-influenced linguist and psychoanalyst such as Julia Kristeva. The *sujet en procès* of Kristeva's early work is thus a subject constantly in the process of *becoming* as a consequence of the shifting and fissuring effects of language, *and* a subject on trial, having to justify and legitimate its claim for subjectivity.[26] Since the subject depends on language, it is alienated from the very beginning, for in coming into being (such as it does), reference must constantly be made to the symbolic dimension of language which always pre-exists and exceeds that subject. This constitutive dependence means that the subject is 'split' by language, inaugurally alienated, and thus 'on trial' in the sense of having constantly to try and legitimate itself by finding a stable, habitable place in language. Such a legitimating project is definitively impossible as a consequence of what Lacan calls 'the play of the signifier', the fissuring effect of language by which 'every signification only ever refers back [*renvoyer*] to further signification'.[27] The authorising function of language for the subject and the question of legitimation implied in Kristeva's formulation of *le sujet en procès*, together with the subjection of the subject to the 'logic of the signifier', explains why both Lacan and Kristeva can refer to the symbolic dimension as the *Law*. Thus subsequent references to the Symbolic Order or to the Law imply the aspects of language determinative of the subject elaborated here.

As the intimately alien force of subjection, language is also the predicate of that domain of otherness which Lacan names the Other. Lacan transforms Sartre's conception of the Other so that it pertains not to another person or individual but to a locus of alterity in relation to which subjective utterance is necessarily oriented. This alterity returns to the subject as something inaccessible to consciousness, as precisely the unconscious: the unconscious is the discourse of the Other. In the psychoanalytic encounter the analyst occupies the place of the Other, is structurally situated in the field of the Other. It is not that the analyst *is* the Other – no person can embody or obtain any kind of control over the function of otherness – but that subjective desire, having to be articulated via the alienating register of utterance, addresses an Other whose place the analyst occupies as a function of the transferential effect. Hence the sense of the patient's utterance as part of a dialogue even if the analyst never says a word (the speech is addressed to the Other as demand). Hence, too, the possibility that literary utterance or cultural signification is dialogically structured, even when the addressee is not immediately apparent. What I mean by the American unconscious is the return of that realm of alterity to the subject of American culture as something unknown; something that is unknowingly and tellingly addressed by the cultural practices – literature, history-writing, ideology-formation, cinema – of American civilisation.

All speech addresses an Other; what counts is both the constitution and locus of that Other, and most importantly, the *orientation* of speech to it. For psychoanalysis, it is always a question of transforming the orientation to the Other of subjective speech (something of which ego-psychology is theoretically incapable as a consequence of its inability to acknowledge the Other or its discourse, the unconscious). Snyder's poetry is culturally signi-ficant because it aims to transform the relation of American culture to its Other, the ground. Reorientation of subject to Other is not therefore necessarily the prerogative of the psychoanalyst (although Lacan's writings provide the most intellectually sophisti-cated and compelling account of the modes, predicate and proces-ses of that reorientation); it is rather a function dependent upon the manipulation of symbols for which the analyst, the poet and the shaman are particularly suited.[28] It is therefore not incidental that Snyder is a trained Zen Buddhist as well as a poet, nor that he typically conceives of the poetic function as analogous to that of the shaman (such as in his early book, *Myths & Texts*, to which we shall turn our attention in the second section of this book). Neither is it coincidental that Lacan has been compared to a shaman and his text to a poetic text.[29]

The Lacanian text, especially that of the *Ecrits*, is indeed like poetry rather than discursive prose or conventional explicatory theory;[30] it should therefore be read with the same attention to formal and rhetorical strategies, to salient figures and characteristic motifs, as poetry is properly read. The oft-levelled charge of obscurantism *vis-à-vis* the Lacanian text (which in a typically indiscriminate conflation of author and text is usually extended to Lacan himself) therefore fundamentally misses the status of the Lacanian text – and, unsurprisingly, consequently finds that text illegible. The Lacanian text is not just poetic for the sake of poetry and its privileges, but instead for the sake of emphasis on lan-guage, on the way in which meaning and knowledge are transmit-ted at the level of the signifier, not just at the level of the statement and its content (the signified). If I have not much introduced Lacanian theory by a method of poetic reading (except in that instance in which attention to the phrase 'strictly speaking' pro-vided for additional – and fundamental – meaning via the sig-nifier), that is a consequence of having to introduce a discourse which is radically new (and hence difficult) to those in American Studies for whom Lacan is unfamiliar.[31]

However, the attention to language evidenced by Lacan's state-ments at both the level of content and of form should make it clear that the employment of psychoanalysis for the purposes of my argument will not have to do with the psychoanalysing of a man named Gary Snyder. Thus Lacan in 1955 addressing his audience of analysts, although the request is equally applicable to literary critics: 'please give more attention to the text than to the psychology of the author – the entire orientation of my teaching is that'.[32] The 'text' to which attention shall be directed here is not just the poetic text signed by a man named Snyder, but also the *cultural text* – the signifying realm of culture, those symbolic processes by which a culture constitutes and comprehends itself. The discourses of historiography, cinema and political science are part of the fabric of that cultural text as well as literature, so my psychoanalysis extends to these discourses too (which is what transforms the status of the account from theoretical literary criticism to properly cultural criticism).

It has been said that Lacan himself extended the object of psychoanalysis to the whole domain of culture. In her book *Figuring Lacan*, whose subtitle, *Criticism and the Cultural Unconscious*, appears germane to my own concerns, Juliet Flower MacCannell writes, 'Lacan speaks about everything under the sun and calls it psychoanalysis', adding 'no analyst was ever more complete in his examination of his patient, which is, in Lacan's case, culture itself'.[33] This is in a sense both correct and incorrect, and after asserting that what Lacan calls psychoanalysis is not 'everything under the sun' but rather his own speech, we should be careful to specify a little more precisely what is at stake in the extension of the object of psychoanalysis to the whole field of culture.

The first problem with adducing that Lacan addresses everything – all cultural phenomena ('culture' in the broadest sense here) – in the name of psychoanalysis suggests not only that psychoanalysis represents a master-discourse empowered to comprehend and diagnose the entire range of cultural formations (psychoanalysis as a version of divine or social omniscience – God or the panopticon), but also that Lacanian psychoanalysis is enabled to do so by its reduction of all cultural phenomena to a single dimension – that of language. Neither psychoanalysis nor any analyst is omniscient. Lacan does not say – or imply – that 'everything is language'. The ineliminable opacity of language represents both the condition of possibility for – and the very limits of – psychoanalysis, which is another way of disallowing psychoanalysis as a master discourse able to comment authoritatively upon whatever it chooses. As both Freud and Lacan realised, the enabling potential of psychoanalysis only serves to highlight its limits – both in terms of epistemology and efficacy.

Secondly, it is somewhat inaccurate and misleading to declare Lacan's patient as 'culture itself', because beyond the implication of culture's homogeneity or univocality in the formulation lies the more pressing question of what it would mean to take the Other as one's patient. The medical discourse of the 'patient' is appropriate since, as I have indicated, Lacan was a doctor who saw hundreds of patients: we may come to him as theorists and critics, but during his life he was a doctor to whom people came to be cured. In this sense, Lacan's patients were people, not something so vague and theoretical as 'culture'. Indeed, when Lacan produces the formulation which I take as this chapter's epigraph – S(Ø) – one thing he was indicating was the way in which culture functions as the Other (O) for the subject of the signifier (S), and it is the subject who is Lacan's 'patient', not the Other.[34] If anything, Lacan as doctor occupies the place of the Other, not his patient. When Lacan writes S(Ø), 'barring' the Other, striking it out, he indicates the subject's fantasy: that the Other can be mastered, that the subject is not subject of – dependent on – the Other (this fantasy is also the one on which ego-psychology and any other number of American therapies depend). The subject of American culture is constituted under precisely this formulation, S(Ø); that is, the foundational fantasy of American culture consists of its belief in its own independence of its cultural Other, the ground and its effects. The American unconscious disrupts this predicative fantasy, returning in various modes to write America as S(O) – as subject of and to the Other. The subject of culture is the patient (in my case, the object of analysis), not culture 'itself' (the Other), even though no analysis can be conducted without acknowledgement of the Other. In other words, we analyse the configuration of its subjective constitution, its orientation to the Other, not simply the Other itself.

A principal condition of the impossibility of analysing the Other as patient, as object of study, is that the unconscious as the discourse of the Other is immune to representation. The unconscious makes itself 'known' by slips, falterings, gaps – the mode of disjunction.[35] As that which is other to consciousness – *unconscious* – it cannot be portrayed adequately in discursive prose (the modernist writing of Faulkner, Stein and Joyce, for instance, together with the disjunctive poetics of Lacan's own text, represent textual instances in which unconscious effect as discourse is legible). The emergence of the unconscious as the return of the

Other occurs at that place and moment when the subject is under the illusion of being at home, being comfortably ensconced within the familiar and the known. Thus it was that Lacan, in his 1966 address to the conference on structuralism at the Johns Hopkins University, provided an *image* for the unconscious as 'Baltimore in the early morning'.[36] Part of the pungency of that image has to do with Lacan's emphasis that the unconscious (and its laws which obey the structure of language) is not something exotically foreign which one might import in small doses from Continental Paris or nineteenth-century Vienna, but that it consists instead of something that has been there all along in homely Baltimore. The visual field of Baltimore in the early morning to which Lacan was referring consisted of the view from the window of Lacan's hotel room, namely, a flashing neon sign tangibly – pulsatingly – fading in the growing morning light. That, he hints, is what the unconscious is like: it flickers in and out of apprehension and is always already disappearing as soon as one perceives its effects.

The unconscious is therefore neither a topography ('below' consciousness) nor a content (a 'storehouse' of archetypal myth-images which Snyder, following Jung, tends to take it to be): it is properly a *structure* predicative of the subject. Hence Lacan in his seminar on 'The Freudian unconscious':

> Freud's unconscious is not at all the romantic unconscious of imaginative creation. It is not the locus of the divinities of the night ... To all these forms of unconscious, ever more or less linked to some obscure will regarded as primordial, to something preconscious, what Freud opposes is the revelation that at the level of the unconscious there is something at all points homologous with what occurs at the level of the subject – this thing speaks and functions in a way quite as elaborate as at the level of the conscious, which thus loses what seemed to be its privilege. I am well aware of the resistances that this simple remark can still provoke, though it is evident in everything Freud wrote.[37]

Without a consideration of the unconscious we only ever get half the story: any 'history of consciousness' is therefore critically inadequate. There is something at the level of the unconscious of the same order as the level of consciousness, and this 'thing' signifies. I hope that by this point in my account the 'resistances' to the dimensions of this notion of the unconscious will be lessened, will have received some answer to their objections, so that the formative history of the American unconscious may now be considered.

BEGINNING THE HISTORY OF THE AMERICAN UNCONSCIOUS: PURITANISM AND LITERARY NATIONALISM

I take SPACE to be the central fact to man born in America, from Folsom cave to now. I spell it large because it comes large here. Large and without mercy. It is geography at bottom, a hell of wide land from the beginning.

Charles Olson[38]

Land as the constitutive feature of the American unconscious is above all a product of history rather than essence or necessity. That is, the American landscape is not *a priori necessarily* unconscious simply because it exists as the literal ground of the nation, because topographically it is 'beneath' the cities and architecture by which we recognise America; rather, it is unconscious as a consequence of the representational relationships which mediate it throughout American history. The history of 'America' – how it has been produced and sustained (not to mention expanded) – is legible not only in textbooks of American history but also in those cultural practices – literature, film, historiography – which symbolise an American subject to and for itself. The history of American land is therefore not only a question of how that land was appropriated from the Indians but also how the land and the Indian have been *represented.* The American unconscious is thereby formed as the trace of representation's excess (what representation cannot contain) and thus can be understood properly as the support of a specifically American consciousness. As such, the unconscious is nothing if not historical, and it is therefore to a history of representation that we must turn in order to read the unconscious in the only way it ever can be read, which is to say, in its effects. This is not only the case because *all* history arrives – as Dominick LaCapra has reminded us[39] – in the form of texts or textualised remainders, but also because America, from the very beginning, has been apprehended via the mediating lens of European representational systems – and subsequently, via the indigenous development of those representational paradigms in the 'New Founde Land'.

It is only possible to outline salient features of that representational history here, for a 'complete' history of the formation of the American unconscious – whatever that might look like – would fill many books.[40] However, psychoanalysis teaches that the subject carries with it as its unconscious support the whole history of its own subjective inscription into the codes of culture, and so any outline of a formative history should be understood as not only the product of a structure (that structure which produces the subject with the unconscious as its necessary prop) but also the *structure of a product* – in which sense 'America' (the 'product') is 'historical' precisely as an effect of its structuring (based on the unconscious). In order to examine the representational strategies by which 'America' was made apprehensible and subsequently 'inhabitable' for a civilised nation, I therefore turn to points in the history of its emergence which are possible to read synecdochially, as parts representing the still-unfolding whole. After the briefest of introductions, I examine the emergence of American *literary nationalism* at the beginning of the nineteenth century, followed by a reading of America's most famous and influential *historical* understanding of itself based on its geography (*The Turner Thesis*), after which I focus in more detail on the mythification of the figure of the *Indian* (the embodiment of the American Other), and then, beyond the question of the West as the site of *myth* itself, to a focus on the twentieth-century Western site of myth's production – Hollywood and its *cinema*. I return finally to a further consideration of literary nationalism as the prelude to Part 2, which focuses more extensively on Snyder's poetry.

Rather schematically, we may divide and group the initial impetus toward colonisation and settlement of the newly discovered continent under two rubrics, each of which precipitates a different representational strategy: first, there are those who consider the land of opportunity in terms of *material* opportunity – America as the place to go to get rich; secondly, there are those who perceive opportunity in *religious* terms – America as the place in which one may practice one's religious devotion in peace. For those driven principally by material interest (the early settlers of Virginia and the Carolinas), the governing representational mode will be *exploitation* (exploitation of the land as a business venture; the production of commodities – cotton, tobacco – for the home market; exploitation of the soil – cotton is extremely soil-exhaustive; the production of new markets in the colonies – the exploitation and escalation of trade and business circuits; extermination of the Red Man who stands in the way of profit; the introduction – and exploitation – of the Black Man to increase profit; exploitation of the *image* of America as the 'land of opportunity' to encourage workers to emigrate from the homeland); for those driven principally by religious conviction (the Pilgrim Fathers, the Puritans of New England, the Quakers of Pennsylvania), the governing representational mode will be *transcendence* (transcendence of every obstacle intervening between the man and his god, whether that obstacle be the severity of geographical and climatic conditions, the Red Man, the Prince of Darkness, the British Crown and Church, or mortality itself). Thus in a sense, although both 'groups' of settlers (who do not, of course, fit the homogeneity I have imposed upon them) view America as the land of opportunity (a place where one can get what one wants), both also view it as a land of *intractability* to be overcome (one does not get what one wants without a struggle). Thus it was initially a question of 'overcoming' – by exploitation or transcendence – rather than a question of inhabiting the ground.

As Puritanism – based on the Calvinist notion of Original Sin ('a hereditary depravity and corruption of our nature'[41]) – declined, the question of *nation* emerged, bolstered by – and substituting for Calvinism – Enlightenment faith in rationality and the perfectibility of Man: the American colonies were to establish themselves as 'The United States', a political experiment in the highest form attainable by civilisation. The notion of 'Man' involved was thus inverted from Man inherently evil – impotent Man utterly dependent upon the mercy of Almighty God – to Man essentially good – independent Man hubristically imagining himself *as* God. Not just one religious sect, then, but the whole land was to become a 'city upon a hill', a new Jerusalem; and the biblically derived rhetoric of John Winthrop's 1630 speech was transformed into a political agenda to which nothing less than the forces of revolution were to be commensurate. And not only God, but the whole world was called to witness the formation of what Charles Olson would later call in his essay on Melville 'the last "first" people'.[42] The extension of the divine into the social is ideologically crucial here for the emergence of nation because it accords the socio-political experiment divine sanction, a strategy of self-legitimation upon which the very *concept* of the United States is based and which, once established, will be henceforth continuously invoked and naturalised in order to authorise every act of expansion and aggression undertaken in the name of the national.

Such legitimation is requisite precisely as the consequence of an unparalleled American self-consciousness. Thus the first document of the new nation, *The Declaration of Independence*, is a self-authorising text which announces its reasons for separation from England, the Mother country, out of 'a decent respect to the opinions of mankind' – not, one may emphasise, from a motivational consideration for mankind itself, but rather out of respect for its *opinions*, its good favour. The most self-conscious nation in the world, then, gazing to observe itself watched as exemplary ('the eyes of all people are upon us', advised Winthrop), monitoring itself through the gaze of an Other constructed by its own mythifying consciousness: no wonder that representation and self-representation quickly came to constitute vital stakes in the nation's formation. Thus although literature is in some sense a conservation of the past, is always *re*-presentation, is defined by and as tradition – the very notion against which America as embodiment of the 'new' rebelled[43] – it soon became urgently apparent that a national literature, founded on its eschewing of tradition, was required as a crucial dimension of the formation of a national identity and consciousness. Yet inevitably, the condition of a demand for a national literature (such as we find Whitman making poetically in 1855 and more directly in 1871) is that the national literary tradition has already begun – it conceives its own cry for invention.

The Puritan poet Anne Bradstreet begins the poetic tradition in America, articulating her best efforts to transcend all obstacles and keep faith with her god. As Snyder's poet-contemporary, Adrienne Rich, has written of the conditions under which Bradstreet wrote:

> Seventeenth-century Puritan life was perhaps the most self-conscious ever lived in its requirements of the individual understanding: no event so trivial that it could not speak a divine message, no disappointment so heavy that it could not serve as a 'correction', a disguised blessing.[44]

Bradstreet's Puritan self-consciousness (consciousness of the self's relation to God) delivers to us a sense of the imperatives of transcendence which is at least two-fold. First, there exists the New England necessity to transcend life's physical deprivations, to persevere in the midst of 'this howling wilderness', to keep the faith no matter what trials the landscape imposes. Secondly, and crucially related, there exists the characteristically Puritan tendency to view the whole world, including the mundane events of everyday life, as symbolically significant: even the uninspiring dimension of life obtains a transcendent realm imbued with spiritual significance, which it was the task of the devoted Puritan to 'read'. Reading the Bible on many levels – for its moral, historical, symbolic and typological significance – Puritans read their lives similarly. Puritan typology ascribes an intentional pattern both to the individual's spiritual career (the specific manifestation of Calvinist Predestination) and to the historical progress and moral health of the community: every event can thus be read as not only an indication of individual status (am I one of the Elect?), but also as instantiating divine approval or wrath *vis-à-vis* the whole social body.[45] The legacy of typology is legible today in United States political policy – both foreign and domestic – whose rationale partakes of a global psychodrama in which good and evil – although secularised – are clearly and absolutely defined, and in which the United States feels *obliged* to intervene on behalf of – and *as* – the 'good'. (In Lacanian terms, the political dimension of the United States thus falls under the rubric of the Imaginary register, which is characterised by the predominance of fantasy and the binary logic of identification and rivalry.)

The Puritan mode of transcendence is exemplified by Bradstreet's meditative lyric, 'Here Follows Some Verses upon the Burning of Our House, July 10th, 1666', in which the initial subjective sense of great loss – 'My pleasant things in ashes lie, / And them behold no more shall I' – is overridden in this instance, not by recourse to the notion of Divine Providence (the biblical platitude, 'I blest His name that gave and took', appears as insufficient recompense early in the poem), but by transferring the attention from the memory of 'my pleasant things' to 'an house on high', the Heavenly home. Adjuring the self in a self-consciously third-person mode of reproof to 'Raise up thy thoughts above the sky', the poem concludes by synecdochially encapsulating the tropological movement of transcendence – the movement of attention from below to above:

Farewell, my pelf, farewell my store,
The world no longer let me love,
My hope and treasure lies above.

The rhyming tetrameter couplet serves to align 'love' with 'above',
thereby accomplishing *formally* the exigencies of subjective spiritual discipline. There is thus less an absolute renunciation of
material wealth than a conversion of the material into the spiritual,
a conversion characteristically accomplished by denigrating the
ground, the 'below', and idealising the transcendent realm beyond
sight, 'above' (or within).

The decline of Puritanism toward the end of the seventeenth
century does not, however, eventuate a corollary diminishment in
the structural potency of its ideology, or 'world-view'. The substitution of Man for God as the organising principle of a compre-
hensively coherent universe proceeds as an effect of Enlightenment thinking, and America subsequently produces a figure like
Benjamin Franklin, who makes individual self-consciousness the
predicate for individual self-improvement (non-theocentric teleolo-
gy), and who combines the two to provide nothing less than strict
guidance for a specifically American way of life. Franklin's *Autobiography* is the significant eighteenth-century textual instantiation
of the assimilation of the religious ethic to the business ethic, a
combination which produces the Protestant work ethic and a
whole ideology whose literary inscription extends to Jay Gatsby's
Franklinesque self-improvement 'Schedule' and beyond (Fitzgerald's *The Great Gatsby*, it will be recalled, *ends* – rather than
beginning – with transcendence 'backwards', to the 'fresh, green
breast of the new world' which 'flowered once for Dutch sailors'
eyes' – transcendence backward toward a spiritually immaculate
materiality, an earthly heaven – nothing short of Utopia itself).

Franklin's fusion of spiritual and material interest reinforces
both the new American religion (individualism) and a condition in
which exploitation of the land couples with doctrines of transcendence to legitimate more effectively the nationalistic activities of the
new nation, particularly with respect to continental expansion. In
order to be new, an immaculately conceived nation, the land and
its effects must be *made* new, made legible as virgin land – hence, to
follow the parallel example, Nick Carraway's concluding fantasy of
'a fresh, green breast', in Fitzgerald's novel, a fantasy which
thereby reveals itself as the *American* fantasy *par excellence*. The
dictum of modern poetry – 'Make it new' – can thus be seen to

have been the American slogan all along, and its literary repetition in the early decades of the twentieth century simply represents yet one more encoding of American ideology – ideology this time as poetic technique. How, then, does one make new what already bears a long and august tradition (literature)? How, also, does one make virgin a land already inhabited by other people? American culture answers those questions in the trajectory of its representational effects.

To move now to the nineteenth-century emergence of a self-consciously *national* literature, we come upon Emerson as the literary embodiment of questions of American originality and transcendence – the foremost proponent of Transcendental*ism*, no less.[46] In relation to our understanding of Emersonian Transcendentalism, the central urgency of the two questions articulated above is what renders pertinent – and symptomatic – here the theory of American poetry developed by Harold Bloom, a theory which plots a lineage beginning with Emerson and which names that lineage American Orphism.[47] Orphism (named for Orpheus, the poet of Greek myth) has to do with wholeness, the desire to include and contain the entire universe in a coherently unified structure whose centre and organising principle is Man rather than God. In the American context, Orphism represents a secular transformation of the Puritan typological world-view, and Whitman is speaking Orphically when he says in 'Song of Myself', 'I contain multitudes': for the Puritan sense of God as container of the universe, Whitmanic Orphism substitutes the body of the man, the corporeal 'I' as the metonymic container. But Whitman is preceded by the Emerson of *Nature*; and so although I find unconvincing for various reasons the tradition of American poetry plotted by Bloom – significant American literature does not begin with Emerson as its founding father[48] – yet Emerson's celebrated 'transparent eyeball' passage is exemplary of the kind of ideologically 'requisite' representational strategy of transcendence which I have been describing.

As the dominant cultural figure in early to mid-nineteenth-century America, Emerson was responsible for importing – via his reading of Coleridge's reading of the German philosophers – European idealism as the epistemological inspiration (albeit vicarious, doubly removed) for a 'belated' American Romanticism. Idealism as a doctrine of substitution – the displacement of the ordinary and visible by the invisible ideal – thus enters American literary Romanticism as itself an effect of substitution – an effect, that is, of one historical series of reading displacements. Continentally derived idealism combines with the domestic legacy of Puritan typology to produce New England Transcendentalism, a doctrine whose paradigmatic literary manifesto is Emerson's 1836 essay *Nature*, in which it is adduced that 'Every natural fact is a symbol of some spiritual fact', the overriding point being that the natural realm exists only to serve our movement through it to the spiritual. Nature's virtue resides precisely in its provisionality, its function as the mediate term between Man and the Ideal (or Emersonian Oversoul). A specific dimension of Nature's mediacy function is language, which Transcendentalist logic neatly characterises thus:

> Language is a third use which Nature subserves to man. Nature is the vehicle of thought, and in a simple, double, and three-fold degree.
> 1. Words are signs of natural facts.
> 2. Particular natural facts are symbols of particular spiritual facts.
> 3. Nature is the symbol of the spirit.[49]

Language is thus an intermediary term, falling between man and Nature, but operating so transparently and with such ortho-correspondency that it does not obscure the equally correspondent, *iconic*, relation which obtains between the world of phenomena and the world of the spirit. This world of the spirit consists of a transcendent dimension which is nevertheless anthropocentrically ordered: 'Every appearance in nature corresponds to some state of the mind, and that state of the mind can only be described by presenting that natural appearance as its picture' (p. 49). The natural image – poetic or pictographic – is the necessary conduit by which intelligibility becomes accessible, just as for the Puritans divine will was never manifested directly but was always to be discovered in some 'beyond' of the visible. As Emerson more elevatedly puts it in 'The Poet' (1844), 'The Universe is the externization of the soul' (p. 266), the neologism, 'externization', being rhetorically symptomatic of the difficult-to-think-directly (because mediate) interrelation.

The Puritan typological system, which remains dependent upon interpretive legibility, is thus transmitted intact to Transcendentalism with only its centre displaced: '[Man] is placed in the centre of beings, and a ray of relation passes from every other being to him' (p. 50). This man is not only always white (black men and red men do not count), but his anthropocentrism extends structural central- ity to qualitative hierarchy: the man is related to, but is also dominant over, the natural realm. The significant ambivalence which obtains when the man is prioritised over that to which he is necessarily and inevitably related becomes evident in those in- stances in which the natural, upon which he could be seen to be *dependent* (as both his relative and his access to the spiritual), becomes his *antagonist*, that which has to be defeated in order to secure his privilege. This ambivalence is negotiated, as we shall see, not only in American literary representations, but also in canonical critical and historical interpretations of the culture, such as *The Turner Thesis* and Henry Nash Smith's *Virgin Land*. But for now we can consider the rhetorical encoding of the ambivalence in a passage from *Nature* which adopts the biblical parable of the industrious ant (Proverbs 6:6) central to Puritan theology for the purposes of Transcendentalist illumination:

> The instincts of the ant are very unimportant considered as the ant's; but the moment a ray of relation is seen to extend from it to man, and the little drudge is seen to be a monitor, a little body with a mighty heart, then all its habits, even that said to be recently observed, that it never sleeps, become sublime.   (p. 50)

The ambivalence is discernible here as an effect of that pathos accruing to the ant which is doomed to be eternally denied sleep but which is considered negligible in and of itself: the insomniac ant's pathos assumes sublime proportions when identified with man, yet without this identification – which is crucially an act of mind, an essentially interpretive gesture – the natural creature merits no attention. The overdetermined precariousness of a condition in which the difference between absolute indifference and infinite significance depends upon an act of transcendent imagination (seeing the ray of relation) is only heightened by the rhetoric of the passage which alludes to both the Puritan authority of biblical parable (and the Puritan emphasis on lessons having to do with life's deprivations – 'the little drudge') and to the newly emergent authority of science (which has recently alleged to have 'proved' the ant's mythic tirelessness – 'it never sleeps'). To invoke traditionally competing discourses – biblical and scientific – is to rhetorically inscribe the ambivalence which the image of the ant *vis-à-vis* man provokes. The figure of scale in the passage, which ranges from the largest to the tiniest, and for which the ant is synecdochial – comprising as it does 'a little body with a mighty heart' – is itself a metaphor for the possibility of proportional inversion, that New Testament trope by which the first shall be last and the last first, the greatest least and the least greatest. Such a threat depends upon the very condition for viewing the ant as infinitely significant in the first place: if each tiny ant's endless labour is seen as sublime, then the possibility is inescapable that the central sublimity of man could be reduced – via the *tyranny* of analogy of which Emerson seems largely unconscious – to ant-like dimensions (partially a penalty, no doubt, for Man's hubris in substituting himself for God at 'the centre of beings').

The potential for inversion, for the overwhelming of man by natural forces, is itself characteristically sublime; and it is no accident that the European idealism which Emerson imports for American Romanticism carries with it the notion of the sublime as the central category of eighteenth-century European aesthetics. One recent compelling account of the sublime has characterised it as a discourse of power[50] (a notion to which I return in Part 2), and here we may note that the inscription of power in the ant passage is significantly doubled: the power of the subjective mind to set itself at the centre of the universe by descrying relations between itself and the phenomena of the natural world is balanced by the power embodied by the ant as a miniature Hercules. Yet since the sublime is ultimately an effect of the subject, empirically unverifiable and immune to exchange (according to Kant's 1790 exposition on the sublime in *Critique of Judgement*), sublimity is best afforded the Transcendentalist subject when the natural realm is completely dissolved by the faculty of subjective aggrandisement. The paradigmatic literary instance of this consists of the passage early in *Nature* when Emerson experiences his famous transcendental elevation on Boston Common – a passage which Bloom calls 'the most American passage that will ever be written':[51]

Standing on the bare ground – my head bathed by the blithe air and uplifted into infinite space – all mean egotism vanishes. I become a transparent eyeball; I am nothing; I see all; the currents of the Universal Being circulate through me; I am part or parcel of God. (p. 39)

The direction of transcendent movement is upward to the sublimity of the infinite, an exaltation which dissolves the boundaries of the self: 'all mean egotism vanishes'. The effect of transcendence is achieved rhetorically by anaphora, the trope of repeated beginning which is characteristic of Whitman and which derives from the oral tradition. Since the repetition here (as so often in Whitman) is of subjective inscription – 'I become', 'I am', 'I see' – the claim for diminished egotism may require qualification: the anaphoric 'I' certainly testifies to the centrality of the self in the transcendent realm of spiritual relations while also supporting Kant's hypothesis of the irrevocable subjectivity of sublime experience. Note also the metaphor of transparency and unimpeded vision which derives from Puritan efforts to read divine effects in earthly phenomena – 'Lord cleare my misted sight that I / May hence view thy Divinity', Edward Taylor characteristically implores his poetic addressee in 'Upon a Wasp Chil'd with Cold'.[52] What I want to draw attention to here is precisely that from which attention is displaced by the Emersonian subject – the bare ground of Boston Common itself, from which Emerson's transcendent vision takes flight. The paradigmatic gaze of Orphic American poetry, when it is functioning at its 'strongest', never sees the ground but instead sees something beyond it. Bloom's endorsement of this instance of American Orphism thus participates in and supports that displacement of attention, one that helps render invisible the exploitative relation to the ground upon which the nation founds itself. Snyder is heretical to this tradition because although his view of the poetic function is an holistic one, concerned with ecosystemic interrelationships (and thus Orphic in that sense), his poetic vision serves always to direct attention back to the ground and to one's relationship with it. Since Emerson, much like Wordsworth,[53] declares the necessary prerequisite for transcendent elevation to be his being alone in the natural realm, the fundamental paradox of American Orphism therefore can be seen to have to do with the status of the natural as *dispensable predicate* of transcendence – the 'bare ground' as that which predicatively conditions transcendent movement, yet also as that which is itself to be transcended. Snyder resolves this paradox by refusing transcendence, a refusal which bears as its corollary the displacement of the mind of man from universal centrality.

In psychoanalytic terms, the refusal or inability to see what is there, namely, the ground – the incessant substitution, that is, of some 'elsewhere' as the object of conscious attention – means that the substitutive mechanisms of the unconscious – displacement, psychic evasion, disavowal – are operative. This is what I mean by saying that the unconscious is always only legible in its effects. The psychic trope of projection is also operative in Emerson's gloss on his transcendent experience when he writes 'Nature always wears the colours of the spirit' (p. 39). The literary strategy by which the natural realm is consistently assimilated to the human and the spiritual has, of course, a long literary history and a specific terminology. In England, John Ruskin first labels this technique 'the pathetic fallacy', denoting the fantasy element which impels the perceiving subject to the conviction that the natural is affectively sympathetic to himself. A predominant version of the pathetic fallacy, by which natural objects – animals, the landscape – are attributed human qualities is known as anthropomorphism, a type of personification. Such representational strategies constitute a strong feature of literary Romanticism, in both its European and American modes – so much so, in fact, that recent theoretical assessments of Romantic poetics have revived an older rhetorical term for the strategy: *prosopopoeia*, which comes from the Greek for 'face-making'. I am thinking here in particular of the later work of Paul de Man (and that of his Yale students) on rhetorics, in which prosopopoeia – the device by which a face and voice is projected outwards, thereby enabling features of the landscape to be possessed of utterance and significance – obtains as its corollary some *defacement* – the inverse operation by which a 'face' is disfigured and a voice silenced.[54] De Man's theoretical concerns, although highly charged with affective pathos, are resolutely linguistic and philosophical; they are not, therefore, directly assimiliable to the discourse of psychoanalysis.[55] Neither is de Man concerned with American Romanticism. I mention his theoretical concepts of prosopopoeia and disfiguration, however, in order to point to an analogy (rather than a homology) between rhetorical effects and unconscious effects (the unconscious tropes of displacement and suchlike) as a way of indicating another dimension of the inevitable *cost* of American Romanticism's poetics of transcendence. When Nature is persistently robed in 'the colours of the spirit', Nature is consequently divested of its own features, is undressed, disfigured, defaced by being made to speak as man's reflection. The relation between these strategies and the typical gendering of Nature as feminine is fairly obvious (and will be considered later); I simply wish to indicate here that the Lacanian insistence on unconscious structure as linguistic structure eventuates the provision for specifying a rhetorics – or *psycho-rhetorics* – of American Romanticism, one which must begin with an assessment of the ground and its figural status.

To pursue the example a little further, we can discriminate between the *modes* of rhetoric's disfiguration of the natural asserted above by reference to Emerson's own figure. My claim – that Nature is 'divested, undressed, disfigured, and defaced' – fails to distinguish precisely between ground and figure: the compounded metaphors of aggression may be differentiated into two groups – first, those figures for disrobing, removing a surface or veil to reveal some essence or body; and secondly, those figures for mutilation which ignore the surface, instead attacking directly the essence of body or face. These two modes of rhetorical operation obtain significantly different statuses, since it could be argued that the removal of a surface appearance to reveal an underlying essence or reality represents the very mode of critical demystification in which Snyder's poetry or my own critical analysis is engaged; whereas, on the other hand, the figure of mutilating a body could be adduced as an effect or cost of the poetics of transcendence which refuses to pay attention to the land or its exploitation. However, these alignments of figural qualities with competing critical and poetic strategies could be *reversed*, since the poetics of transcendence is characterised by its penetration of the visible surface, its casting off of the material, which would then align such poetics with figures of disrobing rather than disfiguring. Emerson's metaphor, 'Nature always wears the colours of the spirit', does indeed suggest an essence behind the illuminating hues of human spirituality, a 'beyond' to which transcendence aspires. Yet, paradoxically, the essential beyond turns out to be the visible surface, since it is not the natural to which transcendence directs itself but precisely the 'spirit', Nature's (projected) outer garment. The Nature of the Transcendentalist thus begins to look like a phantom, something to be passed through and beyond, but which yet remains so insubstantial that no substantive 'beyond' exists. This specifically *rhetorical* paradox is intelligible, I think, not as an effect of undecidability, but rather as an effect of what I remarked earlier as Nature's unacknowledged status in Transcendentalist doctrine as 'dispensable predicate'. It is in precisely this 'unacknowledged' sense that the effects of the American ground constitute the American unconscious. Such effects always return to trouble American consciousness, both literary and otherwise, which is what accounts for the operation of psychic tropes of evasion.

To bring deconstructive methodology into play with a predominantly psychoanalytically motivated account is neither to homologise the two discourses nor to collapse the specificity of their respective analytic methods. It is rather the case, as I have indicated, that the discovery of the linguistic structure of the unconscious allows for the importation of analytic methods which emphasise the peculiarly powerful persistence of figurative language's effects. This, however, typifies American deconstructive concerns (de Man) rather than Continental deconstructive priorities (Derrida), the latter of which, while neither completely identical to nor wholly different from the former, exhibits a tendency to privilege the 'exposure' – precisely, the *deconstruction* – of the binary oppositions which structure all metaphysical thinking – which begins, that is, with philosophy rather than with rhetoric.[56] I mention this elementary (and relative) historical distinction between the work of Derrida and the work of de Man not in order to privilege one over the other as a more 'correct' or more 'original' methodology (such would indeed represent the kind of hierarchical opposition against which deconstruction is mobilised), but instead to suggest the additional pertinence of a deconstructive method concerned with binarism for the analysis of the American unconscious. That is, the tendency of American politics (as I have mentioned above) to operate within what Lacan calls the Imaginary register – the realm of fantasy characterised by oppositional identification and rivalry – means that a critical method or programme which seeks to dismantle such structures of absolute opposition and absolute identification – which seeks indeed to show how such structures inevitably tend to contain their own potential for collapse as the very condition of their possibility – is highly congruent with the project here underway. It is thus to a reading of America's favourite *historical* understanding of itself[57] – *The Turner Thesis* – that I turn now in order to demonstrate the effects of the American unconscious in a paradigmatic historical text as they are produced by a series of conceptual oppositions fundamental to the very notion of the United States itself.

THE TURNER THESIS

The central importance for American history and culture of the
frontier – as historical event or energising cultural myth – has long
been recognised; however, its precise meaning and implications
have achieved no such critical consensus.[58] This case is not least a
consequence of the indeterminacy accorded the notion of the
frontier by its primary exponent, Frederick Jackson Turner, for
whom the term 'frontier' tended to acquire the status of floating
referent throughout his extensive historical writing on the topic.[59]
It is therefore imperative to assess precisely the significance held
by the frontier for Turner as the prerequisite for understanding its
legacy of cultural meaning.

When the Census Bureau declared the frontier officially closed
in 1890, it was referring to the disappearance of a *line* beyond
which American settlement (defined as more than two people per
square mile) had not passed. The fact of settlement at the western-
most point of the continent – California – definitively indicated that
the edge of westward expansion had met the edge of the land: the
'frontier' was therefore no more. The opening paragraph of Turner's famous thesis, 'The Significance of the Frontier in American
History', first delivered at the Chicago World's Fair in 1893,
demonstrates the massive historical significance attached by Turner to the Census Bureau's announcement:

> This brief official statement marks the closing of a great historic
> movement. Up to our own day American history has been in a
> large degree the history of the colonization of the Great West.
> The existence of an area of free land, its continuous recession,
> and the advance of American settlement westward, explain
> American development.[60]

As Benjamin Wright correctly wrote of Turner in 1934, 'His
conclusions begin with his first paragraph and they lack not in
inclusiveness.'[61] The West is named 'Great' as a direct consequence of its making of America (and Americans), which is to say that
the assumption from the very beginning is that American history
depends upon American geography. This is something the 'brief
official statement' is unable to comprehend adequately precisely
because it is official, is of the East, rather than being of the West
and of 'the people'. Before remarking the manifold problems

involved in Turner's easy invocation of 'free land', we should note how completely Turner accepts the terms of the 'brief official statement', how he bases his argument on the Bureau's somewhat arbitrary definition of 'frontier' and proceeds to draw conclusions from that point.

The tone of nostalgia for bygone days of rugged Western individualism and character-making encounters with 'free land', which is apparent everywhere throughout Turner's writing, has recently been innovatively rebuked by a professor of Urban Studies in *The Yale Review* – one Frank J. Popper – who has argued not only the conventional line about the powerful persistence of the frontier in America's mythic imagination, but has indeed claimed that 'the frontier survives to this day as a distinct geographic region – a large remote land area beyond the farthest settlement – across huge stretches of the United States'.[62] The frontier does not merely survive figuratively, but literally as well: 'The frontier never died and shows no signs of dying' (p. 101). Of course, Popper's provision of this argument and supporting evidence in 1986 does not mean that for the purposes of national understanding the frontier had not disappeared: the performative effects of Turner's historicist speech action assured a historiographical and cultural legacy committed to the belief that frontier days were over. It is therefore rather the case that Popper has *resurrected* the frontier in its literal groundedness.

Popper takes the Census definition of unsettled land (less than two people per square mile) and finds that more than a quarter of United States land still fits this definition; this 'frontier land' all lies westward of the 98th meridian. When Popper uses the less stringent nineteenth-century definition of what counts as 'unsettled land' (less than six people per square mile), he startlingly reveals that no less than 45 per cent of American land fits this definition. These findings are graphically illustrated on a map which shows as black 'unsettled' areas: west of the 98th meridian is almost solidly blacked out (with California and adjacent seaboard sections of Oregon and Arizona – named by Popper 'borderlands' – the exceptions). Popper is therefore led to conclude that 'the national frontier line has still not crossed the Great Plains, just as it had not in 1880. Many of the contemporary West's large cities – for instance, Albuquerque, Anchorage, Boise, Denver, and Salt Lake City – amount to urban islands in a frontier sea' (p. 106). There is in Popper's rhetoric a dimension of hyperbole which seeks precisely to *unsettle* the reader: things in the United States are not what you thought; despite technological developments, civilisation has not progressed to the extent where you can feel safe *even at home*, for there are wolves lurking just beyond your urban horizon, exactly as they lurked outside cabin doors on nineteenth-century prairies. The *metaphoric* sense of Popper's argument forces one back to a wild era one thought had been superseded (our conditions are revealed to be like those that obtained in 1880), an era about which one believed one could be comfortably nostalgic (Ah, the frontier made America; things ain't what they used to be) without having to confront its more negative aspects (the danger made apparent by the trochaic figure for being stranded – 'urban islands in a frontier sea'). In so doing, the passage rhetorically enforces upon the reader an unsettling atavism reminiscent of that affect analysed by Freud in 1919 as 'the uncanny' – that which makes the homely (*heimlich*) frightening (*unheimlich*) by bringing to light 'what is known of old and long familiar', which 'ought to have remained secret and hidden but has come to light'.[63] Settlement is unsettled by being suddenly revealed as having been only very precariously settled all along. The rhetorical purchase of Popper's argument derives from just this sense of (temporarily) forcing back the readerly consciousness to an earlier state of civilisation, by rhetorically initiating a readerly 'return of the repressed' for the subject of twentieth-century American culture.

Although we can only speculate about the impulse motivating such affectively resonant rhetoric, we can assert that its *effect* is not diminished by Popper's subsequent rational concessions:

> The frontier is not what it was in the 1870s. It is smaller, less contiguous and isolated, more law-abiding and regulated, less rugged, dangerous, and impassable. It has less free land and no longer provides a safety valve for people who are unwanted or unneeded in cities or settled rural areas. . . . Except for Alaska, the frontier has not for generations been the dream of those who seek a fortune or a new life.   (p. 109)

Thus although Popper disputes Turner's interpretation of the implications of the Census Bureau's proclamation – and indeed disputes the content of that proclamation itself – his own argument is resolutely Turnerian in its epistemology of the West. There are no questioning quotation marks around the Turnerian concepts of 'free land' and 'safety valve'[64] in the passage quoted above, and all the information imparted in Popper's argument is adduced in the service of his claim that 'Because we ignore the survival of the frontier, we repeatedly misunderstand the West' (p. 110). In order to argue against Turner and the political legacy of his thesis for current United States land policy, Popper maintains the Turnerian assumption that the meaning of the West is dependent on the status of the frontier. Such indeed will remain the assumption of my own argument here, except that I shall read Turner against himself at a more fundamental level than Popper's Turnerian anti-Turner account. By 'survival of the frontier' I shall not be referring to still extant 'free land', but rather to the persistence of the *figurative* frontier as a settled, naturalised metaphor which accrues powerful meaning and cultural affect. By 'the meaning of the West' I shall be extending Popper's implication of land policy to the figurative dimension (which none the less obtains literal effects) of the cultural meaning of the West and the ideological function or 'work' that figurative meaning performs in – and for the construction of – American consciousness.[65]

Turner's thesis, as it unfolds from his initial misreading of the 'brief official statement', is organised around a series of binary oppositions: civilisation versus savagery, settlement versus free land, the Great American West versus the Eastern seaboard and Old Europe, emergent American democracy versus the predominance of Old World political institutions, social evolutionary progress versus an inherited status quo – and ultimately, good versus evil. The former term in each pair is associated with the frontier and its effects, so that although the nebulous term 'frontier' appears to cover a multitude of sins in Turner's writing, these 'sins' are in fact peculiarly American virtues. Defining the frontier as 'the meeting point between savagery and civilization' (Turner p. 4) and as 'the line of most rapid and effective Americanization' (p. 5), the frontier becomes the locus of conflict for the oppositional forces, the space of 'versus' in the binary logic which structures the account. The frontier as reified and hypostasised punctum produces 'America' as the effect of its movement: tracing a trajectory of struggle across the continent, oppositionality supports 'effective Americanization' – which is one meaning of Richard Slotkin's analysis of frontier mythology under the title, *Regeneration Through Violence*.[66] Not just *re*generation, though, but the generation of the new American *per se*. And as has often been noted, the consciousness of the frontier's disappearance – more an effect of the Turner thesis than of a geographical condition or 'official statement' – precipitated further American violence on extended frontiers, beginning with the Spanish-American War of 1898 and the subsequent annexation of Hawaian and Phillipine land. Thus when Turner speaks of the frontier as a process rather than a place, he refers to 'successive frontiers', concluding significantly that 'Each was won by a series of Indian wars' (p. 8). If it were not for the Imaginary power of American consciousness, its wholehearted cultural commitment to the claims of myth, it would not need to be explicitly asserted that the price of 'most rapid and effective Americanization' consists of the destruction of Indian lives and culture. To argue that the Turner thesis is written in Indian blood is merely to highlight in an historical way what is written by Turner himself.

It is precisely the foundation of American consciousness upon Imaginary identifications and oppositions that provides for the inflection of Popper's rhetoric quoted above regarding the status of the frontier: when Popper admits that 'Except for Alaska, the frontier has not for generations been the dream of those who seek a fortune or a new life', we may read an emphasis on *dream* which accounts for significant elements of the Turner thesis and its legacy. The frontier was and always has been predominantly a dream, an individual (individualist) and collective fantasy – *the* American Dream, no less. America as the 'new' dreams itself into existence via the enabling metaphor of frontier dichotomies, structural oppositions which precipitate an American subject by a series of identifications with the primary term in each opposition. Indeed, the 'myth' of the frontier is comprehensible as American fantasy, as the exemplary American Dream, by the terms of Freud's conclusion in 'Creative Writers and Day-Dreaming' (1908), that 'myths . . . are distorted vestiges of the wishful phantasies of whole nations, the *secular dreams* of youthful humanity' (emphasis Freud's).[67]

However, as Freud discovered in *The Interpretation of Dreams*, and as subsequent students of psychoanalysis have recently elaborated, the mode of subjective identification characteristic of fantasy is inherently unstable: in Parveen Adams's terms, identification is also always *oscillation*.[68] Similarly (although not identically), Derrida has shown how the development of metaphysical thought based on binary oppositions always involves the privileging of one term at the expense of the other's repression. The *force* deployed to effect such loaded opposition means that the binary hierarchy remains unstable, is potentially reversible, open to deconstruction. It is therefore possible to ascertain more precisely the ways in which Turner's thesis produces American civilisation's value as an effect of its opposite, the 'savagery' which is attributed to the land and the Indian.

The preponderance of evolutionary metaphors in the thesis, which are drawn from the late nineteenth-century discourse of Social Darwinism, indicate the value – and the sense of inevitability – accorded the terms 'civilisation' and 'savagery': 'The United States lies like a huge page in the history of society. Line by line as we read this continental page from West to East we find the record of social evolution' (p. 9). The progress from Old World institutions to superior American socio-political institutions is as clearly and naturally legible as the process of its reading, the scanning of the American continent from West to East like reading from left to right. The frontier, which of course 'moves' from right (East) to left (West), is thus naturalised as inevitable evolutionary progress. Besides the discourse of Social Darwinism, the American ideology of Manifest Destiny supports such a naturalisation as properly inevitable. However, the terms of such rationales are not without their problems. First, the sense of an iron law operative in evolutionary movement hints at a force that significantly exceeds the individual, one so massive that even community must submit to its direction. As such, the rugged individualism of which the frontier was allegedly productive starts to look negligible rather than paramount. If 'Destiny' has made America what it is, then the contributory independence of the frontiersman is exposed as nothing less than imaginary and the frontiersman himself is reduced to the instrument of a higher agency.

Secondly, the importation by Herbert Spencer of Darwin's biologically derived theory of evolution (as put forth in *The Origin of Species*, 1859) into the social realm as an ideology justifying social upheaval and deprivation (the 'survival of the fittest' ethos) produced an emphasis on the savage conditions underlying so-called civilisation. (Thus the turn-of-the-century Naturalistic novels of Stephen Crane, Jack London, Theodore Dreiser and Upton Sinclair concern themselves with the dramas of 'Man versus the [social] environment', a drama in which the environment tends to dwarf human effort. Such a fictional aesthetic indeed represents the inverse of Romanticism: in the Romantic sublime the subject is in excess of the social – is indeed subjectively precipitated as such; whereas in Naturalism the social is well in excess of anything that may count as a subject.) Turner's invocation of 'social evolution' therefore leaves it unclear with which side of the civilisation–savagery opposition the forces of social evolution are aligned.

Related to this is the problem that reading the westward movement as the inevitable product of Nature (Turner's thesis as precisely the naturalisation of this process) competes with the Turnerian emphasis on the pioneer as conquerer of Nature. Nature in the form of the 'savage' Indian and the wilderness landscape requires the mastery of the frontiersman as the foundation for American civilisation. Thus in a supplemental essay to his original thesis, 'Contributions of the West to American Democracy', Turner writes of frontier democracy in a passage replete with the rhetorical contradictions which are the effect of an unacknowledged relation to the land:

> There is a strain of fierceness in their energetic petitions demanding self-government under the theory that every people have the right to establish their own political institutions in an area which they have won from the wilderness. Those revolutionary principles based on natural rights, for which the seaboard colonies were contending, were taken up with frontier energy in an attempt to apply them to the lands of the West. No one can read their petitions denouncing the control exercised by the wealthy landholders of the coast, appealing to the record of their conquest of the wilderness, and demanding the possession of the lands for which they have fought the Indians, and which they had reduced by their ax to civilization, without recognizing in these frontier communities the cradle of a belligerent Western democracy.   (p. 33)[69]

The 'strain of fierceness' and recognisable belligerence again render it unclear whether frontier democracy derives from the civilised or the savage. Although this democracy is sufficiently civilised to be possessed of a 'theory', it is a theory that is doubly contradictory: first, because it claims the philosophical doctrine of 'natural rights' (which – although not directly referring to the rights of nature – bases its authority on the privilege of the natural, the sense that the natural realm obtains a law deriving from divine ordinance) in association with claims which refer to the destruction of the natural realm (via the synecdoche of the axe) as support; secondly, because it appeals for precedence to the revolutionary legislative procedures instituted by the East *against* which it is claiming institutional autonomy. The 'theory' of frontier democracy is therefore based upon twin 'dispensable predicates': Eastern institutions and the natural realm.

Since the central problem is therefore once again revealed to be the relation to the ground, the question of mastery which obtains between man and ground may be clarified by this passage from the thesis which pictures mastery as the effect of a dialectical process:

> The frontier is the line of most rapid and effective Americanization. The wilderness masters the colonist. It finds him a European in dress, industries, tools, modes of travel, and thought. It takes him from the railroad car and puts him in the birch canoe. It strips off the garments of civilization and arrays him in the hunting shirt and the moccasin. It puts him in the log cabin of the Cherokee and Iroquois and runs an Indian palisade around him. Before long he has gone to planting Indian corn and plowing with a sharp stick; he shouts the war cry and takes the scalp in orthodox Indian fashion. In short, at the frontier the environment is at first too strong for the man. He must accept the conditions which it furnishes, or perish, and so he fits himself into the Indian clearings and follows the Indian trails. Little by little he transforms the wilderness, but the outcome is not the old Europe, not simply the development of Germanic germs . . .   (p. 5)

The allusion to 'germs' here – besides adding to the rhetorical comedy of the passage in which one ends up having to speak of 'Germanic germs' – is to be understood as a reference to the 'germ theory of politics' propounded by Herbert Baxter Adams, who was Turner's teacher at the Johns Hopkins University, and against whose position Turner was writing. Adams's 'germ theory' argued that American political institutions were traceable back to earlier Teutonic political customs – that is, he offered an historical predicate for American specificity. In contrast, Turner provides an account of American specificity which is unhistorical precisely because it makes America look ultimately like the product of an immaculate conception: the question of America's origins and predicates is thereby converted into a tautology – because America itself is pictured as generative of – precisely – America itself.

Initially, the relation of mastery is inverted on the frontier: 'The wilderness masters the colonist.' The rhetorical combination of anaphora (syntactical repetition of 'It'), a passive masculine subject (grammatically mastered by the gender-neutral wilderness), and the short sentences cataloguing the series of Americanizing operations performed on the pioneer, produces the comic tone. It is as if the wilderness were a mother meeting her little boy at the station, taking him off the train, changing his clothes and putting him outside to play; once there the child comes into his own, taking upon himself of his own volition what had initially been imposed from without: 'Before long he has gone to planting Indian corn'. The condition of masculine dependency can afford to be perceived as comic, to look faintly ridiculous, because hyperbole ('he shouts the war cry and takes the scalp in orthodox Indian fashion'[70]) reveals it as both frighteningly necessary ('He must accept the conditions . . . or perish') and merely temporary ('the environment is *at first* too strong for the man') – just as, of course, masculine dependency on the maternal is alarmingly requisite (we are all 'of woman born'), is reassuringly offered the promise of rapid obliteration by the Oedipus complex, and is the source of much cultural comedy (the return of this repressed consists of the figure of the *mother-in-law*, the mother reinstituted as Nemesis).

How the initial relation of mastery – in which the frontiersman is subordinate – is reversed is far from clear, for from what looks like an 'orthodox' Indian comes the piecemeal transformation of the 'wilderness'. What may after all constitute the Americanising effect is the displacement of the Indian, which is rendered here in *figurative* terms: the pioneer *becoming* the Indian as an effect of the land – it 'runs an Indian palisade around him'. Indeed, one account of 'The Frontier West' argues that 'The replacement of the Indian by the white man was one of the most important features of the cultural process that defined the Frontier West';[71] and what is significant about the Turner passage is that its rhetoric produces the impression that this figurative displacement (an historical *replacement* – not just shifting the Indians elsewhere but actually eliminating them) is brought about by Nature itself, is occasioned almost against the will of the frontiersman whose activity is grammatically rendered as passivity before the irresistible claims of Nature. Such an impression is of course an effect of the frontier ideology, is produced with Turner as its most prominent rhetorician; it constitutes not only an example of the mythifying process by which historical event is converted into ideological or mythic representation, but also obtains an extended dimension in which fantasy is naturalised as historical fact. Thus, for instance, in the later and more rhetorically high-flown essay, 'Contributions of the West to American Democracy', in which the escalation of paeans of praise to the West is inversely proportional to the attention paid to historical events, Turner projects his own idealism and historiographic intentions into the past to account for events which might otherwise appear suspiciously exploitative: 'Western democracy has been from the time of its birth idealistic. The very fact of the wilderness appealed to men as a fair, blank page on which to write a new chapter in the story of man's struggle for a higher type of society' (p. 43). What is most striking here, beyond the ahistoricism which essentialises democracy as eternally idealistic via the metaphor of biology – beyond even the reference to the most overtly ideological element (blank wilderness) as 'very fact' – is the way in which the historian's desire – 'to write a new chapter in the story of man's struggle' – is converted into the American people's desire while itself simultaneously transforming the land into 'a fair, blank page' on to which that historiographic conversion may then be written.

In his classic account of the mythic dimension of the West, *Virgin Land* (1950), Henry Nash Smith noted the ambivalent status of Western land as representing both the enemy to be conquered by the pioneer and beneficent Nature, the source of spiritual value responsible for transforming the pioneer into the ideal democratic American.[72] Nature as nurturant mother is very apparent in the rhetoric of this poetic passage from the conclusion to 'Contributions of the West to American Democracy', a passage in which fantasies of mastery are significantly absent:

> Into this vast shaggy continent of ours poured the first feeble tide of European settlement. European men, institutions, and ideas were lodged in the American wilderness, and this great American West took them to her bosom ... she opened new provinces, and dowered new democracies in her most distant domains with her maternal treasures and with the ennobling influence that the fierce love of freedom ... furnished to the pioneer. (pp. 47–8)

The paradox of the frontier is that the land represents at once 'savagery' as an earlier, more primitive stage in social evolution to be mastered, and yet simultaneously the natural source of American democracy – and hence progress on the social evolutionary scale. That such an insoluble paradox, such a source of hermeneutic difficulty, should be overtly gendered and figured here so strikingly in terms of a maternal feminine sexuality is a significant feature of the American frontier myth to which we shall return.

THE INDIAN

When Turner repeatedly declares that 'The most significant thing about the American frontier is that it lies at the hither edge of free land' (p. 4), the vital significance of the frontier remains crucially indeterminate as a consequence of the ambivalence with which the relation to the land is invested. Furthermore, it remains uncertain whether or not the land is 'free', a golden opportunity and 'free gift' (pp. 27, 43), as it is later termed (a gift either from God or from capitalist Providence – 'The Lord helps those who help themselves'), or whether the wilderness is in fact neither virgin nor unoccupied but instead has to be *won*, wrested from another occupying agency. It hardly takes enormous feats of heroism to take a free gift or to settle 'vacant lands' (p. 34); thus what Turner's rhetoric of 'winning' that which is freely and bountifully dowered manages to both hide and reveal is the presence of the Indian, the extent to which the land was neither unoccupied nor free.

It is not that the land *belonged* to the various Indian tribes situated on it, since their cultures possessed no comparable notions of ownership: land was not something to own, master or exploit, but rather something with which one had an interdependent, reciprocal relationship, something which one could no more possess than the air. Writing in the 1930s, Luther Standing Bear (1863–1939), Chief of the Oglala Sioux, described the metonymic relation between Indian and land in which each is intimately related as parts of a larger whole:

> The American Indian is of the soil, whether it be the region of forests, plains, pueblos, or mesas. He fits into the landscape, for the hand that fashioned the continent also fashioned the man for

his surroundings. He once grew as naturally as the wild sunflowers; he belongs just as the buffalo belonged.[73]

The pathos of the passage depends upon the possibility that nature is always almost about to precipitate into culture, thus initiating a fall from innocence: although the Indian counts as part of the natural realm, 'is of the soil', he may in fact fall victim to cultural corruption – indeed extinction – if his natural status is analogous to that of the buffalo. The vulnerable status that accrues to the natural when it is isolated from its natural ground is endemic to the lapsarian rhetoric of the passage via its usage of the Christian myth of the Fall and the Puritan diction of the creator's 'hand'[74] – its utilisation, that is, of cultural codes recognisable not only as derivative of that culture which exterminated the buffalo (and hence the Plains Indians' food supply), but recognisable also as cultural codes *per se* – and therefore as the signs of that corrupting fall into culture which the passage reluctantly laments.

The perception of the Indian being 'of the soil', part of the natural wilderness landscape, was acknowledged by Whites and exploited for their purposes; and thus, paradoxically, the assimilation of Indian to landscape indeed precipitated the illusion of 'virgin land' – land free, unpossessed and uninhabited. Invoking the religious discourse which framed America as a new Eden, Bernard Sheehan has commented on this recursive relationship between ground and original figure:

> as part of the landscape of Paradise, the Noble Savage reflected a unidimensional image. Rather than standing aside from his surroundings as did civilized man, the Noble Savage blended into the surface of Paradise. In effect, he could not be differentiated from a natural resource, and the White Man tended to treat him as such.[75]

Compare Sheehan's assessment with this passage from Turner, in which the Indian is reduced to a natural hazard to be overcome:

> the Indian trade pioneered the way for civilization. ... The trading posts reached by these trails were on the sites of *Indian villages* which had been placed in positions suggested by nature.... Thus civilization in America followed the arteries sug-

gested by *geology*. . . . The *wilderness* has been interpenetrated by lines of civilization growing ever more numerous. It is like the growth of a complex nervous system for the originally simple, *inert* continent. . . . The maps of the census show an uneven advance. . . . In part this is due to *Indian resistance*, in part to the location of *river valleys and passes*.   (pp. 11–13; emphases mine)[76]

The identification between Indian and landscape – and the assimilation of one to the other for the purposes of exploitation – is evident here and is rhetorically accomplished by the functionalist analogy of the land as biological organism: although 'geology' has made natural 'arteries', the continent remains 'inert', not an organism because devoid of life; its invigoration is a consequence of the production by civilisation of 'a complex nervous system', a production which is naturalised as 'steady growth' and which substitutes civilised life for Indian inertia. The alignment of Indian with 'inert continent' in opposition to the alignment of civilisation with 'a complex nervous system' rhetorically implies that the Indians were incapable of feeling, that their exploitation and extermination were not coterminous with anything resembling human suffering.

The equation between Indians and land is not restricted to the historian, for Emerson himself viewed the aboriginal inhabitants of the land via a similar ideological perspective:

The man of the wood might well draw on himself the compassion of the planters. His erect and perfect form, though disclosing some irregular virtues, was found joined to a dwindled soul. Master of all sorts of woodcraft, he seemed a part of the forest and the lake, and the secret of his amazing skill seemed to be that he partook of the nature and fierce instincts of the beasts he slew.[77]

The extent to which the Indian '*seemed* a part of the forest', making the difference between man and beast barely distinguishable for Emerson, testifies to the distortive power of the perspective through which he was viewed. An essentially recursive figure, the Indian blends in with his surroundings. If I use a diction drawn from painting and the visual arts here – perspective, recursive, figure, blends in – it is to highlight the way in which the Indian was above all the product of European-derived *imagery*. As Robert F. Berkhofer puts it in his excellent study, *The White Man's Indian* (1978), 'American attitudes to the Indian have been influenced more by European images than American realities.'[78]

The very term by which the aboriginal inhabitants of the American continent are known is, of course, a misnomer deriving from Columbus's initial error. Yet to refer to Indians as 'Native Americans' or 'Amerindians' seems to me a corrective strategy that is always in danger of repeating the original imposition of (mis)-naming as an act of White power. Since the American aborigines never conceived of themselves as a single race and were in fact composed of disparate tribes and clearly distinct *nations*, the designation of these various social groups by any single unifying label will always represent an inaccurate and more or less arbitrary colophon of white colonialism. By retaining the name 'Indian', as I do here, we are at least reminded – simply by that momentary but necessary distinction of *which* continent of Indians we are speaking about – of the power of naming and the historical abuse of that power by Whites. We are thus more likely to avoid the illusion that a new name will evaporate the historical problems and their persistent implications of responsibility for the present.

Referring to Fenimore Cooper's complicated misrepresentations – at once idealising and scapegoating – of the Indian in his Leatherstocking novels, D. H. Lawrence wrote in the first psychoanalysis of American culture – his *Studies in Classic American Literature* – in 1923, that 'men see what they want to see: especially if they look from a long distance, across the ocean for example'.[79] It is possible to extend the significance of Lawrence's criticism by reading it as a metaphor for the ways in which the Indian has not only been apprehended *through* the lens of European mythology and iconography but has indeed been *constructed* as an object of the Eurocentric colonial gaze. Lawrence employs the hyperbolic metaphor of looking across the Atlantic through the reverse end of a telescope to describe the distorting effects of Eurocentric matrices of apprehension (p. 56), yet we should remember that Lawrence himself was looking in a sense 'across the ocean' toward the American literary scene, and he is indeed not exempt from participation in this cultural construction of the phenomenon of the Indian Other. Having censured Cooper for 'see[ing] Apollo in the young Mohawk', Lawrence proceeds to naturalise the Indian as feminine rather than as classically Grecian:

As if any Indian was like Apollo. The Indians, with their curious
female quality, their archaic figures, with high shoulders and
deep, archaic waists, like a sort of woman! And their natural
devilishness, their natural insiduousness.   (p. 55)

Indians are apprehended as 'feminine' – with the enormous freight
of cultural meaning which attaches to the feminine gender accompanying the designation intact – because they *look* feminine. As
image without depth, 'unidimensional' figure devoid of interiority,
the Indian is gendered feminine (and hence Other), while simultaneously being accorded powers ('feminine wiles') whose status is
indeterminately ranged between the natural and the supernatural
(the oxymoronic 'natural devilishness').[80] The metaphors of vision
with which the Indian is persistently associated therefore indicate
that the Indian is not merely a product of the imagery by which its
figure achieves cultural meaning, but that the Indian is also –
ultimately – signifiable and apprehensible *only as image.* The
meaning of 'Indian' is the meaning of imagery itself. That such a
condition should be directly analogous to the status of the woman
and her sexuality as exposed by Lacanian theory – 'images and
symbols *for* the woman cannot be isolated from images and
symbols *of* the woman ... it is the representation of sexuality
which conditions how it comes into play'[81] – is by no means
coincidental. Imagery conditions how 'the Indian' comes into play
– in so far as s/he is ever allowed *agency* in the processes which
produce cultural meaning (including her own cultural meaning).
As Vine Deloria, one of the most politically forceful and articulate
Indian spokesmen, put it in 1969, 'To be an Indian in modern
American society is in a very real sense to be unreal and
ahistorical.'[82] This tyrannical *power* of the image is echoed by
Berkhofer in his book's Epilogue: 'what began as an image alien to
Native Americans became a reality to them'.[83] The hold obtained
by the Imaginary dimension over a subject, particularly a collective
subject, is tyrannical to the extent that it produces the real as an
effect of the Imaginary, that it makes what could theoretically be
known as unreal the most compellingly real of all.[84]

It is therefore to a necessarily brief archaeology of Indian
imagery that I now turn, extending analysis of frontier mythology
into examination of the dualistic iconography of cannibalism and
the Noble Savage which has dominated representations of the
Indian. Perhaps the most significant feature for an account of the

American unconscious that emerges from analysis of such representations is that the Indian is consistently mobilised as the
opposite – the *Other* – of the Euro-American subject.[85] The Indian
therefore stands as the figurative *embodiment* of the American
unconscious – not that Indians, any more than women, *are* the
Other, but that they are *figured* for the subject as if they were. As
embodiment of the American unconscious, the Indian is therefore
– both literally and figuratively – the support of American consciousness, culture and civilisation. The opposing myths of cannibalism and Noble Savage indicate not an Indian fiction (the Indian
as mythically dangerous) against an Indian reality (the Indian as
really rather decent), but rather the dialectics by which the Other
precipitates a subject as the effect of a *process*.[86] These opposing
myths can also be read as an extension of the ambivalent relation to
the land and Nature discussed above: the benevolent, nurturant,
maternal dimension of Nature, which gives rise in Turner to the
frontier virtues of rugged individualism and American democracy,
also precipitates the Noble Savage – natural man as the ideal
because Nature is ideal. On the other hand, Nature as the enemy to
be overcome by the pioneer, as the domain of savagery, gives rise
to the image of the Indian as cannibal, demon or enemy. As will be
discussed below, these oppositional images of the Indian are
historically specific, contingent to some extent upon actual Indians' status *vis-à-vis* the American nation.

Thus the first broad representational convention to note is the
tendency to describe Indian life in terms of its deviation from white
standards, its substantial *lack* when compared with European
culture, rather than considering the possibility of specific and
independent cultural norms and terms which would provide for
description based on an Indian (or tribal), rather than European,
framework of perception.[87] Hence, for instance, Emerson's reference to the Indian's 'dwindled soul' in the passage quoted above,
in which the standard by which something as insubstantial as a
soul might be measured is subsequently revealed to be that of
Protestant Christianity: 'the hunters of the tribe were found
intractable at catechism', says Emerson. The possibility that resistance to the Christian catechism might, on the contrary, indicate a
'soul' sufficiently developed and committed to its own version of
spirituality so as therefore to be *immune* to the Christianising efforts
of the settlers is never considered.

Concomitant with the Euro-American ethnocentricity that

judged the Indian as deficient was the censure that usually accompanies the registration of difference: cultural absolutism preceded moral absolutism. The ready availability of the Indian as an object of censure provided justification for any number of white strategies ranging from *transformation* in the forms of religious conversion and education to *elimination* in the forms of massacre and removal. As Other, the Indian was susceptible to the violent psychic mechanisms of *splitting* and *projection*: 'splitting' as the effect by which a subject makes itself presentable to consciousness by casting all negative elements outside itself – 'projection' as the mechanism which accomplishes this 'demonisation' of the Other – and splitting of the Other itself into a *beneficent* dimension (the Noble Savage) with which the subject might identify and which it idealizes, and a *maleficent* dimension (the cannibal) whose relationship to the subject is one of negative identification (binary structure is once again noticeably operative). And thus we can recognise the elements of cultural fantasy in all their violence in this caption accompanying a 1505 engraving of Indians:

> They go naked, both men and women. . . . They have no personal property, but all things are in common. They all live together without a king or government and everyone is his own master. They take for wives whom they first meet, and in all this they have no rule. . . . And they eat one another. . . . They live to be one hundred and fifty years old, and are seldom sick.[88]

As Hayden White correctly notes, this description refers to the violation of at least five European taboos: nakedness, common property, lawlessness, sexual promiscuity and cannibalism. From the mixture of horror and delight which pervades the tone of the description (all that freedom, including sexual license – and no 'penalties' of ageing or sickness to boot!) it is difficult to know whether to characterise the mythic description in Freud's terms as the effects of a cultural dream or a cultural nightmare. No doubt the excess of pleasure which accrues from the realisation in fantasy of repressed desire is itself experienced as horrific, a horror which may indeed account for the image of cannibalism as the wholesale engulfment of the subject by its own excessive bliss, a rapture which overwhelms to the point of annihilation the subject of refined and strictly regulated culture.[89]

Leslie Fiedler has even gone so far as to suggest that 'Indian' was synonymous with 'cannibal' for the post-Columbus Latin mentality. In his treatment of the topic in *The Return of the Vanishing American* (1968) – a title which could be inflected as a play on the Freudian concept of 'the return of the repressed' and whose grammatical formulation is strikingly analogous to the Lacanian imagery of the unconscious: the return of a *vanishing* (as opposed to *vanished*) entity suggests the flickering of the entity between the visible and the invisible – Fiedler notes that the name of the villain, 'Caliban', in Shakespeare's *The Tempest* is anagrammatic of *cannibal* (the play was allegedly composed around the time of the first permanent English settlement of a colony at Jamestown, Virginia). As the monstrous embodiment of an excessively violent, bestial sexuality, Fiedler suggests that Caliban's characterisation – as a metonym for the Indian so recently revealed to a startled European consciousness – is an effect of projection on behalf of a European subject stifled by the demands of Christian marriage and the seventeenth-century hegemonic cultural codes of courtly love.[90]

Cultural projection on to a safely remote, monstrous Other may be legible as an effect of the profound unassimilability of New World phenomena to Old World epistemological paradigms.[91] Snyder himself commented on this in a 1967 essay, 'Poetry and the Primitive' (to which I shall be referring in more detail later), in relation to the frontier:

> Much has been said about the frontier in American history, but overlooking perhaps some key points: the American confrontation with a vast wild ecology, an earthly paradise of grass, water, and game – was mind-shaking. Americans lived next to vigorous primitives whom they could not help but respect and even envy, for three hundred years. (*EHH*, p. 119)

'Mind-shaking' may indeed be the lay term for the kind of psychic disruption experienced by the Euro-American subject, and such a disturbance certainly accounts for the mobilisation of modes of psychic defence that I have been elucidating with reference to American rhetorical strategies in various textual genres. However, it is apparent from this passage that Snyder is not immune to the mythological legacy which initially compensated for the 'mind-shaking' encounter, for his reference to 'an earthly paradise' inevitably alludes to the Edenic myth, one of the earliest European matrices imposed on the 'new founde land'.[92] It is also clear that the inevitable affects of envy and respect attributed to the settlers constitute more an effect of Snyder's participation in the romanticising revival of the Noble Savage myth than an effect of earlier historical events (Snyder goes on to discuss the Noble Savage later in the essay).

To refer first to the Edenic myth and its secularised extension, Manifest Destiny, we may register the severity of theological disruption afforded fifteenth-century European culture by the discovery of a whole continent – and peopled withal – of which the Bible made no mention and which therefore was not supposed to exist. The dominant Christian ideology, which was based on a relatively literalist interpretation of Scripture, and which postulated the origin of all peoples from a single source (named Adam and Eve), was forced to accommodate itself to an incontrovertible phenomenon which contradicted one of its most fundamental tenets.[93] One explanation offered was that the Indians comprised the Lost Tribes of Israel, in accordance with which seventeenth-century apostles fondly imagined themselves to be 'penetrating the wilderness to restore the Old Testament to those to whom it properly belonged'.[94] This notion is consistent with that of the Indian as Other, because the Other is typically attributed a desire based on the subject's constitutive orientation to it rather than on any 'evidence' from the place of the Other. Because the Other as an effect of language is resistant to meaning, subjective interpretation is accorded the 'free' license of signifying play. In other words, Europeans could make of the Indian what they wished – and what they made of him was precisely conditioned by culturally determined, partially repressed *wishes*. The European dream of a new Eden – and hence the possibility of a new start, an opportunity to be restored to a state of grace – to, in short, *relinquish history* – constituted precisely an effect of wish-fulfilment (in the sense that psychoanalysis reveals that 'Every dream is the fulfilment of a wish').[95] The legacy of the dream of a New Eden persisted into early American writing – indeed, persists to the present as Snyder's rhetoric indicates – and combined with the exigencies of the New Republic (the politics of Jacksonian democracy) to produce the ideology of Manifest destiny, the ideology that impelled the aggressive dissemination of the joint gospel of Protestant Christianity and Republican Democracy across the entire North American continent.

The Noble Savage myth, which seems to me the most perni-

ciously obstinate representational frame by which the Indian
continues to be viewed today, derives in part from the typing of
the Other as benevolent – the Indian as merely requiring the
Gospel in order to be restored to the inexplicably lost state of grace.
That is, the concept of the Noble Savage posits an innate dignity
and virtue; it focuses more on the noble dimension than the savage
and consists of an idealisation of natural man released from the
trappings of civilised culture. It will therefore be clear that the
tendency to associate the Indian with the landscape, to assimilate
one to the other, makes the Indian exemplary of natural man, for
the Indian represents less man *in* nature than man *as* nature.

The concept derives from the eighteenth-century revival by
Rousseau of an earlier French tradition which could be said to have
begun with Montaigne; it is, however, a particularly Romantic
notion which obtained political effects in the Romantic era. As
Hayden White in a remarkable essay, 'The Noble Savage Theme as
Fetish', argues, the concept could be invoked by French radicals
such as Diderot and Rousseau to denigrate nobility and its social
privileges via the logic that if the savage was innately noble then
the social benefits accruing to French aristocracy could legitimately
be extended to other social classes.[96] To an extent, then, the
'redemption' of the 'savage' via the concept was merely a secondary effect of its deployment. Idealised natural man vitiated the
cultural claims for the transmission of wealth, power and status via
genetic inheritance; the natural thus functioned as that which was
to be *appropriated* for the services of culture (or at least a certain
politically identified section of culture). Herein lies the meaning of
the Noble Savage myth and its recurrent potency: it is the means
by which an image of the Indian can be appropriated by one
disenfranchised section of the culture to be 'used' as armature
against the cultural hegemony, and this typical political condition
accounts for the recurrence and potency of the myth and its
invocation (it is in this sense – as a powerful synecdoche for
political causes and their justifications – that the myth acquires the
status of a *fetish*, an overdetermined signifier on to which various
highly charged meanings, or signifieds, can be displaced). It is in
precisely this way that the Noble Savage myth re-emerged with the
vengeance of fetishism in the United States of the 1960s as a
specific feature of counter-cultural discourse. And this is the
function of its rhetorical purchase in Snyder's essay, 'Poetry and
the Primitive', when he suggests, 'One of the most remarkable

intuitions in Western thought was Rousseau's Noble Savage: the idea that perhaps civilization has something to learn from the primitive' (*EHH*, p. 120). Aside from the dimension of idealisation operative here, and against the claim that Snyder is appropriating the Noble Savage myth for counter-cultural purposes like any other number of 1960s 'hippy' discourses, we may adduce here Snyder's extensive knowledge of North Pacific Indian culture, his study of authentic Indian discourse and mythology, his lifelong (not faddish) commitment to finding non-exploitative modes of inhabiting the American ground: if Snyder finds a model for such non-exploitative possibilities in 'primitive' Indian cultures at a moment which coincides with a significant counter-cultural resurgence of interest in anything Indian, then we may look to the history of his poetic and ethical work as a measure of his difference from standard counter-cultural appropriations of the Indian.

However, the extent to which the idealisation of the Indian as Noble Savage is simply one half of a psychic strategy which splits objects into good and bad elements means that the Noble Savage myth precipitates a cannibalistic demon as its inevitable effect. Another version of this splitting (besides the one provided above) consists of the way in which the appeal of the archaic, the desire for the Indian's 'primitivism', is dialectically related to the desire to impose 'progress' in the form of European civilisation upon the Indian, to bring primitive cultures 'up to date'. To the Enlightenment European mind, devoted to the ideology of Progress via technological development, the Indian was precisely *retarded*: lagging behind on the teleological scale of historical time. Primitivism denoted the social origins of man which had to be superseded in order to achieve the sophisticated social organisation of civilised culture. Although there was a specific theological appeal to the primitive – the return to a prelapsarian state of grace – the sense of necessary Progress was divinely sanctioned and was therefore to be accommodated – hence 'the machine in the garden', the importation of technology into Eden, the incursion of the frontier into 'virgin land', the obligations of Manifest Destiny – spread the Word, the political system and the superior culture.[97] The frontier and its advance has always been connected with new technology, and so in contemporary American society the frontier is associated with science – the frontiers of outer space (new territory to map and explore) and biological engineering (nothing less than the transformation of the species).

The Noble Savage could thus become an object of nostalgia as the Indian was destroyed and accommodated by technology to White ways (various diseases, alcoholism, scalping, horses, all were introduced into Indian culture by the settlers). The Noble Savage emerges in the eighteenth century as actual Indian numbers are drastically reduced and gains wider popularity in the United States during the late nineteenth century as remnants of Indian tribes are removed to reservations. As Bernard Sheehan passionately declares, 'Ultimately, the white man's sympathy was more deadly than his animosity. Philanthropy had in mind the disappearance of an entire race.'[98]

As a representational effect of psychic processes that are themselves primitive, the Noble Savage image has been particularly amenable to visual representation – both iconographic and cinematic. That is, the Noble Savage myth partakes of the Imaginary dimension, characterised as I have noted by identification and opposition; it is therefore disposed to appear in the form of visual images. Eighteenth-century European painting gives us many images of this kind, in which cultural identification with the Indian figure is achieved by depicting the Indian according to the visual codes of classical and Christian iconography. The Indian in these paintings is usually Europeanised to a certain degree, yet left sufficiently 'exotic' so that the figure may still function as Other, as 'nature' to European 'culture'. An excellent example of this mode of representation is Joseph Wright's *The Indian Widow* (1785), which may be viewed in the Derby Museum (see Plate 1).

The canvas is divided into two planes, foreground and background, the division running from bottom left-hand corner to top right-hand corner. At the centre of the foreground visual field sits the Indian widow, her clothes in disarray (one breast is naked) and one hand to her forehead as a gesture representing grief; yet her anguish is ordered, not wild: elevated by her classical, flowing attire and the sublime cloudscape which frames her head like a halo, the figure appears contemplative, stoic. She sits on the hillside which fills the foreground with her back to a blasted tree and her back three-quarters to the viewer (in Michael Fried's terms, the image is thus *absorptive*, autonomous from any beholder, framed as if the viewer did not exist, and thus an image for its own – rather than any subject's – sake).[99] The blasted tree, somewhat larger than a stump, is hung with an Indian tomahawk and sheaf of arrows – her dead husband's possessions, the mark of his masculinity and tribal status. The tree is roughly the height and width of a man; destroyed by nature and hung with the brave's weapons, it is thus legible as a metaphor for the absent Indian warrior. From the broken tree-stump a thick branch protrudes at a 45-degree angle into the light background space of sky and clouds. The light is so angled that the tree and woman are almost in silhouette, her upper body and the branch starkly contrasting with the heavenly realms of profusive light and foaming clouds in the background. The image is precisely iconic, a recognisable symbol, an image assumed to have a significance identical with itself: the tree as visual metaphor for dead hero is also a visual and linguistic metonym for the Cross, and the whole image is thus replete with the Christian iconography of *Stabat Mater*, the Latin hymn commemorating Mary's maternal grief at the crucifixion of Christ. *Stabat mater dolorosa*, begins the sequence, 'Stands the grieving mother': into this classic European icon of Christian devotion the Indian is fitted, ennobled and spiritually elevated by the painter's insertion. The reference to hallowed sentiment thus indicates that the Indian as Noble Savage, even without sacramental knowledge of Christian doctrine, is naturally reverential, affectively devoted to God even in ignorance of His Name and ordinances. Familiarity with the religious iconographic tradition which literally *frames* the Indian enables the participation of the European viewer in Indian affect, thereby facilitating a projective (and idealising) identification with the represented figure's tragic plight – which is in fact precisely a consequence of the representational operation by which the figure has already been identified with the devoted subject of European culture.

The over-determined iconographic features of the painting, together with the Indian's absorption in grief, also mean, however, that the viewer's identification can only ever be partial, substitutive, several times removed. The absorptive grief of the *Stabat mater* is itself iconic in the sense that the maternal meditation on the dead son represents an exclusive affective encounter which is dyadically self-contained in the way that the child's initial Imaginary relation with its mother is. No third term intervenes when such a relationship obtains: there is temporarily no room for a third subject, for the mediation of language, the Law of the Symbolic (paternal) function (which will come later). Such absorption – and here I am introducing a 'third term' (named Lacan) between Fried's notion of absorption and my use of it – is the more hermetic and replete when the *object* of absorption is absent, invisible, internal. Thus although the Indian warrior's masculine effects remain in the painting's field of vision, they are not the widow's focus of attention: they are merely signs for the viewer who has no direct identificatory access to the widow's object of meditation. Indeed, the widow's status could be allegorical of *cultural* mourning if the object of her meditation consists of the historical passing away of the Indian in general, rather than a specific Indian. Her eyes are closed as if in prayer; her absorptive 'object' is completely internal, and thus an *object* in the Freudian sense. That mediatory distance stands in the eighteenth century for the whole cultural difference between Europe and what can be seen or known of America.

HOLLYWOOD WESTERNS

I have said that the Noble Savage – and the image of the Indian generally (we are talking about a hypostasised myth of Indian here, not about Indians 'themselves') – is a product of the European subject's Imaginary, and it is therefore in that most Imaginary of culture's representational apparatuses – the cinema – that images of Indianness are circulated and obtain their dominant cultural meaning in the twentieth century.[100] The Imaginary power of the cinema depends not least upon the illusion that what occurs on the screen is 'real' in the way that what goes on in books manifestly is not: the Imaginary guarantee of the cinema thus depends upon the body of the actor, the Star, for that body in motion on the screen can have reference to the body of the viewer in the audience, and hence appear immediately, visibly, palpably, sensually real.[101] And in view of the twentieth-century dominance in the United States of the cinema as the cultural form obtaining most representational exposure (now superseded, of course, by television and video culture), any examination of mythic phenomena or subjective consciousness in the United States cannot afford to ignore film. In short, American people cannot be said to refer their subjectivity to their sociality by the reading of poems in the way that they understand themselves as American at the movies. It is thus symptomatic of American culture that the reference to 'Western' constitutes a reference not immediately decidable: are we referring to cinema or geography, the Imaginary or the real? The undecidability, or rather the conflation of the two, is symptomatic precisely of the means by which the West is typically apprehended, which is via the representational matrix produced at that most mythic of Western sites – the site that stands as the metonym for all Western myths and thus as the metonym for *myth itself* – Hollywood. This symptomatology has been played out most graphically recently not merely in politics broadly understood but in American party politics itself, in the very White House, no less: having made the West synecdochially equivalent to national virtue ('what made America great'), and having made Hollywood Westerns insepar- able from the meaning of the West, America twice votes a cowboy of the cinema for President of the nation – not, we may add, just a cowboy in the sense of a man really close to nature in the West, but a man hyper-really part of nature.[102] The transformation thus comprises less the conversion of history into myth (as, for instance, Clark's account articulates it) than the precipitation of cinema into the real, into historical and political events. The image is consis- tently more compelling than narrative because there is a way in which simultaneity is more effective than seriality. It is not the case that the cinema *is* – or *is equal to* – the real, but rather that the cinema *precipitates* a real as one of its effects.

It is therefore to an examination of three classic Hollywood Westerns that I now turn: *The Iron Horse, The Searchers, The Man Who Shot Liberty Valance*. These cinematic texts represent stages in both the career development of their auteur, John Ford, and the development of the genre itself, whose features Ford's work helped shape. Their significance exceeds the elements of both auteurial and generic histories, however, and derives for my purposes from their pivotal participation in the construction of Western myth: their cumulative and most cogent meaning is that of producing a meta-myth of the West which claims itself (as meta-myth) as the real.

> 'This is the West, Sir. When the legend becomes fact, print the legend.'
>
> (*The Man Who Shot Liberty Valence*)

There runs throughout the Western genre an appeal to truth in the form of history which aims to exemplify the real of the historical

American development of the West beyond the necessary fictional treatment – in literature and the cinema – which vests history. This Western myth – the myth of meta-myth – is precisely the one whose effects produce the history of the West as meaningful only in so far as it is mythic. 'West' here is metonymic for America as a whole: as two commentators have noted, 'In 1607, when the Virginia Company initiated the first successful English settlement, all the continent outside Jamestown was the new settlers' Frontier West.'[103] It is as America itself that the West ultimately gains its meaning – 'America' as equivalent, in the ideological equation, to 'free land'. More precisely, the cultural chain of substitutions precipitative of an American subject runs: West – America – freely *contestable* land. It is for this reason that the paradigmatic landscape of the Western is Monument Valley, a landscape which purports to be purely natural, immune to history. Unlike the farmstead, small town or city (in the latter of which generic features of the Western metamorphose into the gangster movie), a landscape which can be viewed as bearing no historical inscription (being seamlessly natural) constitutes the ideal surface on to which can be cinematically projected the desired version of history, history as one imagines it (in which America is Great). As the quotation above might suggest, with the West synonymous to the whole continent, a primary preoccupation of the genre is land appropriation.[104] Exemplary in this respect is Ford's *The Iron Horse* (1924).

The *ideological* success of films like *The Iron Horse* can be measured by referring to the comments of contemporary film scholars. Thomas Schatz, for instance, writes of such early Westerns in his study of Hollywood genres:

As cultural and historical documents, the earlier silent Westerns differ from the later Westerns. In fact, these earlier films have a unique and somewhat paradoxical position: Although they were made on the virtual threshold of the Modern Age, they also came at a time when westward expansion was winding down. Certain early cowboy heroes like 'Bronco Billy' Anderson and William S. Hart did lay the groundwork for the heroic and stylized mythology of movie Westerns. But many other films, like *The Covered Wagon* (1923) and *The Iron Horse* (1924), were really historical dramas, depicting as accurately as possible the actuality of Western expansion.[105]

The effect of later Westerns is to make earlier ones look as if they were depicting an historical event. Schatz completely misses the historical meaning of the early Westerns; his analysis is thus based on the Western myth as a version of historical fact and therefore cannot be anything but a critical perpetuation of that myth, a mere footnote to the genre's ideological narrative. As 'cultural and historical documents', such early Westerns (like *The Iron Horse*) emerged when technology combined with historical demand to provide what was required for the production and validation of the American myth after the closing of the frontier and several international wars. The cinematic apparatus was that technology and the myth it secured was the West.

Ford's epic concern in *The Iron Horse* was the nineteenth-century building of the transcontinental railroad. The central representational technology of the twentieth-century thus focuses in an important stage of its historical emergence on one of its technological predecessors in the American context: if in the nineteenth century the railroad was what both made America (girding it from coast to coast) and made it great, in the twentieth century the cinema *remakes* America, commemorating and securing its prestige through the myth of new technology and the technology of revitalised myth. Thus far from being generically unsophisticated, as Schatz implies, a text such as *The Iron Horse* reveals a complex mode of reflexivity from the very beginning. Indeed, the image of the railroad is the paradigm for the *shock* of cinema's new technology, as those stories of the first cinema audiences who fled from the auditorium in response to the projected image of an oncoming locomotive suggest. Such stories not only exemplify the novelty of the representational apparatus together with the historical shocks associated with the novelty of the railroad – the hysteria it induced as a consequence of its speed, 'train-brain' as a somatic protest against supernatural speed[106] – they also testify to the Imaginary *power* of the technology which, once assimilated, we forget. The reflexivity upon which the Western genre is founded is therefore not just reflexivity of the purely generic kind (in which later, more 'generically sophisticated' Westerns encode references to earlier examples of the genre), but instead has to do with the self-consciousness of a technology of story-telling, the displaced acknowledgement of narrative's generative effects.

As an instance of relatively early, perceptibly evolving cinematic technology – specifically pre-'sound' – *The Iron Horse* constructs a spectacle of technological advance which culminates when 'East meets West' in the form of the railroad spanning the continent. The triumphant version of two sides meeting and becoming one has, however, at least two darker models in the film, and I would suggest that these problematic – even horrific – versions of 'two sides meeting and becoming one' function ideologically in the narrative to drain off all negative aspects from the railroad meeting so that national glory can be constituted as both natural and immaculate. Interrupting the labour of railroad building are, of course, the Cheyenne Indians, who represent a type of 'natural hazard' the pioneer heroes classically have to overcome. In this instance, the Indian is precisely an obstacle to Progress. And lest the spectacle betray the Indian as a direct and unmitigated *cost* of Progress – an image which might threaten to tarnish the production of national glory – the image of the Indian is split (again in the classic mode, which should be familiar from my analysis above) into good and bad. Two Indian stereotypes are imaged: the villainous Cheyenne, wearing headdresses, living in tepees, dancing round totem poles – evil figured *as* Indianness (such stereotypical accoutrements were not, in fact, typical of Cheyenne culture); and the benevolent Shawnee, who help the pioneers against the Cheyenne and who fit the Noble Savage mould – a striking, lingering, affective image is of a Shawnee Indian lying dead while his dog lies on his chest licking its dead master's face. The pathos of such an image depends upon the Noble Savage as *naturally* noble and good (recognised so by nature, by his dog who mourns the loss) and, crucially, upon the emergence of the Noble Savage myth as Indian numbers are decreasing (nostalgia for what is perceived as evanescent and impotent). The image 'fits', seems natural and proper, because it is nothing less than the cinematic validation (which can be read as irony only *now*) of the old American adage that 'The only good Injun is a dead Injun'.

The good Indian killed by the bad, the bad Indian subsequently 'justly' killed by the pioneer, the 'one' (the Indian) is thus split in 'two' (good and bad) in order that 'two' (Indian and pioneer, savagery and civilisation, the primitive and Progress) may meet and 'become' one (the new nation, becoming unified by the railroad) by the *elimination* of the other. The elimination of the Other is also deemed proper by the cinematic narrative by being translated into sexual terms, terms which draw on a primitive horror of the Other – specifically, miscegenation – and by analogy thereby insist on the necessity of the Other's annihilation. The cultural horror of miscegenation, which has a particularly prominent history in the United States as a consequence of slavery – the slave-owner's sexual abuse of his female slaves which in time led to the birth of children who 'looked' white but were 'officially' black – is above all a function of the image, the horror occasioned by the image's trickery, its fooling of the senses.[107] (There is, of course, an inverse to this horror in the cinema, in which white actors play the roles of Indians and Blacks – an inversion which only strengthens the sense of the image's unreliability). In *The Iron Horse* the threatened miscegenation, which adds import to the romantic sub-plot, is prevented when the white heroine's fiancé, Deroux, is revealed as a half-breed Cheyenne masquerading as White and immediately killed. The horror is a consequence of the prospect of savagery – primitive, animalistic sexuality – about to 'become one' with civilisation – the pure white woman – *without one being able to readily distinguish* (and therefore prevent) it. That is, the Indian as claimant to the 'human' privileges of the pioneers is revealed as duplicitous, rapacious, contaminatory – and therefore the denial of his access to human status and his elimination is affectively justified. The founding and consolidation of the American nation based on its expropriation of Indian land is therefore displaced on to a sexual problem in which the projected spectacle of white woman mating with little more than a beast produces the kind of unequivocal response which the question of land theft could not so easily generate.[108]

The myth of the Western encounter between 'savagery' and 'civilisation' is also represented in highly charged sexual terms in Ford's later, and perhaps most famous, Western, *The Searchers* (1956), in which John Wayne plays a character named Ethan Edwards, the movie's hero, who although he eventuates as more 'savage' than his main Indian enemy, Scar (played by blue-eyed, non-Indian Henry Brandon), is ultimately the hero of civilisation as a consequence of the rescue of his niece, Debbie (Natalie Wood), from her life as Scar's wife. To the extent that women function in this movie completely overtly as objects of exchange between men – paradigmatically, Debbie as mediator for the Edwards–Scar relationship – and as a consequence of the fact that the opening sequences are shot from the woman's point of view, the viewing subject (the cinema audience) is thus also positioned spectatorially 'between men' – between, that is, the poles of savagery and civilisation.[109] The whole dialectic of the spectacle occurs within this subjective space and inevitably produces via the cinematic code a subjective commitment not only to the representative of civilisation, but more importantly, to the *content* of the category of the 'civilised'. In being constructed by the apparatus as spectator – spectatorship as a subjective possibility manufactured as synonymous with civilisation – one's subjective allegiances are enlisted for every act committed under the rubric of the civilised, no matter how savage.[110] The alternative viewing position (dependent upon a recognition that the deeds of civilisation are unconscionably savage) entails eventual identification not only with the Indian but also with the sexual barbarity with which the Indian comes to be associated from the start of the film. Spectatorship is thus presented very much as an 'either/or' condition since the identities of the civilised and the savage are so close that no middle ground or alternative option exists. The audience positioning is thus doubly a case of 'beween men', for the space of between is constructed as impossible for occupancy: hence the imperative of *choice* – choosing between the two men, Edwards and Scar, as Debbie must do at the film's climactic conclusion.

The Searchers opens with a shot of Monument Valley framed by the silhouette of the farmstead and angled from the domestic point of view of the woman, who stands on her porch and looks out across the desolate valley with the camera poised behind her back. We thus view savagery from the point of view of an island of civilisation, looking with – and at – the woman gazing. From the wilderness of the West rides the Western hero, Wayne, moving alone from the domain of the savage with which he is intimate into the realm of the civilised: the farmstead is his brother's and the woman, Martha, his sister-in-law. The film closes with a similar sequence in reverse: Wayne riding out of the wilderness toward the homestead, shot by the camera approaching the civilised from civilisation's point of view; he deposits the woman on the porch and then rides off into the sunset, framed by the doorway of the farmhouse. This pattern represents the classic Western paradigm by which the hero enters the realm of what we can know and see at the film's beginning and exits in reverse style at the film's close. The doorway as frame for these sequences operates doubly metaphorically – first, architectural doorframe functioning as celluloid shot-frame; secondly and following this first, operating by its archaic function as threshold or beginning, meeting point of distinct geographies, the boundary marking off civilisation from savagery – precisely, the frontier. Therefore, opening the film with woman in doorway indicates that the film will take place within the space of the frontier, with all the mythic dichotomies which structure that space. More significantly, aligning the viewer with the woman in doorway means that the spectatorial subject is constructed from the outset as one hovering between civilisation and savagery, a point of uneasy oscillation which will require resolution by commitment to one side or the other. As I have suggested, the film constructs no other option for the spectator than to commit to the 'civilised', and the narrative of its mythic 'work' – the cinematic work of the Western itself – consists of nothing other than the projection of this ideological commitment for its viewing subject. The 'choice' between men, between the civilised and the savage, is not 'ours', for the film makes it on our behalf; to be subject of its cinematic gaze is to be subject *to* that gaze and hence to be in the process of making that choice, that American commitment.

Thus Martha gazing, Wayne arriving, and the following day another emissary from the realm of the savage: the farmstead is attacked by Comanche Indians, the building razed in Wayne's temporary absence, and the woman sexually violated prior to her murder. This we learn but do not see. What we see is from the point of view of the women – Martha and her two daughters, Lucy and Debbie – in the farmstead on the fateful evening: their growing sense of unease, their alarm when an Indian owl-sound is heard – the language of the savage which is legible as language yet barely translatable; the translation of that sound into Lucy's hysterical scream when she realises her mother's unspoken fear; the growing sense of helplessness and vulnerability; the hustling out of Debbie, the smaller child, to hide in the family graveplot yards away from the house, with her blanket and the doll she refuses to leave behind, delaying agonisingly; then, from Debbie's anxious but uncomprehending viewpoint, the shadow which overtakes her as she ineffectually tries to hide, the silent pan up to the head and torso of Scar – man as beast. The cinematic effect of this sequence depends upon the development of suspense by which nothing is seen or heard, nothing sighted or directly spoken – the growing sense that what is imminent is horrible beyond language or representation. The Indian is thus initially Other by being barely accessible to conscious apprehension, savage beyond human thought: he can only be seen from the point of view of childhood innocence – and from the point of view of Hollywood stereotype, with painted face, feathers in his hair and next to no clothing.

He is, however, notably handsome, with blue eyes and the look of a Hollywood star, evidencing the kind of primal masculinity depicted today by the heroes of many popular romances. I mention this in order to note not simply Hollywood conventions of using handsome actors and of using Whites to play Indians, but also to indicate that *The Searchers* allows a measure of attraction to the savage for its viewing subject. If the savage were utterly repellent from the start, the cinematic narrative would lose much of its force, its 'work' would be easier, its subject pre-constructed rather than requisite of enlistment. Allowing the savage some lure also allows for the potential conversion of Wayne's savagery into attractive masculine heroics – something posited as essentially masculine for the Western man: it may seem a little rough at first, ladies, but it's what makes real men, and it was with real men that the West – and America – was won. The familiarity of this line indicates the importance of the American West for the construction of American masculinity. Thus, via the Western, masculine dominance can be seen to be closely related to national political dominance – because as Jane Tompkins argues in a useful essay, 'The fact that the seventy-five-year period during which Westerns flourished coincides with America's dominance as a world power suggests that the genre is intimately tied to the country's sense of itself, both politically and psychologically.'[111]

Savagery may be allowed sexual allure, but the prospect of indulging that allure, of surrendering sexually to the savage – the prospect, that is, of miscegenation, framed (as in *The Iron Horse*) as white woman and Indian man – is what sets the narrative in motion: having discovered his sister-in-law not only dead but sexually violated too, Wayne sets off on his search for his nieces and for revenge. The civilisation/savagery opposition about which the filmic subject will ultimately have to decide is thus complicated by being presented as inseparable from not only racial questions (White versus Red) but also sexual questions, sexual questions having to do with masculine anxieties about feminine purity and contamination, masculine potency and possession, and the mediating function of women between men. To elaborate: the pioneer hero is definitively a man without women, a man pitted against other men, whose masculinity – defined in terms of *physicality* – is always at stake. The price of rarefied masculinity is uncertainty regarding what one's women may be up to, whether or not they might be succumbing back on the range to the lures of the exaggerated version of civilised masculinity which is nothing other than savagery, the Western hero's evil twin. Specifically, in *The Searchers*, it is hinted that Wayne had harboured an illicit desire for Martha, his brother's wife; it may have been the case that Martha married the brother because Wayne as hero was always off riding the West. As such, Wayne's masculinity, although enhanced by Western solitude and physical achievement, is compromised by not getting the woman. Martha may ultimately function as little more than mediator of desire between brothers, and so her violation by Indians – a further instance of Wayne's impotence and failure of possession – becomes the feature of displacement by which her daughter's violation, realised as miscegenation, motivates Wayne. Debbie takes her mother's place in the Western hero's masculine psychic economy, and Scar takes the brother's place, this time as overt sexual rival for the White woman. In this way, Scar becomes Wayne's double in the film, so that the civilisation/savagery opposition flirts dangerously close to simple mirror reversibility. Figuring the question of civilisation versus savagery in highly charged sexual terms converts and elevates the stakes, so that it is not only the categories of gender which are at stake, but the very boundaries – incest, miscegenation, rape – which legislate the sexual in order to secure it are also at stake. And within this configuration, the difference which charges both the sexual and the frontier dichotomies is the racial question, the irremediable alterity of the Indian that makes difference too different, makes it undesirable.

The sexualisation of this paradigmatically racial question is weighted by the camera, which is to say that just as White destruction of Indians is shown in frame while Indian attacks on Whites remain consistently off-frame, so the question of miscegenation between White man and Indian woman is treated not as a source of horror but as an occasion for comedy. Thus when Martin Pawley, Edwards's search companion, accidentally buys an Indian wife, the prospect of their relationship together is source of much mirth for Wayne: the spectacle – uncomprehending woman eagerly following the men, Pawley embarrassed, Wayne guffawing. The disjunction between Pawley's expectation – he is trying hard to be a serious, single-minded, 'man's man', worthy of Wayne's companionship – and what his ignorance of Indian culture eventuates is offered as the source of the scene's comedy for its spectator; but behind the mirth is the myth generative of the more profound disjunction: that contrast between the sanctioned attitude toward miscegenation of White man and Indian woman as opposed to Indian man and White woman, the latter of which only death can sanction.

For it is the primitive code of revenge – death for death – according to which the Edwards character operates: the crimes of sexual violation, murder and miscegenation require the death of both Scar and Debbie. Edwards's failure to kill Debbie at the movie's close is accountable by the long exchange of looks between them, from which the resemblance of Debbie to Wayne's old sweetheart can be registered. It is thus significant that by this penultimate scene the spectatorial subject is viewing from Wayne's point of view – we register the resemblance, and with it the memory of desire, as Wayne registers it: the 'work' of the movie is over when the viewing subject identifies with Wayne – not in spite, but *because*, of what he has done.

The engineering of this identification is indeed 'work', because in the early part of the movie it starts to look as if Wayne is of the realm of the savage rather than the civilised: he disrupts the social rituals of funeral and marriage by which the White community sustains itself; he knows – and violates – the codes of Indian culture too by shooting out the eyes of an unburied Comanche, thereby consigning him to eternal wandering between this world and the spirit world (according to Indian belief); he disregards the ties of Indian marriage by separating Debbie from her life as Scar's wife (a life in which she appears to be happy). Not only does he seem more savage than savagery in his disruption of civilised ceremonies and social forms, but he also resembles the Indian via his knowledge of the landscape and of Indian customs and culture. He is thus able to think like an Indian, and small details like the fringe of his rifle make him look like an Indian: his oscillation between the poles of what counts as civilised and what counts as savage produce the film's interest and several consequences, not the least of which is the perception that civilised and savage are less different than one might originally have thought. For instance, when Edwards and Scar finally meet, after years of Edwards's dogged searching, the confrontation is represented by an exchange of over-the-shoulder shots which is rare at this point in the generic development of the Western, since it encourages a measure of identification with the Indian's point of view. The point, however, is not, as Schatz implies, to produce audience sympathy for the Indian viewpoint, but rather to secure *despite* a modicum of attraction to the Indian the ultimate identification with Wayne and what he represents. Thus although the illusion of a temporary perception from the Indian viewpoint is allowed, and although we clearly see that Debbie has been seeing things from Scar's point of view for years (the echo of an anonymous warning from one outpost along the way of the search that White women kidnapped by Indians as children grow up as if they were Indian and cannot therefore be saved), such commitments to the side of the savage make the ultimate commitment to the side of the civilised all the more effective: recognising the *cost* of civilisation – the savage destruction of a culture that seems at points not so bad – and yet aligning oneself with civilisation despite that cost constitutes the securing of the dominance of the civilised. The inexorable logic in which savagery is ultimately annihilated (even though savagery may temporarily dominate by annihilating islands of civilisation in the wilderness) means that to commit to savagery is to commit suicide, to privilege the death drive over civilised life. As Tompkins notes, 'To go west, to go as far west as you can go, west of everything, is to die.'[112] The price of Western civilisation's establishment is thus revealed as the most savage of all: the old choice between killing or being killed. Debbie makes that choice at the movie's close, and the difficulty of her choice means the commitment she makes is all the more binding. The Western announces that America is founded upon the difficult necessity of such a commitment: the price is high, but will always be paid.

If the comparative exposure of the Western's ultimatum seems a little too harsh, then a movie like *The Man Who Shot Liberty Valance* (1962) secures the myth in a different and even more subtle way by claiming to completely expose it: the myth of this later Ford classic is precisely the demystification of myth. This film evidences an enlarged self-consciousness about narrativity and hence presents itself as metacommentary on the Western myth: 'This is the West, Sir. When the legend becomes fact, print the legend', urges a minor character at the movie's close. The myth is that myth's exposure necessarily undoes that myth: metamyth is thus myth revitalised, for ideology does not have to be either unconscious, static or free of contradictions to achieve its ends.

By 1962 the United States no longer holds political world

dominance as it once did, and its myth about itself as represented by the Western therefore requires modification. The end of an era, the kind of era depicted and constructed by *The Searchers*, is registered at the opening of *Liberty Valance* by the death of the classic Western hero, Tom Doniphon, played by none other than John Wayne. This 'end' which begins the movie – the whole narrative space of which obtains the dimension of nostalgia by being shot as an extended flashback (a relatively rare narrative device in the Western) – is also signalled by the villain's name: Liberty Valance (played by Lee Marvin) can be decoded as a reference to the frontier itself, defined as 'free land', land at *liberty*, which is on the fringe, or *valance*, of territory claimed by civilisation. Having Liberty Valance as the film's villain suggests that traditional frontier values have been historically outmoded: the 'law of the hired gun' which Valance and Wayne represent has been replaced by the civilised law of community as represented by Ransom Stoddard (James Stewart), the timid lawyer who is the new, unassertive hero. Stewart's substitution for Wayne, which also obtains a sexual dimension in the movie's romantic subplot, relies on narrative sophistication in the form of cinematic intertextuality: Wayne's coffin as the focus of the opening sequence's attention stands for the death of the Western genre as it was known – both Wayne and the genre for which he stood have gone as far West as they can go. Yet despite the acknowledgement that a new code prevails in the West, that the West and the Western (and by extension the United States) are not what they were, the film as flashback disavows this recognition and fantasises its own past, nostalgically lingering over 'the good old days'. In this way, the Western 'law of the hired gun' is subtly revalorised and retained. To achieve mutually contradictory aims constitutes the film's ideological success and represents a measure of the ideological *power* of the cinema, the structure of disavowal by which the Imaginary characteristically operates (we know the West is not really that way any more, but let's pretend that it is). The effects of such fantasy are not limited to the movie auditorium, for Reaganite politics operate by the logic of a similar nostalgic fantasy (which is what I mean by saying that the cinema precipitates a real, that fantasy is not without its political effects).

The achievement of this ideological contradiction – ideology as precisely the erasure of contradiction – is above all a *cinematic* achievement, a function of the possibilities of the frame (what the camera selects to represent and what it refuses to show) and of cinematic narrative (how it orders what it shows). Thus the film begins with the arrival of Stoddard and his wife by train for Doniphon's funeral: the new hero enters the small Western town by train rather than horseback – the railroad as the emblem of civilisation's progress – and leaves by train at the movie's close, replicating the classic Western opening and closure with the substitutive difference being not only that of the railway's replacement of the horse (and the visual signs accompanying such a change – different attire for the hero), but also the direction from which the hero arrives. Stoddard emerges not from the realm of the wilderness, the domain of savagery, but from a larger town, the state capital, and he appears not as a solitary figure but with his wife, the masculine tie to the domestic. In ideological and temporal terms, his movement is thus not forward (from savagery to civilisation, as is Wayne's in *The Searchers*), but backward, away from the emergent form of social organisation – the city – back to the small-town America of the nineteenth century. The narrative of nostalgia thus leaves it unclear whether 'forward' remains synonymous with Progress or whether the nineteenth-century teleological model of Manifest Destiny might not have gone into reverse as a consequence of subsequent political developments.

At Doniphon's coffin, the question of his legacy – which can be understood as nothing less than the Western's legacy, the legacy of the West itself – prompts the flashback that narrates the answer to the question, 'Who shot Liberty Valance?'. The question is itself interpretable as 'What ended frontier days?', and the ambivalence of the film, its self-contradiction, depends upon the different resonances that accrue to the larger question of the frontier's supersession. Liberty Valance had been the embodiment of the threat of savagery to civilisation, the 'law of the hired gun' gone wild. Valance is Edwards of *The Searchers* trespassing the boundary which divides civilised from savage, the example of how the masculine law of 'kill or be killed' which supposedly 'won the West' becomes outmoded when it threatens to institute a new brand of savagery all its own, compromising the civilisation it is supposed to secure. The spectacle presents the image of the classic shootout between Valance and the inexperienced Stoddard, in which the law of order triumphs over the law of the wild. Stoddard shoots Valance to his own and everybody else's amazement, and is thus able to institute more effectively the legal codes of civilisation.

That is, the lawyer replaces the cowboy and is able to legislate the social, substituting for the materiality of the bullet the abstraction of symbolic law.

However, this is not as easily effected as it appears: so much depends upon the myth of the West that it is not to be outmoded so readily (in the larger ideological sense, the whole paraphernalia of American political identity and American gender identities are at stake). Thus a subsequent expansion of frame reveals Wayne in the picture, and as the fatal shootout is re-enacted (a flashback within a flashback), we see Wayne's bullet kill Valance, rather than Stoddard's. The frame is composed so that Stoddard occupies centre-left of frame, facing Valance; when the frame deepens, extending vertically downward, Wayne is revealed at bottom-left of frame, *supporting* Stoddard. Wayne is thus a supporting character in every sense, and the re-enactment – itself a metaphor for the culture's replaying of its own Western myth, the revision in fantasy of the national myth – reminds the American subject of what it wants to hear, which is that the West, America, is indeed founded on the Western hero one knows and loves (Wayne as the embodiment of that hero), despite appearances to the contrary.

This fantasy is then itself subject to revision by a further expansion of frame which encloses the flashback narrative within the filmic narrative, thus reminding the audience that the long flashback was itself merely a product of mind, an elaborated fiction. Just as the image is revised to show Wayne as original hero, so it is revised to show Stoddard as new hero, thereby calling attention by narrative dexterity to the fictional dimension of the Western, its status as myth. The final revelation – that the narrative has been just a recollection – thus makes a claim for legitimacy exceeding myth; it claims, that is, itself and its exposure as narrative truth. As Stoddard and his wife make their return journey by train, the train porter refers to Stoddard as 'the man who shot Liberty Valance', thereby revealing the persistence of the Western myth, and confirming the truth-value of the earlier utterance, 'This is the West, Sir. When the legend becomes fact, print the legend.' These utterances combine to produce the illusion of demystification: we know who really shot Liberty Valance and therefore we also know that the West is a place devoted to myth and legend, that, indeed, the Western is the American mythic genre *par excellence*. This cinematic knowledge is offered to us as truth beyond myth; yet that 'truth' depends upon the image of

Wayne as the man who shot Liberty Valance. That is, this new truth has recourse to the oldest Western myth upheld by *The Searchers* – a sense which is compounded by the closing nostalgic remark of Stoddard's wife, Halle (Vera Miles), who gazes at the passing landscape and says, 'It was once a wilderness; now it's a garden.' The transformation of the West from mythic wilderness (where civilisation confronts savagery) into mythic garden (Edenic haven of civilisation where murder is outside the law) simply depends upon the metamorphosis of one myth into another, a transformation that is subtly revealed to have reference to Wayne and the old law as its predicate by the image of the cactus plants blooming in the desert which prompts Halle's remark (her tone is audible as nostalgic precisely by recalling that the cacti upon which she gazes are bigger versions of a smaller potted cactus once given her by Wayne when he was her suitor). The hint of submerged love for the old hero suggests that although the old law has been superseded, it was not outmoded by *but actually produced* the new law: the old heroics of Western myth are thus carefully reinscribed by the film as *indispensable* predicate of Western life, a reinscription which achieves its powerful appeal to credibility by existing concomitantly with the sense that the myth has been exposed. It is in this sense that the Western myth of *The Man Who Shot Liberty Valance* conforms to the notion of myth as metalanguage described by Roland Barthes: for Barthes, myth as metalanguage consists of a discourse which claims separation from and objective privilege over the phenomena it distorts.[113] By providing the cinematic appearance of a metalanguage able to comment on the Western potential for mythification, *Liberty Valance* utilises cinematic technique to produce a far more sophisticated myth of the West, one whose mythic power depends upon its looking like narrative truth. It is therefore in the cinema that the formation of an American unconscious as the support for an American *image* of nation in the twentieth century has been centrally operative.

AMERICAN WESTERNISM

The dependence of the nation upon images of the West became apparent, as Richard Slotkin has lately demonstrated, in the political policies and rhetoric of Vietnam. Slotkin begins a recent article by asserting that 'Myth is the primary language of historical memory',[114] and argues (as I am doing) that when the American nation comes under threat – when, that is, the concept of the national is at stake – the characteristic rhetorical recourse is to the West of cowboys and Indians, the cinematic West which the United States is perpetually 'winning' at the movies. The West becomes synonymous with the act and concept of winning itself, and therefore can be invoked in defence against the scandal of Vietnam. Snyder himself linked the image of the Indian with the war in Vietnam in his essay of the late 1960s, 'Passage to More than India': 'The American Indian is the vengeful ghost lurking in the back of the troubled American mind. Which is why we lash out with such ferocity and passion, so muddied a heart, at the black-haired young peasants and soldiers who are the "Viet Cong"' (*EHH*, p. 112). As Snyder's metaphors of the national psyche suggest, the defeat in Vietnam constituted a significant national 'return of the repressed'.[115] The image of the Indian as Noble Savage could then be appropriated to stand protest against the inhumane actions being perpetrated upon the Vietnamese, which is the allegorical function of the Indian in, for instance, Arthur Penn's movie *Little Big Man* (1970), although the tradition of having white Hollywood stars play Indian parts continued, representing an appropriation supplemental to the cinematic appropriation of the Indian image as such. The filmic protest against the abuse of the Vietnamese – an abuse which was partly *symbolically* motivated on the United States' behalf – thus finds a disturbing analogue in the film itself, in which the Indian is appropriated and 'used' by the film for its own symbolic purposes.

The foundation of the nation based on its historical exploits in the West was invoked in other ways in the 1960s as a rhetorical strategy designed to secure the political basis of the national identity. For instance, J. F. Kennedy famously invoked 'the new frontier' in his Inaugural Address of 1961 to herald an era of renewed American expansion, both economic and imperial. Poetic discourse on the frontier was enlisted at the same event in order to add cultural sanction to both the Presidential figure (Kennedy as an intellectual) and to the maintenance of the American national plan – expansionism as an updated version of Manifest Destiny. When Robert Frost read 'The Gift Outright' at Kennedy's inauguration, poetry became indistinguishable from political discourse on the level of content if not on the level of form. (The success of Frost's reading on that occasion can be measured by his subsequent appointment by Kennedy as ambassador to the Soviet Union.) Frost's delivery of 'The Gift Outright' (first published 1942) was prefaced by 'For John F. Kennedy: His Inauguration' – made in rhyming couplets for the occasion – which is not only a weak poem but is replete with the various dimensions of nationalist sentiment I have been describing.[116] Hence the depiction of American history as an unblemished narrative:

> Some poor fool has been saying in his heart
> Glory is out of date in life and art.
> Our venture in revolution and outlawry
> Has justified itself in freedom's story
> Right down to now in glory upon glory.

The past is idealised and made continuous with an immaculate present. But the transparent weakness of Frost's 'preliminary history in rhyme' need not detain us; instead I reproduce here the text of 'The Gift Outright'.

> The land was ours before we were the land's.
> She was our land more than a hundred years
> Before we were her people. She was ours
> In Massachusetts, in Virginia,
> But we were England's, still colonials,
> Possessing what we still were unpossessed by,
> Possessed by what we now no more possessed.
> Something we were withholding made us weak
> Until we found out that it was ourselves
> We were withholding from our land of living,
> And forthwith found salvation in surrender.
> Such as we were we gave ourselves outright
> (The deed of gift was many deeds of war)
> To the land vaguely realizing westward,
> But still unstoried, artless, unenhanced,
> Such as she was, such as she would become.

Frost is still the national poet (despite the initial appointment of Robert Penn Warren to the recently opened position of American Poet Laureate), although I do not know if 'The Gift Outright' is taught in American high schools with the pedagogical fervour accorded 'Stopping by Woods on a Snowy Evening', or if and when it is taught, to what extent its virulent nationalism is naturalised or questioned. Although the poem's title suggests an unconditional gift, the American relation to the land is clearly revealed to be one based on possession, possession contested not between Whites and Indians but between Americans and the land itself, which is characteristically gendered female. Since Americans possessed the land before 'she' possessed them, the land cannot be said to be figured as Mother Earth, just as England is not figured as the colonial Mother country. The sibilant repetition of forms of 'possessed' generates a slightly sinister impression of supernatural possession, as if the people had to surrender their souls to the land in order to become its people properly. The relationship may be supernatural, but it is resolutely secular (unlike the nationalist diction of 'For John F. Kennedy', which invokes traditional divine sanction for the political experiment), such that the religion becomes nothing other than democracy itself: the people alliteratively save themselves (a highly appealing American notion) – 'And forthwith found salvation in surrender'.

The parenthetical admission that 'The deed of gift was many deeds of war' is interpretable, however, as an acknowledgement that more than surrender to the land was at stake: the many wars were the Indian wars, the massacres (not just revolution against the English Crown); and the semantic shift from 'deed' as legal term settling land ownership to 'deeds' as acts, specifically violent acts, indicates that American entitlement to the land was a function not of 'surrender' but of victory over a dispossessed people. America legitimates itself as such on the deeds of violence; to characterise such a process as a 'gift' testifies to the ideological effect of Americanist rhetoric, for the gift outright consists of nothing other than stolen property.

Inseparable from this myth of the gift is the Turnerian myth of 'free land', land represented here as 'vaguely realizing westward' because the concrete particulars upon which the nation is formed are inadmissible to national consciousness: knowledge of the land is 'vague' so that geography can safely be imaged as virgin, untextualised – 'still unstoried, artless, unenhanced', 'artless' connoting innocence and unsophistication (the uncivilised) as well as the dearth of culture. Just like the Indian, who is described in terms of his lack of white says, so here the land is figured – by the negative prefixes and suffix ('un', 'less') – as deficient, as a continent awaiting its landscape. The caesurae of the concluding lines lengthen the cadence, slowing the rhythm to the measured grandeur of the national process, the future infinitive: 'But still unstoried, artless, unenhanced, / Such as she was, such as she would become.'

The poem encompasses the nationalising movement itself by beginning at the colonial beginning and ending with a gesture toward the future, thereby poetically 'storying' America as a process still unfolding, one in which all American people properly participate (including poets). As one historian put it with reference to the Turner thesis later in the 1960s, 'Turner's greatest practical achievement may well be that he made every community feel it had contributed to the shaping of American democracy, for the thesis brilliantly related the average man and his past to national history and the national character.'[117] One is not born American, one is made American by occupying a standard subjective position *vis-à-vis* the social, a position designated individualist and productive of the illusion that one is master of one's destiny, just as the United States is – or should be – political master of its continent and the international field. Individualism thus denies or minimises the social in the same way that the national political identity denies or minimises its geographical predicate and its international interdependence. The paradox of the American subject is thus that it is at once subject of an unfolding, glorious history named the national (which indeed it has helped produce), while also being subject of itself as sovereign, socially independent.

2

The Real Work: Inhabiting the Ground

There is work to be done in the matter of knowing where we are, the old American quest, which I share with all of you, for an identity, a sense of place. (OW, p. 79)

From the discussion of 'the American unconscious', it should be evident that the modernist dictum 'Make it new' constitutes not only a methodological imperative for poetic technique but also an ideological imperative upon which American culture is founded. Since 'Make it new' has been the imperative all along for American literature too, the question of how an American poet begins a poetic career, how s/he finds a new voice, thus becomes considerably overdetermined – and, as a consequence of this difficulty of beginning, becomes a matter of great interest.

For Harold Bloom, the question of beginning – or poetic priority – represents *the* question of modern poetry (ever since Wordsworth).[1] In Bloom's terms, the modern poet necessarily experiences a sense of belatedness, a sense that the poetic field is overcrowded and that all the best poems have already been written: the new poet thus has to clear a space for himself by repressing his knowledge of poetic precursors via an Oedipal struggle with poetic 'fathers' (as in the classic Freudian model). Noting the overt masculinist bias of Bloom's model of poetic influence opens the possibility of alternative models of poetic inception, the principal labour of discovering which has been undertaken by feminist critics, particularly Black feminists. Thus Alice Walker, for example, has used as a metaphor for the Black woman writer's sense of an *empty* poetic field (the tangible *absence* of precursors) her own search for her mother's unmarked grave: 'In search of our mothers' gardens' thus becomes the sign by which writers whose tradition has been suppressed seek to reconstruct that tradition as a source of inspiration for their writing today.[2]

This development – by poets or critics – of alternative literary traditions (White versus Black, male versus female) means, however, that writers who 'fit' neither tradition continue to be excluded from consideration. Thus although Snyder's poetry has been classified as part of the Beat movement of the 1950s and 1960s, or as part of a Pound–Williams objectist tradition, or as part of the tradition of American Romanticism, or as central to ethnopoetics, his work significantly exceeds these stereotypes and therefore does not easily fit into any pre-established literary tradition (including Bloom's American lineage).[3] Literary criticism seems unable to think without its developmental notion of tradition (or literary history), but when we consider carefully the work of a poet like Snyder which does not fall readily into preconceived categories, we may be able to modify the models of tradition – or even the notion of tradition itself. (This, it seems to me, is what the best feminist literary criticism achieves: not just the generation of a supplement to the canon or an 'alternative' women's tradition, but a radical reconception of the very concept of literary history itself – a challenge to what counts as the literary and what counts as history.) By arguing for Snyder's central significance for American literature, the tradition of that literature is necessarily revised. I therefore begin this part of the book by examining Snyder's poetic beginning in the 1950s and 1960s, focusing on his first two remarkable books, *Riprap* (1959) and *Myths & Texts* (1960) – not the least remarkable thing about which is the great difference of one from the other.

RIPRAP

The man pictured on the cover of Snyder's first book of verse, *Riprap*, does not look like a poet, or even a literary man of any kind (Plate 2). Yet the book, when it was reissued in 1965 with added translations by Snyder of ancient Chinese poems, advertised itself explicitly as poetry: its title, *Riprap & Cold Mountain Poems*. I am reminded here of a first volume published by an American poet just over a century earlier, probably the single most important volume of poetry published in the United States in the nineteenth century. I am referring, of course, to Walt Whitman's first edition of *Leaves of Grass*, about which, when it first appeared, the reading public was not even sure whether or not it constituted poetry as such.

Unlike the standard daguerreotypes of literary men of the nineteenth century – portraits such as those of Emerson or the members of the long-running Bostonian Saturday Club, which showed dignified men formally dressed and usually seated[4] – Whitman places a highly unconventional image of himself opposite his book's title page (Plate 3). The figure is shown from around the knees upward, slouching rather than standing, his right hand on his hip, his head cocked almost defiantly to one side. The man is not dressed in a respectable suit of the kind sophisticated Boston literary men wore; instead, he wears a working shirt open at the neck and has a hat perched on his head: he appears as a labourer or a man of the street – precisely, a man of the people. His book has a common title – what could be more prosaic than grass? – and it even goes so far as to suggest that the book is something organic, hardly a literary product at all: one is not holding leaves of a book, but leaves of grass (this is an outdoors kind of author, not a library man). There is indeed no name on the title-page, no claim to authorship, just the odd title, *Leaves of Grass*, and the place and date of publication: 'Brooklyn, New York: 1855' (this is not a book made in Boston). Substituting a body for a proper name, the immediacy conveyed by photography over the mediacy of symbolic appellation (proper name as Law, of the Symbolic, precisely what gives the Author authority), adds to the desired impression of unliterary, non-Symbolic, untutored presence: we are presented here with a man rather than with an artefact of civilisation.

It is to be assumed that the rough-looking character on the facing page made the book, but it is only when the reader has negotiated no less than five hundred lines of the strange book that one is offered a name:

Walt Whitman, an American, one of the roughs, a kosmos,
Disorderly fleshy and sensual . . . eating drinking and breeding,
No sentimentalist . . . no stander above men and women or apart
   from them . . . no more modest than immodest.

Not Mr Whitman, Author, or even Walter Whitman, but Walt, familiar, informal – 'one of the roughs', as he would have us believe; but first and above all 'an American'. Disorderly, yes: the absence of poetic meter and rhyme – the conventions which make poetry recognisable – apparently testify to that; and yes, one can imagine the rude character pictured doing the bodily things he proposes, just as well as – better even – than one can imagine him as a poet. Unless, that is, poetry has come to mean something new – a new kind of lyricism appropriate to a new land, a different society.

This is poetic democracy (one does not have to have read the Classics to read Walt Whitman), and it is Whitman representing himself as the democratic poet, the American poet. Whitman's artifice worked and continues to work – hence Gary Snyder in 1964: 'Whitman is the *American* poet'.[5] Whitman's artifice depends upon representing itself as precisely the *absence* of artifice, as natural: just a regular guy speaking to and for the people, speaking without meter or rhyme or allusion, without stanzaic forms, without even titles separating his poetic utterances in the first edition. The illusion is thus that one is not holding a book and reading poetry but that one is touching a man and being addressed with the immediacy obtained by speech as full presence. The effort, which appears as effortless, is to speak naturally, directly, as American people speak, without correct punctuation, with a specific idiom, and with poetic discourse functioning all-inclusively, excluding no objects as unacceptable for the field of the poetic – functioning analogously, that is, to the American socio-political ideals of equality and democracy. Whitman's experiment brought something absolutely new to poetry; it made poetry modern somewhat before its time, and it exists as an innovation of the kind that would enable Gertrude Stein (another literary innovator as radical as Whitman) to declare that America must be the oldest country in the world because it had started on the twentieth century long before anybody else had. Stein was correct, of course; and it was not only moderns like herself and Picasso who had irrevocably precipitated America into the modern and the new, but it was also the Whitman of 1855.

I produce this brief analysis in order to point to both Snyder's comparable representational innovation and also – inevitably and paradoxically – the tradition of which that self-representational strategy is a part. The man pictured on the front of *Riprap & Cold Mountain Poems* is a little younger than the one pictured on the first page of *Leaves of Grass*, but this man is bearded too and looks like a working man. He is not wearing a suit, shirt and tie, as a Mr Eliot, a Mr Stevens or a Dr Williams would be pictured wearing; he is not even shown in 'bust' head-and-shoulders form like a Mr Pound; rather, he is shown in full, crouching on his haunches, possibly in the mode in which an Indian would position himself at leisure.[6] He is crouching in a field, no less, in front of a barbed-wire fence, and he is clad in the kind of garb one would expect a man in a field to be wearing: an old sweatshirt, jeans and a fringed, patterned-weave waistcoat, which also looks Indian. This man looks like a man of action, the outdoors-type, a man who would have some idea of what to do in a field or on a mountain (what can one imagine Mr Eliot doing in a field?).

Indeed, facing the title-page is another photograph, somewhat out of focus, showing the man on a mountain – or more precisely, showing him lounging in the doorway of a mountain lookout station: 'Sourdough Mountain Lookout, Summer 1953', the legend beneath the photograph reads. The man is not posing as a mountain lookout, he *is* a mountain lookout (Plate 4). But neither is he posing as a poet: as in Whitman, there is every effort to eschew the literary, to avoid artifice and speak naturally. Of course, the two photographs introducing the new poet to us are devices calculated to have a specific effect, and are therefore in that sense completely artificial, rhetorical. However, as in Whitman, the effect required is that of no effort, no literary straining or learning (there are no literary epigraphs in any language, classical or otherwise): the man is presenting himself as natural man, man in Nature *working* (not man in Nature meditating on himself as a transparent eyeball or as the centre of natural relations). Because there is the sense of work being performed – physical, not intellectual or poetic, work – there is not a lot of transcending going on: this is not a man who would set up a Brook Farm without knowing what he was doing regarding the tending of plants and animals, not a man unused to getting a little soiled. Thus the book is not dedicated to those parties to whom books are usually dedicated – the parents, the beloved, the mentor; instead 'This book is dedicated to' – and hence follows a list of masculine names, including what look like nicknames (Speed McInturff, Blackie Burns, Spud Murphy and Crazy Horse Mason – the latter sounding like an Indian name) – 'In the woods & at sea'. Dedicated to comrades in physical labour, the book appears as the product of 'one of the roughs'.

As if cued by the frontispiece photograph of the man in his lookout cabin, the opening poem is entitled 'Mid-August at Sourdough Mountain Lookout'. And 'cue', a figure drawn from the discourse of the theatre or the cinema, is indeed the appropriate term, not only for its connotation of direction – the image as preparatory for the word – but also because both photographic

images function conditionally, predicatively: the frontispiece operates like a filmic establishing shot, setting the scene of viewer in
lookout whose range of gaze the first poem will then survey. The
photograph of the man in the lookout doorway is shot from a low
angle: we are looking up at him from below. The book's first poem
is 'shot' from above, gazing down from the lookout, and the initial
absence of any speaker (no first-person pronoun 'I') means that the
man is out of frame because the shot is from his point of view. The
photograph is thus not merely illustrative, it is indeed part of the
poem's composition, although as framing device it obtains the
curious status peculiar to any frame, being both inside and outside
the text at the same time.[7] But there is more to the image and the
poem than this relation, since the image frames the man in at least
two ways: as a bounded visual space within whose field he is
represented, and via reference to his positioning with the terms of
the image – standing in a doorframe. As we deduced about the
figure of Martha (in Ford's *The Searchers*; see pp. 69–70) standing in
the wooden-frame doorway gazing out on to the landscape at the
beginning of that cinematic narrative, such a positioning represents a traditional beginning (Janus as the classical deity of
doorways and beginnings), but also a beginning as a boundary, the
space of between (between civilisation and savagery literalised by
positioning between two men in Martha's case). I would suggest
that this framing has a triple significance with respect to Snyder's
first book.

First, it simply represents a beginning, the location of the
speaker in a space from which a narrative will proceed – be that the
narrative of a poetic career, the emergence of a new lyric voice or
the narrative of a man in the mountains, an American kind of
Western narrative. Secondly, as a consequence of the fact that,
unlike the establishing shot of *The Searchers*, we are not looking
'with' the woman – that is, although we are looking at the man
looking we do not have the same objects in view as we would were
the camera stationed behind him – and so our readerly identification is not being enlisted in the same way. Of course, identification
does not operate identically in the reading process as it does at the
cinema, although the emphasis on the visual at the start of
Snyder's book partially justifies the analogy. The point is that we
are not being encouraged to look at objects in a certain way as the
more ideologically urgent text of *The Searchers* encourages us to do
– which is not to say that there is no poetic ideology operative but

rather that Snyder's motivation in this text is not based on a demand for readerly commitment (although that kind of more overtly political motivation is at work in later books such as *The Back Country*). Thirdly, the preparation for the *possibility* of a demand for commitment – that is, the possibility for highly motivated rhetoric – is achieved at the outset by the immediacy which the photographic image conventionally arrogates for itself, its illusion of immediate access to the real. This is important not just because an enhanced sense of the real can make rhetorical demands more pressing (that is, more rhetorical), but also because *Riprap* operates to make the business of poetry itself seem like work analogous to the physical work of mountain lookout, or the work of chopping trees and making trails. By way of qualification, however, the *text* of the frontispiece photograph – its grainy texture and homemade effect of fuzziness (not a professional photograph) – functions *against* the photograph as measure of the real by enhancing its status as representation (it is a compositional artefact, something somebody has made). Thus the effects of representation intrude even as the mediacy of representation itself is sought to be abolished.

With the status of the visual image and its relation to the first poem (and the first book) in mind, we can now read that opening poem:

Mid-August at Sourdough Mountain Lookout

> Down valley a smoke haze
> Three days heat, after five days rain
> Pitch glows on the fir-cones
> Across rocks and meadows
> Swarms of new flies.
>
> I cannot remember things I once read
> A few friends, but they are in cities
> Drinking cold snow-water from a tin cup
> Looking down for miles
> Through high still air.

Although the failure to remember – especially in the form of a willed forgetting – represents for a critic like Bloom the central trope of poetic innovation,[8] the first line of the second stanza does not provide occasion for a Bloomian field-day as much as it measures the distance of the speaker – who is subjectively articulated in this line only and who is associated via the only polysyllabic word in the poem, 'remember', with the failing of subjective history – from the ties of the civilised. The effort is to distance the self from the human and situate it in the natural realm, and so the smoke haze of the opening line is immediately revealed by the second line to be of natural rather than human origin (and is thereby implicitly contrasted with distant, unspecified 'cities'). The situation is directly opposed to the Romantic situation of transcendent self-realisation in which the subject (whose proper name may be instanced as Emerson from the earlier example) seeks solitude in the natural realm in order to dramatise his subjectivity. Instead, Snyder's poem situates the subject in the natural realm in order to show it as just one part of that realm: the 'I' does not order or dominate the landscape in any way (not even in a metonymic fashion analogous to the Stevensian subject which sets a jar in Tennessee in order to observe the jar coagulate the landscape around itself as centre), but neither does the landscape dominate the subject as an occasion for sublime experience.

If the first stanza is characterised as purely descriptive and the second as more reflective and meditative, then we may emphasise that the relation between the non-centralised 'I' (which appears at the mid-point of the text but not as the central focus or meaning of the scene depicted) and its distance from the civilised realm consists of a proportional relation which insists that civilisation as culture – texts, friends, cities – aggrandises the self (the American doctrine of individualism) while nature compensates that aggrandisement by diminishing the 'I' to its proper size. Nature precisely puts the self in its place, modifying its status as just one among many natural phenomena, yet also according it a sense of place within the variegated phenomenal field, denominating a proper habitat (a function of which the city is incapable).

There is thus the sense that the gazing subject has been there for quite some time ('Three days heat, after five days rain'), that he is content to remain there looking and thinking, that he is alone (the few friends are in cities), and that the object of his attention is the natural place in which he is situated: we are told first the direction of gaze ('Down valley'), then we are offered a broad descriptive stroke which conveys the general look of the valley ('a smoke haze'), then comes the explanatory source of the haze ('Three days heat, after five days rain'), then the gaze moves in to focus more specifically upon details of the scene, principally further effects of the light ('Pitch glows on the fir-cones' and clouds of flies contribute to and animate the haze). The attention then shifts in the second stanza to the situation of the viewing subject as consciousness reflecting upon the scene, but this is not the point of the scene or of its description, because from memory and its lapse the attention shifts to what the man is doing ('Drinking cold snow-water from a tin cup') and ends by encapsulating the image, the composed elements of the scene, rather than concluding anything about the subject's meditation. The ultimate concern is not with what he thinks or how he perceives himself or his place in the scene but instead with the sufficiency of looking, the repletion of the medium itself:

> Looking down for miles
> Through high still air.

That closural image connotes an atemporality which lends the natural a sense of permanence and priority over the civilised life of cities (the latter of which is apt to be forgotten as a consequence of its impermanence). The dimension of height which has situated the poem's beginning (by its opening words, 'Down valley', and the preliminary photograph) is taken up again by 'high still air' and combines with the dimension of latitudinal distance – 'Looking down for miles' – to gesture toward the infinite, that which exceeds measurement (miles of air).

Although this sense of atemporality is developed in other poems toward a sense of sublimity, the hint of the infinite is contained in this instance by the compositional structure of the image. The poem's symmetrical shape thus achieves formally a balance between its elements which works to constrain any tendency toward either a sublimity in which the landscape would be in excess of the subject or a transcendence in which the subject would be in excess of the landscape. To persist with the metaphor of the camera, the symmetrical poetic structure may be characterised as starting with a zooming in from the hazy expanse of valley-scape to the minutiae of fir-cones and flies, which is then reversed by moving from the figure and the elemental detail of 'Drinking cold snow-water from a tin cup' back out to the motionless gaze which not only takes in a great distance but which also looks for a long time (this latter is connoted by the participial verb forms and the assonanaic lengthening of enunciation in the last two lines).

It needs to be noted that such neutral patience in the natural realm is not typically a characteristic of civilised man: an Emerson in Nature is a man busy reading and interpreting everything around him, organising the natural into a system which has man at its centre; a Whitman in Nature is a recorder and a cataloguer, constantly shifting attention and persistently making objects of perception into parts of the self; a Huck Finn in Nature is a lad transforming the land into an adventure – romancing as the literary version of landscaping. The kind of subjective attention we find in 'Mid-August at Sourdough Mountain Lookout' – which is characteristic of Snyder's poetic attention at its best in this first book, and which extends to the more recent *Axe Handles* – is the kind of gaze of which a wild animal or an Indian may be imagined to be possessed. The 'I' is just drinking, waiting and watching – but waiting and watching for nothing in particular: the motionless attention is an end in itself, is not strictly purposive. Looking is not subsumed here to any other function – be it political, didactic or the function of the pleasure principle.

The sense of subjective disinterest (which is not to be mistaken for *lack* of interest) can be read in one of two ways. The conventional interpretation (I'm presupposing a conventional reading here since, although this has not always been said about Snyder or the poem, what follows is 'conventional' in so far as it would be made within the framework brought to American poetry in which acts of mind – *à la* Stevens – constitute the ultimate critical referent[9]) would most likely make something of the appearance of purposiveness without purpose by having more or less explicit recourse to a Kantian notion of aesthetics (from which the diction of purposiveness is drawn) in order to make the appearance of purposiveness without purpose legible as a poetic operation by which *the lyric subject transforms itself into an aesthetic object*. To borrow Michael Fried's term once more, I would suggest that a conventional reading would valorise the poem by interpreting its speaker as absorbed in his attentiveness as a consequence of which the poem itself is rendered *absorptive*, as productive of the impression of being without audience, independent of reader – that is, not a text that exists as a function of any reception. Although Fried's vocabulary is not quite the currency of literary criticism, its terms and priorities seem to me roughly analogous, for instance, to

Bloom's notion of poetic strength – the poem is 'strong' to the extent that it successfully disavows its precursor text and announces its originality and independence, that is, its aesthetic autonomy.[10] The notion of absorption also seems eventually analogous to Hillis Miller's privileging of 'the linguistic moment' as the textual point at which the poem is absorbed to the extent that it focuses on its own medium, language, and thus appears autonomous as a consequence of self-reflexion.[11] Such critical recourse to a more or less Kantian notion of the aesthetic is conventional in the sense that it insists on privileging the text that most successfully concerns itself with itself, with its manner and means of production and resolution – which is not to say that there are not more and less sophisticated versions of this convention of reading American poetry (Bloom and Hillis Miller constituting the more accomplished versions).[12]

I do not think we get very far reading either American poetry or the work of Gary Snyder in this way, primarily because I think something other is more fundamentally at stake in these texts, something which I have indicated to be the land, the ultimately inescapable *grounding* of any American aesthetic. And as my earlier discussion of the land as always mediated by representation should have made clear, the repudiation of an aesthetic-centred criticism in favour of an ultimately political critique concerned with the predicates of a national culture does not eventuate in any nostalgic recourse to an unproblematic and immediate real such as we find in most critical accounts that are derived from various Marxisms and which name the locus of the real as either history, the forms of social relations or the human body. We have no part of this because the unconscious undermines all these forms of the real, making the real impossible. Against the emphases of these other accounts, then, I am suggesting that the most appropriate method of reading American poetry, and particularly Snyder's writing, is that method implied by Snyder's poem – that is, a method attentive to the landscape as that which houses the subject, in which the subject must find a place no matter how provisional.

The landscape as an effect of sign-systems, as the always-already-represented, means that housing will never be permanent but will instead be subject to substitution; it is thus a question of inhabiting the ground by orienting one's relationship to it in a particular way – the kind of orientation which is developed in

'Mid-August at Sourdough Mountain Lookout' and which is irrevocably dialectical and therefore has to be laboured at: inhabiting the ground is always a process (it is not an easy either/or question of inhabiting or not inhabiting). It is in this sense that the motionlessness of the subject at the end of the poem is not stasis but rather a non-transcendent orientation of consciousness, consciousness acknowledging rather than disavowing its predicates – predicates that include rocks and meadows but not essentially books or friends or cities.[13]

This, then, is the emphasis brought to bear on the poetic enterprise by Snyder as he sets out as an Americañ poet. It is noteworthy, however, that there is no direct reference to the nation in the poems of *Riprap*, no passionate Ginsbergian invocations of 'Amerika', even though the poems are legibly at odds with the dominant cultural imperatives of the period in which they were written (the 1950s characterised as a decade of cultural and political consensus[14]). And yet, despite Snyder's association with the Beats – the dominant literary expression of cultural dissent in the 1950s – the kind of jeremiads declaimed against the culture which we associate with the Beats (say Ginsberg in *Howl*) and the development of counter-cultural alternatives (say Kerouac in *On the Road*) also connected with that literary coterie are basically absent from the lyrics of *Riprap*.

To characterise the poems of that first book in a fairly general way before turning to elaborate the literary situation of the 1950s in more detail, we can adduce at least three categories of poems and the loose narrative into which they are set. First, there are the poems of work and man-in-nature of the order of 'Mid-August': these poems comprise the first two-thirds of the book, are each around one page long (often much shorter) and are generally, to my mind, the best poems. Some of them, the ones to which I shall return, instantiate the Snyderian sublime. They are ostensibly 'about' Snyder's manual work in the Western mountains, drawn from his various working experiences of the early 1950s when he was in his early twenties. This section of poems (which is not formally designated as such by any rubric within the volume) ends with a transitional poem, 'Migration of Birds', which is dated April 1956, and which pictures Snyder living with Kerouac, and metaphorises his preparations prior to leaving for his first visit to Japan. This is the textual juncture at which the loosely structured personal narrative obtrudes most overtly; it is the least important aspect of the book, although 'Migration of Birds' is an interesting poem. Thence follow four poems about Japan, the first three with titles comprising Japanese names, and the fourth a longer poem whose four parts metaphorise (not completely successfully) the four islands of Japan and which names Japan in its title 'A Stone Garden'. Three poems of work 'at sea' follow, topically based on Snyder's travels as a merchant seaman; and the book closes with the title poem 'Riprap', which we shall read later as a formal statement of aesthetic conviction, an innovative and superbly successful poetic manifesto.

The second half of the 1965 version of the book comprises Snyder's translations of Han Shan's ancient Chinese poems on 'Cold Mountain'. Although it will be interesting to consider the relation between *Cold Mountain Poems* and *Riprap* which occasioned their link and which produces additional meaning for both sets of poems via the technique of juxtaposition, the principal hold on our attention must derive from the short, descriptive, partially meditative, undisguisedly autobiographical poems of the first third of the book, and from the statement of aesthetic intent whose significance is partially evident from its lending its name to the volume as a whole. Before relating the character of the book to the history of its emergence (the cultural scene of its writing), and prior to further detailed analysis of individual poems, I would like now to contrast *Riprap* to the volume published just one year later, *Myths & Texts*, which was written simultaneously (or in parallel), but which represents at once a rather different mode of beginning and the claim to a wholly other poetic.

MYTHS & TEXTS

Published in 1960, *Myths & Texts* constitutes a poetic achievement of the order of the major long poetic cycles of modern American poetry: Eliot's *The Waste Land* and *Four Quartets*, Pound's *Cantos*, Crane's *The Bridge*, Williams's *Paterson*, Zukovsky's *A*, Olson's *Maximus Poems*, and HD's *Helen in Egypt* and *Trilogy*. This comparison does not mean to reduce the texts here mentioned to analogies of each other or to elide their considerable differences; neither does it wish to situate Snyder's poem within the category of Modernist writing; rather, it is to indicate that *Myths & Texts* must be judged a great poem by the prevailing standards which canonise these modern American epics (some are privileged more than others, of course[15]). It is also to suggest the difficulty and complexity of Snyder's poem, to advise that one must needs be versed in a certain body of textual and cultural knowledge in order to read its densely interwoven allusions.[16]

According to Snyder's retrospective comment in 1977, the title of his book derives from 'the happy collections Sapir, Boas, Swanton, and others made of American Indian folktales early in this century; it also means the two sources of human knowledge – symbols and sense-impressions' (*MT*, p. vii). Besides noting that this book is quite definitely based on the *memory* of 'things I once read', we may also note that the designation of *myth* as symbol is a significant Lévi-Straussean notion (to be analysed later), and that the alignment of *text* with 'sense-impressions' lays emphasis on text as *textuality*, structured experiential texture, which seems remarkably close to the Derridean sense of text.[17] Myths and texts are therefore acknowledged by Snyder to be both the products of reading and research but also, more importantly, the experiential and epistemological effects obtained as a consequence of reading the world according to what one has gleaned from one's reading of history and aboriginal culture. Representation is thus adduced as dialectically related to life: it is that which mediates experience and that which arises as an effect of experience (which includes reading). Once again, what counts as the overriding factor is the direction or orientation of this representational dialectic, one part of which consists of the records of Indian culture, another part of which consists of Snyder's *Myths & Texts*, and the ultimate goal of which is the effort Snyder articulates regarding his book as the effort 'to make sense, and to find somehow a way to actually "belong to the land"' (*MT*, p. viii). *Myths & Texts* thus provokes the central question of this second part of my book, which is: How can poetry help us 'belong to the land'? Snyder's poetry points toward the answer to this question while also effecting its desire; but before elaborating this function (and answering the question), it is necessary to distinguish both between *Myths & Texts* and *Riprap* and between *Myths & Texts* and the modern epics to which I have compared it.

First, *Myths & Texts* is structured as a poetic cycle, a set of poems internally linked and coherently ordered to create a single whole, as opposed to *Riprap*, which is structured as a series of basically unconnected short lyrics. However, within this difference there exists the similarity of structure by which the juxtaposition and placing of poems in *Riprap* generates meaning (they do not form just any old series), and in which the three sections of *Myths & Texts* ('Logging', 'Hunting', 'Burning') are comprised of relatively loosely linked short lyric or narrative poems whose *juxtaposition* generates their significance. In both volumes, then, the relation *between* poems functions almost as importantly as the relation between elements *within* each individual poem for the production of meaning. For this reason, Snyder's poems, particularly those of *Myths & Texts*, do not anthologise well; neither is it easy to appreciate the totality of their significance when they are excerpted within the critical context. The technique of juxtaposing both poems within the book and elements within the poems also means that significance is not immediately or easily apprehensible: this is one dimension of the difficulty of reading Snyder. It consequently means that the poetry is not aesthetically replete, autonomous or absorptive, since meaning increasingly becomes a function of reception: the reader has to do the work in the production of sense. Furthermore, this technique has political effects in so far as the situation of the reader internal to the poem analogises the situation of the reader with respect to the phenomenal referents symbolised by the text: that is, just as the reader has to work to understand and get meaning from the poetry of the landscape, so the reader has to work to situate him or herself within the landscape itself. This is one sense in which reading Snyder constitutes training in inhabiting the ground.

Secondly, despite the similarities of juxtapositional technique between the two books, a marked difference exists on other levels. Where *Riprap* demands no training in the reading of allusions (unless it is the kind of *internal* allusion which consists of understanding elements of one *Riprap* poem in order to fully appreciate the poem subsequent to it – this being an effect of juxtaposition), *Myths & Texts* makes more formal demands upon its reader, requiring that one have some idea of both Indian cultural myths and practices as well as the myths and religions of Eastern cultures. In this sense, *Myths & Texts* is less 'democratic', for certain kinds of learning are necessary for its reading. However, this version of poetic élitism is distinguishable from that evidenced, for instance, by Eliot's *The Waste Land*, in which it is the classics of the Western tradition in which one needs to be schooled (the Bible, Shakespeare, Dante), as well as the tenets of Protestant Christianity (this latter is particularly requisite in the case of *Four Quartets*), in order to read the poetic text. By contrast, Snyder's reader does not need to have had a classical or privileged education to read *Myths & Texts* (Snyder himself has not had this kind of education); instead, the ideal reader of the book needs to know something about Indian cultures (particularly those of the Northwest Pacific) and just a little about Buddhism (the various notes can help with this). It is noteworthy that although Snyder's canonical marginalisation could be justified by comparison with Eliot as a consequence of his use of relatively unfamiliar allusions and mythologies (as opposed to Eliot's more traditional utilisation of canonical mythologies), such an argument weakens when we compare Snyder's technique with Pound's in *The Cantos*, since Pound finds models for civilisation in non-Western cultures. (It should be added by way of qualification, however, that the dominant mythological framework of *The Cantos* does derive from the Western literary tradition – indeed, it derives from the perceived source of that tradition's beginning in Homer – in the sense that Pound's great poem represents a version of *The Odyssey* made for modern times.)

Further objections may be raised against Snyder's use of unfamiliar mythologies by referring to his own comments on the accessibility of the allusive register within which the poetic of *Myths & Texts* operates. Thus in a 1973 interview, Snyder declares to Ekbert Fass that he 'probably know[s] as much about myth as anybody', adding that 'Probably Duncan is the only poet who has studied myths as much as I have'; yet a few moments later in the interview, he expresses some surprise that not everybody 'knows about Shiva and Parvati'. The later comment is made among – and gives rise to – laughter, and so it is difficult to tell how seriously it is intended. Seriously, Snyder adds, 'I don't put any prime value on obscurity, it's not my intention to appear overly learned.'[18] I would characterise that last comment as a fair assessment of his own conscious intention regarding his poetic method, and yet the laughter around the question of allusiveness seems interpretable as the effect of uncertainty regarding the extent to which one can allude to a body of uncommon knowledge without limiting or alienating the audience.

Against such an objection, however, it is important to stress the function and place of mythological allusion in *Myths & Texts*, since the references to other cultural traditions are made in the service of an appeal to a certain relation to the ground, are subordinate to that appeal, make sense only within its context, and are thus ultimately subordinate to the project of ground-inhabiting for which *Riprap* and my own critical argument have prepared us. Despite the apparent difference of *Myths & Texts* from *Riprap*, then, beginning in *Myths & Texts* is in fact constructed in terms of nature (here as a consequence of the planetary cycle) rather than in terms of culture, the latter of which is figured in the book by various forms of violence and artifice mobilised *vis-à-vis* the natural.

However, nature is not arraigned against culture as an absolute good against an absolute evil, for Snyder is aware that humans only live in social arrangements (this is not least a consequence of language) and that therefore the Romantic ideal of situating the self in an uncontaminated natural realm is both delusional and impossible. It is therefore not a question of culture versus nature but rather a question of one kind of culture versus another. By privileging the natural realm and its mode of organisation, *Myths & Texts* suggests that those cultural forms which are able to harmonise the social with the natural (which is not the same as naturalising the social) are preferable over those cultural forms which instigate the social at the cost of the natural. Nature is offered as the model for social organisation by emphasising its networks of interdependence, its mutuality. Snyder's version of nature is thus in a fundamental sense *more* social than the individualistic social organisation of the United States.

United States politics is connected with the religion of Protestant Christianity in *Myths & Texts* and is opposed to what might be called an aboriginal politics of inhabitation, which is in turn associated with Indian religions and connected to the Eastern beliefs of Buddhism. Thus the book's epigraph is biblical:

> *So that not only this our craft*
> *is in danger to be set at nought;*
> *but also the temple of the great*
> *Goddess Diana should be despised,*
> *and her magnificence should be destroyed,*
> *whom all Asia and the world worshippeth.*
>
> Acts 19: 27

The connection here between the maintenance of a religion and the perpetuation of an economy ('our craft') is identified as the necessary predicate of the destruction of Diana's temple; this connection and predicate is then offered as a metaphor for the foundation of the United States – its politics, culture and economy – upon the desecration of the land. In ancient times, Diana was the name given to the Italian goddess who inhabited wooded groves and whom the Romans made their goddess of hunting and the moon (her Greek equivalent was Artemis). Diana's 'temple' is thus not a building so much as it is the woodlands in which she was worshipped; the name is thereby associated with trees and with the natural cycle (via the figure of the moon), but also with hunting – with, that is, the natural law by which elements of nature destroy other elements as a necessary part of the natural process. We can thus already begin to see the significance of Diana for the book whose cover-picture shows a cross-section of tree-trunk (the chopped-down grove), whose middle section is entitled 'Hunting' and whose first section is entitled 'Logging'.

The second poem in that first section begins with another biblical quotation, this time from the Old Testament, which reinforces the sense of the book's epigraph by indicating the continuity of the destructive ideology in opposition to which the poem is written as an alternative myth or text: 'But ye shall destroy their altars, break their images, and cut down their groves – *Exodus 34: 13*'. The emphasis is not just on the destructive, violent dimension of Christianity, but on the way in which it demands the annihilation of nature as well as of other gods' altars.[19] Poem 2 of 'Logging' runs:

> The ancient forests of China logged
>   and the hills slipped into the Yellow Sea.
> Squared beams, log dogs,
>   on a tamped-earth sill.
>
> San Francisco 2X4s
>   were the woods around Seattle:
> Someone killed and someone built, a house,
>   a forest, wrecked or raised
> All America hung on a hook
>   & burned by men, in their own praise.

Snow on fresh stumps and brush-piles.
The generator starts and rumbles
    in the frosty dawn
I wake from bitter dreams,
Rise and build a fire, . . .

'Pines grasp the clouds with iron claws
like dragons rising from sleep'
250,000 board-feet a day
If both Cats keep working
& nobody gets hurt

The juxtapositional technique is evident here and affords the opportunity for the generation of significance *even without necessarily knowing* the context of the biblical epigraph, the historical details about China, or the original textual source of the final stanza's quotation. Although the poem begins by referring to the destruction of trees in other, ancient cultures, the second stanza's curt denotation of 'San Francisco 2X4s / were the woods around Seattle' links the traditions of the earlier cultures to contemporary America and to American capitalism, which can only view woods in instrumental terms, as material for exploitation, commodification and the production of economic profit. However, this general indication becomes individualised in the long third stanza in which the speaker is implicated in the destruction by his job as a logger. This implication is reinforced by the internalisation of accusation as 'bitter dreams'. And just as the generalised forest of the second stanza is 'burned by men' who are at once both anonymous and representative of the nation ('All America hung on a hook'), so the speaker rises to build a fire himself: his actions parallel those of the men who are the objects of poetic censure. There is a less obvious connection between the 'fresh stumps' of newly cut trees and – via the partial humanisation of the destruction as killing ('Someone killed and someone built') – the ominous possibility of somebody getting hurt at the end of the poem (as if 'stumps' prefigured dismembered limbs). This connection is developed by the juxtaposition of starting the Cat, the machine for chopping, with the fantastic personification of pine trees grasping the sky 'like dragons rising from sleep': just as the machine is started, so the trees shake off their inertia and appear aggressive, an analogy whose likenesses are compounded by the abbreviated name given the machine, which makes it seem like a fantastic giant animal about to do battle with dragons. The prospect of somebody getting hurt thus begins to appear as less the consequence of a machine fault than a consequence of the revenge of the trees, the delayed response of nature to the violence wreaked upon it. 'All America' implicitly operates by the logic of this destruction as a national necessity, as something to be praised, something elevated to the status of the patriotic; yet against this logic is the logic of nature, whose emblem is revealed by the following poem, number 3, to be the regenerative potency of the pine-cone: nature responds to destruction not in the manner of dragons but in a more survivalist, cyclic, interpenetrative manner (which is precisely the implicit model for the social offered by the book).

Poem 3 begins with a quotation from some botanical text whose significance derives from its metaphoric extension, an extension which is dependent upon the connotative power of juxtaposition, and which makes legible the possibility for transformation of every end into a new beginning, since nature as cycle allows no destruction to function as an absolute terminus:

> 'Lodgepole Pine: the wonderful reproductive
> power of this species in areas over which its
> stand has been killed by fire is dependent upon
> the ability of the closed cones to endure a fire
> which kills the tree without injuring its seed.
> After fire, the cones open and shed their seeds
> on the bared ground and a new growth springs up.'

In its poetic context, this denotative passage acquires several highly charged connotative meanings. Indeed, its importance can be registered initially by its lineation: not only is it excerpted whole and placed within the poem, it is also arranged in lines so that it looks itself poetic. That is, not only is botanical discourse indicated to be wholly acceptable for inclusion within poetic discourse, but the botanist's praise of 'the wonderful reproductive / power of the species' is considered to obtain a special lyric status of its own which allows it to form lines of verse. It is as if the 'fir-cones' of 'Mid-August at Sourdough Mountain Lookout' were metaphorically inert underground, just waiting to emerge charged with poetic significance by this other poetic sequence. In this way, the natural life and significance of the pine-cone is interpretable as analogous to its poetic career and significance.

To elaborate on the image's connotative potency: first, the reference to temporal sequence, 'After fire', will remind the reader who has read the book at least once that the book's final section, 'Burning', must therefore return the reader back to the beginning ('a new growth starts up'). The poem therefore seeks to imitate the natural cycle by being structured as a cycle or circle, and this natural cycle – which bears the special kind of seed as its emblem – is also made analogous to the cosmic cycle, since the very first poem opens with the line, 'The morning star is not a star', and the very last poem ends with the line, 'The sun is but a morning star' (which is also the last line of Thoreau's *Walden*, written a century earlier and constituting another text concerned with the connection between one's relation to society and one's relation to nature). Seed and star are metonymically related, both as synecdoches for their respective and analogous cycles, and because both are linked to goddesses: the morning star is not a star because it is a planet, the planet Venus, and although Venus is not the same goddess as Diana, they are related as a consequence of Venus's connection to spring as the time for her worship and her sacred connection to the myrtle tree. In Roman mythology, Venus was also the goddess who presided over gardens, and gardens are interpretable as nothing other than culturalised versions of the wooded groves in which Diana might properly be found.

We can thus read poem 3 as comprised of five juxtaposed fragments or images whose implied connection itself implies the mode of cyclic connection that makes of every end a beginning and that enables survival despite the destruction wrought by the business of logging. Following the botanical text quotation the poem runs:

> Stood straight
> > holding the choker high
> As the Cat swung back the arch
> > piss-firs falling,
> Limbs snapping on the tin hat
> > bright D caught on
> Swinging butt-hooks
> > ringing against cold steel.

> Hsu Fang lived on leeks and pumpkins.
> Goosefoot,
>   wild herbs,
>   fields lying fallow!
>
> But it's hard to farm
> Between the stumps:
> The cows get thin, the milk tastes funny,
> The kids grow up and go to college
> They don't come back.
>   the little fir-trees do
>
> Rocks the same blue as sky
> Only icefields, a mile up,
>   are the mountain
> Hovering over ten thousand acres
> Of young fir.

These four sections following the botanical quotation are spoken in different voices, although no speaker or 'I' is apparent anywhere to identify this. Besides the content of the continued narrative of operating the tree-chopping machine, the language of the first fragment quoted above alerts us to the voice of the logger, because 'Limbs snapping' recall the images of dismemberment in the previous poem, while the juxtaposition of 'piss-firs falling' with 'Limbs snapping on the tin hat' echoes the elements of 'grab my tin pisspot hat' in the antecedent poem. 'Piss-firs' is the name given (one may assume) by loggers to the small trees, fir saplings, which get broken and destroyed as the main work of felling mature trees proceeds. This contrasts with 'the little fir-trees' of the next-but-one fragment, which are implicitly cherished as a consequence of their analogy to children, and with the 'young fir' of the final line which represent the triumph of natural regeneration over human destruction. As logger, the speaker expresses nothing but contempt for the new growth by the term 'piss-firs', but as poet he expresses respect for the meaning of that new growth.

The Oriental example of Hsu Fang is offered in the third fragment as a counter-model of a man living close to nature and living off nature without interfering with or disrupting its cycle; yet the subsequent fragment of colloquial American discourse suggests that the time has passed when such a solution might have been tenable for the United States: 'it's hard to farm / Between the stumps'. The poem is not counselling a return to the American ideal of Jeffersonian agrarianism, which was the earlier model for the individual relation to the land and the basis for political democracy, since the implication is that the time for that is also past. There is a cost to the people for the logging (thin cows, irregular milk, the rupture of the farming cycle – the children do not return to carry on the work of their parents), and although that cost includes natural cost (the failure of cows), nature is not beaten in the same way that the people are, since the 'little fir-trees' return where the children do not.

The imagery of the final lines pictures nature's reciprocity – which provides for regeneration – in the figure of the mountain; natural resistance thus allows for the conversion of vulnerable 'piss-firs' into the impassive solidity of the mountain, since the mountain reflects the sky by its colour and also functions protectively with regard to the 'young fir' whose resilience can be measured by number: 'ten thousand acres'. The mountain is imaged as an intermediary term between trees and sky; it mirrors the sky and watches over the fir-trees, mirroring their expansive power with its own immovability, the implication of that final image being that one might as well try to destroy the sky or eliminate a mountain as try to annihilate the trees.

Within the context of this imagery and its resonances, the condensed allusiveness of the section's first poem becomes much more accessible:

> The morning star is not a star
> Two seedling fir, one died
>> Io, Io,
> Girdled in wistaria
> Wound with ivy
>> 'The May Queen
> Is the survival of
> A pre-human
> Rutting season'
>
> The year spins
> Pleiades sing to their rest
>> at San Francisco
>> dream
>> dream

> Green comes out of the ground
> Birds squabble
> Young girls run mad with the pine bough,
>   Io

This poem is particularly powerful because each of its images obtains several connotations which allow for the weaving of significance between elements. Just as natural elements can only function properly within their cycles and proper contexts, so this text can only signify fully within its context (it is for this reason that it is necessary to devote extended attention to these initial poems in the volume). For the new reader, the poem appears hermetic, inaccessible, only partially signifying; but for the reader acquainted with the book and with Snyder's poetic technique, the poem fairly reverberates with meaning. Within its few short lines, the poem connects the planetary cycle with the natural seasons and with natural and human cycles of generation. Morning is connected to mourning in the opening lines, but also to rebirth, to spring, and the image of the Pleiades waning which opens the second stanza links autumn to night-time ('dream / dream') which then completes the cycle by giving way again to images of spring ('Green comes out of the ground'). Howard McCord's notes inform us that Io represents part of the planetary constellation, yet the sign also functions poetically as a ritual refrain, part of the song of the natural cycle which is echoed in 'Pleiades sing'. The way in which this sign can signify meaning with reference to the stars yet also with reference to the human dimension of cyclic composition indicates that the natural cycle and its seasons are enhanced and facilitated by the human rituals which include those cycles' poetic representation: there is thus the chanting of 'Io', the allusion to the May Queen as a vestigial trace in contemporary culture of archaic spring sexual rituals, and there is the final image of girls intoxicated with the worship of Dionysus and carrying pine branches. These images of feminine generativeness are reinforced by the pictured relation between other plants – wistaria and ivy – and the pine tree: wistaria and ivy clothe the tree as a woman – say the May Queen – might be clothed ('Girdled'). These feminine elements also implicitly invoke Venus and Diana as goddesses associated both with trees and with sexuality, thus making the fertility of the woman a metaphor for the cyclic generativeness of the planet itself. Nature is thus not only sexualised but also gendered in a constellation of imagery to which it will be necessary to return.[20]

For now we can begin to read a whole system of links developing: links between poems, between sections, between images drawn from different textual and cultural registers, between different cultures' deities, between versions of the natural cycle (including the woman's monthly cycle) and versions of the cosmic, planetary cycle – and ultimately, between beginnings and ends. It is thus in the cycle or circle that we find the organising principle of *Myths & Texts*, a principle which extends beyond the poetic to the political, so that just as the lodgepole pine-cone can function as a metaphor for a heavenly planet (the great reflecting the minute), so the poem can function as a metaphor for the world – textual organisation providing the model for social organisation. Poetry becomes intimate with politics rather than utterly separate from it when we acknowledge that poetic structures are potentially analogous to social structures. It is thus far from a question of the substitution of the natural for the social; it is rather a case of acknowledging the interdependence of the natural and the social, and of acting consequentially in relation to this acknowledgement.

However, neither the model of the cycle nor the figure of the circle are without either their American literary tradition or their epistemological problems.[21] There is not only reference to Thoreau in the diction of stars and yearly cycles (*Walden* is structured according to the seasons), there is also important implicit reference to the Emerson of 'Circles'. In the transcendentalist vocabulary of his somewhat later essay ('Circles' appeared in 1841), Emerson declares that the circle 'is the highest emblem in the cipher of the world', an emphasis whose figuration posits world as coherent text merely requiring decoding.[22] The circle achieves its status as most privileged emblem because – from the Renaissance onward – it represents the completion of order and coherent organisation; it is a figure for balanced totality, exhibiting neither lack nor excess, and having no beginning or end. Hence Emerson introducing his essay's topic:

> The eye is the first circle; the horizon which it forms is the second; and throughout nature this primary figure is repeated without end. It is the highest emblem in the cipher of the world. . . . One moral we have already deduced in considering the circular or compensatory character of every human action. Another analogy we shall now trace, that every action admits of

being outdone. Our life is an apprenticeship to the truth that around every circle another can be drawn; that there is no end in nature, but every end is a beginning; that there is always another dawn risen on mid-noon; and under every deep a lower deep opens.   (Ziff (ed.), *Selected Essays*, p. 225)

We can register the similarity between Emerson's conception of the circle and Snyder's use of it as an organising principle by noting the reference here to the circle as figure for compensation, which Snyder deploys as an index of regeneration. The difference between Emerson and Snyder derives from Emerson's positing of the subjective eye ('I') at the centre of circles, which contrasts with Snyder's positioning of natural elements – the pine-cone and the star – as the focal points of concentric and analogous cycles.

The dimension of figuration announced as the object of the essay's analysis – concentricity – itself represents both the compensatory potential and the limit of Emerson's transcendentalist economy of figuration. The concentric circle is a compensatory figure in so far as it provides the solution to the possibility of rupture or the failure of inclusion: if one circle either breaks or is unable to contain all that it should, one simply imagines another circle around it. In this way the infinite regress of an endless series solves the problem of heterogeneity and the apparent absence of pattern. Yet the extent to which such a structure must necessarily be provisional, must always necessitate further expansion in all directions (upwards, downwards, backwards and forwards), imposes upon the subject at the centre of expansion the impossible and vertiginous prospect of registering circles forever. Delineation of structure, and consequently the job of interpreting 'the visible world as the dialplate of the invisible' (as Emerson refers to it elsewhere), is an endless, always unfinished task. This can be a source of exuberance, but the possibility remains that it may overwhelm its subjective centre, with the implication that the collapse of the centre might call into question the whole system. It is in this sense that the concentric circle represents, paradoxically, the limit of the Emersonian enterprise: its limitlessness determines precisely its limit. This allows for the inflection of the diction of 'apprenticeship' in a somewhat more negative way than it may originally appear: one's life is bound to a terrifying propulsion of endless outward expansion, which it is not clear the subject can tolerate in moments of doubt or exhaustion.

A passage later in the essay may be read as the Emersonian defence against any problems associated with his propositions. The defence consists of the paradoxical invocation of provisionality as authority:

> But lest I should mislead any when I have my own head and obey my own whims, let me remind the reader that I am only an experimenter. Do not set the least value on what I do, or the least discredit on what I do not, as if I pretended to settle any thing as true or false. I unsettle all things. No facts are to me sacred; none are profane; I simply experiment, an endless seeker with no Past at my back. (Ibid., p. 236)

Provisionality is used here to disavow responsibility and to generate the illusion that concentricity provides for a measure of autonomy. Earlier, concentricity was adduced as a 'truth' to which subjective history testifies as a consequence of being subject to that 'truth' ('Our life is an apprenticeship to the truth'); but here the profession of truth is disavowed in a gesture of absolute freedom: the 'I' as 'endless seeker with no Past', which is nothing other than another inscription of the American Dream. The conviction that one can relinquish history does not accord with the figure of concentricity since each circle depends for its production on the one preceding it; yet the provisionality which derives as a consequence of concentricity is motivated to deny dependence. Against the explicit avowal ('No facts are to me sacred; none are profane'), this logical slippage functions in the service of the need to hold some facts sacred and deem some profane – that is, it reverts to self-serving pragmatism when it is a question of preserving some 'facts' (say, American political ideals) and dispensing with others (say, the rights of certain bodies of people to certain areas of national land).

Snyder's poetic is not imbued with the ideology that the speaker represents 'an endless seeker with no Past at [his] back'; rather the opposite is the case, because *Myths & Texts* operates to identify and produce continuities, to show the dependencies and interrelations of all phenomena – including the myths of cultures which differ from each other both geographically and historically – as opposed to positing their independence. Far from this structure of mutual dependency representing symbiosis or a set of absolute limits, the cyclic organisation guarantees freedom, growth and movement by its images of expansion and persistence in the face of all obstacles. Thus the enigmatic opening line of the poem, 'The morning star is not a star', becomes by the end 'The sun is but a morning star', a transformation which implies the possibility of an enlarged future for even the very source of earthly life itself. This notion of expansion is saved from any tendency toward transcendence, however, as a consequence of the resolute rootedness of the system which finds its centre not in any subjective visionary dimension but in the ground itself and its natural effects.

As I have been suggesting all along, an essential part of this natural system and its history is the trajectory of its representation. This is not least the case because human representation – whether it be ancient social rituals consisting of dancing and chanting, or the production of various religions and cultural myths, or even the practice of commemorating these in poetry – functions to remind society of its historical continuity, a continuity whose basis is the ground. This archaic task is the poetic function whose responsibility is claimed by the speaker of Snyder's poetry. It finds its authority in ancient models from many different cultures, one example of which closes the 'Logging' section of *Myths & Texts*. Poem 15 recalls the structural thematic of regeneration by beginning:

> Lodgepole
> > cone/seed waits for fire
> And then thin forests of silver-gray.
> > in the void
> > a pine cone falls

Just as the single cone/seed is sufficient to being new growth, so the single nominative, 'Lodgepole', has by this point in the sequence achieved sufficient poetic resonance to fill by itself a whole poetic line with meaning. This resonance is echoed by the image of a single pine-cone falling in the void: the cone is a natural sign capable of original signification; it has the power to inscribe the abyss with meaning and life. The poem then ends by foregrounding the question of representation, indicating that the wait in the void can be supplemented and its end result actually *prefigured* by the image-maker's art:

> Pine sleeps, cedar splits straight
> Flowers crack the pavement.

> Pa-ta Shan-jen
> (A painter who watched Ming fall)
>   lived in a tree:
> 'The brush
> May paint the mountains and streams
> Though the territory is lost.'

There is a reference in the second line quoted here to the American poetic tradition besides the Chinese one. The allusion is to William Carlos Williams's 1944 poem, 'A Sort of a Song', in which the dictum proposed for modern poetry is 'No ideas / but in things', and in which the image for this poetry is that of a flower breaking apart rock: Williams's poem ends, 'Saxifrage is my flower that splits / the rocks'. Therefore Snyder's two lines, 'Pine sleeps, cedar splits straight / Flowers crack the pavement', obtain as one referent the tasks of modern poetry, while also synecdochially signifying the whole process of natural destruction and rebirth – the personification of the dormant period, 'Pine sleeps', the alliterative and somewhat onomatopoeic image of destruction, 'cedar splits straight', and the emergence of the natural within the interstices of its own immolation, 'Flowers crack the pavement'. (Note also the dimension of poetic organicism by which the word 'splits' enacts the line-break in both Snyder's and Williams's poems.)

This highly poeticised diction – use of personification, alliteration, onomatopoeia and rhythmic meter – together with the submerged reference to another poem, foregrounds the extent to which regeneration is a consequence of its representation. (This link between poetics and a flower splitting rock also obtains resonance with respect to Snyder's own early statement of poetics in 'Riprap', which will be discussed below.) Thus the immediately subsequent lines of poem 15, the section's final lines, may be read as a summary of the three images (pine, cedar, flowers) and their relation, a summary which analogises art and nature – the image reclaims what has been lost just as the pine-cone is able to compensate the destruction of trees (and the flower reclaim the landscape). The fact that this poetic coda and interpretation of the image-sequence should consist of a quotation points to the interdependence of representation itself, as well as the source of alternative models of inhabitation in other cultures. The allusion to an ancient Chinese artist is made further explicit by the parenthetical gloss on the unfamiliar name (that is, the explanation converts it from an allusion to a quotation); nevertheless, the detail about the painter – denoting the identity of the quotation's source – does not prevent the connotation of his figure as a tree-spirit. The connotation makes the painter, who lives in a tree, analogous to the pine, which is personified as sleeping, by humanising the natural and naturalising the human. Finally, the analogy between the preservative and regenerative dimension of both art and nature – which are significantly not pictured here as competitive but as complementary – is compounded by the potential for a pun on 'brush', since the sign denotes both the artist's instrument and the natural growth which Snyder will use as the dominant metaphor for land-rehabilitation in *Turtle Island*.[23]

The section entitled 'Logging' therefore ends with an emphasis on the regenerative potency of representation itself, which is structurally fitting because the following section, 'Hunting', begins with an important poetic meditation on the social function of poetry, its mythic power. If Snyder were not convinced that poetry has a social function with identifiably beneficial effects, he would not be in the business of making poems. Snyder has often referred to the practice of poetry as the production of 'healing songs', and in a 1976 interview he said, 'Poetry within the civilized area of history is the fragmented attempt to recreate a "healing song" aspect of the shaman's practice' (*RWork*, p. 175). The poetic function for Snyder is therefore analogous to the shamanistic function; and as further investigation will reveal, it is also analogous to the psychoanalytic function.

Shamanistic lyricism 'heals' by making whole; as shaman, the poet restores the cultural and the natural to a holistic relationship of interdependence – just as the psychoanalyst may 'cure' by provoking the subject to accede to his lack which is a consequence of sociality: the subject of a psychoanalysis is cured when s/he achieves the proper orientation to the Other, acknowledging the subjective degree of *subjection* to the Other as Symbolic function, the representative of the social. The homology between psychoanalysis and Snyder's vision of the poetic function is only partial, however, because where Snyder sees poetry as a making whole, Lacanian psychoanalysis views one primary task of analysis as the subject's acceptance of an inevitable impossibility both of wholeness and of independent subjective integrity. And yet to the extent that wholeness for Snyder represents not the individual's integrity but the enmeshing of the individual as part within the

1. (*above*) Joseph Wright, *The Indian Widow* (1785).

2. (*left*) Cover photograph of Gary Snyder, from *Riprap & Cold Mountain Poems* (1965).

3. (*left*) Frontispiece daguerreotype for Walt Whitman's
   Leaves of Grass (1855).

4. (*right*) Sourdough Mountain
   Lookout, Summer 1953,
   frontispiece to *Riprap & Cold
   Mountain Poems* (1965).

(*right*) Frontispiece to Gary Snyder's *A Range of Poems* (1966).

(*below*) Albert Bierstadt, *Among the Sierra Nevada, California* (1868).

7. Ansel Adams, *Moon and Half Dome*, Yosemite National Park, California, 1960.

whole of sociality – represents, indeed, the ultimate impossibility of wholeness when one insists upon individual independence – then the emphasis of Lacanian psychoanalysis upon the subject's predication by the signifier (and its effect, the unconscious) can be seen as analogous to the Snyderian insistence upon the emergence of proper sociality as only ever a consequence of the relationship to the natural as the necessary predicate. Hence Snyder in 1978:

> That specialized variety of poetry which is the most sophisticated, and is the type which most modern poetry would aspire to be, is the 'healing songs' type. This is the kind of healing that makes whole, heals by making whole, that kind of doctoring. The poet as healer is asserting several layers of larger realms of wholeness. The first larger realm is identity with the natural world, demonstrating that the social system, a little human enclave, does not stand by itself apart from the plants and the animals and winds and rains and rivers that surround it. Here the poet is a voice for the nonhuman, for the natural world, actually a vehicle for another voice, to send it into the human world, saying there is a larger sphere out there; that the humans are indeed children of, sons and daughters of, and eternally in relationship with, the earth. Human beings buffer themselves against seeing the natural world directly. Language, custom, ego, and personal advantage strategies all work against clear seeing. So the first wholeness is wholeness with nature. (*RWork*, pp. 171–2)

Snyder's conception of poetry as 'healing song' is not idiosyncratic or eccentric because it is alleged as the implicit conception of the poetic held by the best modern poetry. Indeed, despite Eliot's later disavowals of *The Waste Land* (claiming it to be just his 'personal grouch'), it is clear that the poem is intended to do more than just register cultural disintegration and decay: it is intended to make good that decay, to shore poetic fragments against the ruins, to renew the mediaeval myth of the Fisher King in order to effect an analogous renewal of postwar European culture. Similarly, Pound's *Cantos* can be read on one level as desiring to effect a cultural rejuvenation, and whether or not one would want to endorse some of the measures advocated in the poem to effect the poetic–political purpose, the poem's characteristic status as epic labour performed in order to purify culture remains unaltered.

What is most significant about the shamanistic, healing function of the poet is that it depends not upon the voice or person of the poet but rather upon something other operating through the speaker. Giving voice to the Other is precisely the function of the analyst in psychoanalysis: as Lacan's persistent interventions on the misunderstood topic of transference never ceased to emphasise, it is not what the analyst says that counts but what of the Other is allowed to speak through him. Thus in answer to the question about the point at which psychoanalysis begins to 'work', Lacan says, 'When does transference really start? When the image which the subject requires becomes confused for the subject with the reality in which he is placed.'[24] Transference begins when the figure of the analyst (the 'reality' of the psychoanalytic situation in which the subject 'is placed') becomes indistinguishable from the Other (the 'image' required by the subject as constitutive recipient of his demand). And for Snyder, like Lacan, it is not the ego to which poetry directs itself (Lacanian psychoanalysis does not attend to the ego other than as a resistance to the treatment); instead, the ego is recognised as a barrier to the acknowledgement of the Other, in whose field both shamanistic poet and psychoanalyst aspire to situate themselves.

Occupying the place of the Other means that one's discourse articulates the unconscious, and although Snyder's conception of the unconscious differs from Lacan's (according more with a Jungian version of the unconscious), it is precisely the unconscious as an Other discourse to which the shaman-poet provides access. Thus Snyder continues his 1978 meditation:

> The poet as myth-handler-healer is also speaking as a voice for another place, the deep unconscious, and working toward integration of interior unknown realms of mind with present moment immediate self-interest consciousness. The outer world of nature and the inner world of the unconscious are brought to a single focus occasionally by the work of the dramatist-ritualist-artist-poet. That's another layer. Great tales and myths can give one tiny isolated society the breadth of mind and heart to be *not* provincial and to know itself as a piece of the cosmos.   (*RWork*, p. 172)

The unconscious is represented here in topographical rather than structural terms and is characterised by the metaphors of depth (below consciousness), interiority and occlusion – as something hidden deep within requiring lyric utterance to seduce it out and up into consciousness. However, the unconscious is not individualised – is not, that is, interior to a single person; rather, by being made analogous to the exteriority of the natural world, the unconscious is more generalised than personalised. Indeed, in an earlier essay, 'Poetry and the Primitive' (1967), which addresses similar questions of the poetic function and its context, Snyder makes the analogy explicit: 'Outwardly, the equivalent of the unconscious is the wilderness' (*EHH*, p. 122). Thus the poet who gives voice to the repressed relation to the land is indeed articulating the American unconscious, and this giving voice may 'heal' by identifying the distortions worked upon the American subject's relation to the land and subsequently remaking that relation. And so a little later in 'Poetry and the Primitive', Snyder refers directly to the father of psychoanalysis in the context of shamanist poetics, declaring that 'Freud said *he* didn't discover the unconscious, poets had centuries before' (ibid.) – which is not to render Freud's discovery redundant but rather to emphasise the link between psychoanalysis and a certain kind of poetic practice. It is also, crucially, to imply that which Snyder does not say about the relation between poetry and the unconscious which marks the difference between the poetic 'discovery' and use of the unconscious and the Freudian discovery, which is that although poetry may have discovered the unconscious before Freud it was not conscious of this fact. This assertion has two consequences, the first and less important one being that the Freudian theory of the unconscious is therefore necessary and not in the least bit redundant, since poetry is unable to provide a theory of the unconscious (being itself unconscious of its discovery); the second and more significant consequence being that not only is it not absolutely necessary that poetry's audience completely understand the operation of the shamanistic poetic function, but also that it is not necessary the poet understand it either. Just as what counts in analysis being the analyst's occupation of the place of the Other *vis-à-vis* the analysand rather than anything the analyst may or may not know about the patient's subjective or family history (Lacan groups the analyst's knowledge of this kind under the rubric of *counter*-transference), so what counts for the effective restorative function of poetry is the place occupied by the poet rather than his conscious knowledge of what he might or should be doing. It is for this reason that Snyder insists, in accordance with Zen Buddhist teaching, upon the reduction of the poet's ego. The correct attitude for the shamanistic poet is very similar to that counselled by Lacan for the analyst: both must become blank surfaces (screens rather than mirrors) ready to register – and return to the subject – something of the Other.

Thus it is that the speaker of the first poem of the 'Hunting' section of *Myths & Texts* is pictured engaged in the pursuit of this egoless state; and indeed, the extent to which the speaker of Snyder's lyrics achieves this state as prerequisite for any poetic articulation may be measured by the relative absence of the first-person pronoun from the lyric utterance. For Snyder, there is but one mode of access to the required state: meditation. In an essay of the early 1960s, he goes so far as to claim that 'whatever is or ever was in any other culture can be reconstructed from the unconscious, through meditation' (*EHH*, p. 93), which confirms a later statement made about healing and the unconscious that makes the latter sound very much like a Jungian collective, transhistorical and transcultural unconscious:

> Healing on many levels but not really psychotherapy – healing primarily on the level of continually bringing back in the dream-lore, myth-lore, free-floating/international themes and motifs as concentrated in their place, bringing it back into the consciousness of everybody, to show everyone who they are, and to give people a place.   (*RWork*, p. 176)

Snyder is right to distance the healing of shamanistic poetry from psychotherapy, since psychotherapy (as opposed to psychoanalysis) is concerned with bolstering rather than minimising the ego. He is also correct to emphasise the end result of poetic healing as having to do with inhabitation, the achievement of a sense of place, a knowledge of the proper relation to the American ground. However, although Snyder registers elsewhere the inadequacy of a Jungian notion of the collective unconscious to account for the mythic function,[25] the logic of mythology proposed in this instance is Jungian in so far as it is characterised by 'free-floating/international themes and motifs'.

For Jung, the unconscious is neither topographical (as it is developed in Freud and implied above by Snyder) nor structural (as for Lacan); instead, it is universal – transhistorical and transcultural – and therefore peculiar to no individual yet pertinent to all. Most crucially, for Jung the unconscious consists of a *content*, a reservoir of symbols or archetypes – hence Snyder's analogous 'themes and motifs'. Jungianism is problematic in so far as it is unable to provide any coherent account of the relation between the archetype, the individual and the social order, a problem which is important for the Snyderian poetic practice because it is in the reworking of relation that poetic healing consists. Posited as wholly transcendent, the archetype derives neither from the individual nor from any socio-historical context, which raises as a first question the constitutive origin of any and all archetypes. On the level of artistic production, a Jungian psychoanalytic account seems initially attractive because by focusing on the reverberation or reactivation of the archetypes in the poet or the audience, meaning is made a function and effect of *reception* (either the poet's reception of the archetype, his mediation of a universal language, or the audience's reception of the textual product of that mediation), and is therefore dissociated from neurosis (as opposed to vulgar Freudian accounts which focus on artistic *production* as an effect of individual sublimation). However, the practice of meditation is inadequate to account for the transmission of archetypes, partly because poetry's audience is not required to meditate to receive its beneficial effects (that is, to experience the archetype's reverberation), and partly because meditation cannot account for the manifest possibility of radically divergent responses to archetypes. It is insufficient to answer that different responses may be elicited as a consequence of different arrangements of archetypes within individual psyches, because the corollary possibility that certain psyches may not contain certain archetypes throws the fundamental dimension of universality radically into question (any history of different arrangements also undermines the status of universality and collectivity). The representation of archetypes as transcendent eliminates the crucial psychic dimension of *intersubjectivity*, which then severely constrains any account of literary reception. The disavowal of intersubjectivity as the area of intersection between the subject and the social is therefore the point at which Jungianism cannot be sustained. That area of intersection is also that within which the shamanistic poet operates and which it is his function to reorient; its exclusion from the Jungian account is therefore catastrophic with respect to the development of any theory of poetic effects based on mythological manipulation as the characteristically Snyderian technique.

This problem may be partially ameliorated here by recourse to

Lévi-Strauss's anthropological theories of myth's structure and the power of symbolism (from which – in combination with structural linguistics – Lacan develops his account of the unconscious as a structure). In 'The Effectiveness of Symbols', Lévi-Strauss subjects to structural analysis a myth recorded from a South American Indian tribe and performed by the tribe's shaman to facilitate difficult childbirth. One of the conclusions this analysis enables Lévi-Strauss to draw is that all myths 'can be reduced to a small number of simple types if we abstract, from among the diversity of characters, a few elementary functions'.[26] Lévi-Strauss adds that 'the myth *form* takes precedence over the *content* of the narrative' (ibid.), so that although the form is not autonomous or transhistorical, it does provide a structural model or grid according to which an impressive range of disparate myths can be read and interpreted. It is in this sense that the structural (Lacanian) unconscious can be differentiated only *relatively* – rather than absolutely – from a collective unconscious possessed of a content (as in Snyder and Jung). Indeed, Lévi-Strauss's anthropological conclusions are delivered within the context of a comparison between psychoanalysis and shamanism, adducing what would come to represent a characteristically Lacanian emphasis, namely, the precedence of form over content and a consequential decrease of emphasis on the importance for psychoanalysis of remembering the acual content of subjective history as opposed to the form of memory's reconstruction (and subjective reorientation).[27]

According to the anthropologist, symbols are effective – for the shaman, the psychoanalyst and the poet – because they provide a vocabulary without which something extremely difficult, some insurmountable obstacle, could not be negotiated by the subject in whose service the symbolism is manipulated by the healer. In each case, the difficulty has to do with what is unconscious; it is therefore not primarily to consciousness that symbolism is directed. In other words, it makes little difference whether the Indian woman in labour, or the analysand, or poetry's audience ultimately understands *how* the technique operates to effect a cure; rather what makes the difference is the *unconscious effect* obtained by the handling of the symbolic – not direct – influence. In Lévi-Strauss's words, 'the [shaman's] song constitutes a *psychological manipulation* of the sick organ, and it is precisely from this manipulation that a cure is expected' (p. 192). Since it is both a question of manipulation rather than control and of indirection rather than immediacy, it is also not requisite that the shaman-analyst-poet have absolute mastery in terms of complete knowledge regarding his own function: what counts is that he know the procedure of the ritual, how to function as mediator or Other. The shaman provides a vocabulary through which the sick woman can express and negotiate what would otherwise remain inexpressible and impossible; the psychoanalyst provides a kind of screen against which the patient's subjectivity can be renegotiated; and the poet provides a mouthpiece and conduit for the rehabilitation of relation – both between past and present cultures, and between one dimension of componential organisation (the social) and another dimension (the natural).

The provision of such poetic power requires training, requires the kind of ritualistic self-situation in the natural realm characteristic of the shaman or the initiate Indian brave. The first poem of 'Hunting' pictures this situation:

first shaman song

In the village of the dead,
Kicked loose bones
         ate pitch of a drift log
         (whale fat)
Nettles and cottonwood. Grass smokes
            in the sun
Logs turn in the river
         sand scorches the feet.

Two days without food, trucks roll past
         in dust and light, rivers
         are rising.
Thaw in the high meadows. Move west in July.

Soft oysters rot now, between tides
         the flats stink.

I sit without thoughts by the log-road
Hatching a new myth
watching the waterdogs
         the last truck gone.

                          (*MT*, p. 19)

This constitutes the first shaman song because it details metonymically the meditative preparation undergone by the shamanistic
subject in search of a vision or myth. Thus although the present
tense is adopted by the end of the first stanza and continues
throughout the text, the poem is not a process but a product, a
record and effect of meditation. However, since representation is
not without its effects, and since I am discussing the aspect of
regeneration that obtains as a consequence of representation, the
relationship between the poem and meditation can be seen to be
dialectical. It is in this respect that the metonymic technique of
composition allows for the poetic product – the poem – to be
experienced as a poetic process – analogous to meditation. In this
way, the shaman's song functions by engaging its audience, an
engagement which occurs at the level of the unconscious as a
consequence of associative displacements. That is, metonymic
displacement constitutes, according to Lacan, one of the primary
operations of the unconscious; in classically Freudian terms, the
patient's 'free association' provides an index of the subjective
unconscious by pointing to the structure of displacements operative at the level of speech. Conceptualising the unconscious as
structured linguistically means that the rhetorical trope of metonymy – substitution by name, term or word, rather than by resemblance (as in metaphor) – is particularly prone to engage unconscious mental operations rather than conscious ones. In other
words, the more metonymic poetic discourse becomes, the more it
engages – and can manipulate – the structured subjectivity of its
reader-recipient. Thus for the critical reader of Snyder's poetry,
which consists of a highly metonymic poetic discourse (often
tending toward the minimalism of the list), three categories of
response are available: first, one can refuse to engage – or be
engaged by – the text, in which case there will be a dearth of
meaning produced; secondly, one can be engaged by the text, in
which case certain undeterminable but none the less consequential
effects will be precipitated (the principal effect which Snyder
intends being that of the holistic restoration of a natural–social
interrelationship); or thirdly, one can engage the text (and be
engaged by it) in order to produce meanings that can be assessed
and differentiated by consciousness. One cannot, however, receive
a predetermined meaning from the text. (I consider it highly
unlikely that reading ever operates in a way that allows for the
reception of predetermined meaning, but my point is that some

texts determine and confine the range of textual meanings and effects available to a far greater extent than Snyder's poetry, whose meaning is intentionally pushed toward existing only as a function of its audience.)

The highly metonymic poem tends in its disjunction toward resembling the dream (it has no clear beginning or end; one is always somehow in the middle of it, without explanation); and thus the poem as dream is offered here in order to encourage a dream-like state of altered consciousness – although not, one should emphasise, the dream as fulfilment in fantasy of an unconscious wish. The alternative state of consciousness desired by the poem is a meditative, egoless one in which the subject is open to receive impressions in a different way, open to vision. For the speaker of this poem, as for many Indian cultures (including the Papago of Arizona and most of the Plains tribes), the dream or vision is regarded as the highest reward for an individual's efforts. By contrast, the highest individual reward in the Western tradition, beginning with Homer, has always been what the Greeks called *kléos*, or imperishable fame. *Kléos* was accorded the hero via the commemorative power of lyric, and the supplementary function of *kléos* was to accord glory not only to the object of lyric (the hero) but also its subject (the poet-singer). Classical poetry thus immortalised the poet as a secondary consequence of its immortalisation of another. This contrasts with the Snyderian conception of lyric, as it partially derives from Indian cultures, because the dream as reward institutes an economy in which glory is accorded the subject as a consequence of the Other's discourse (the unconscious) rather than as a consequence of the subject's commemorative discourse about another. The dream or vision thus comes to be seen as more 'real', more a consequential effect, than a representation which seeks to preserve presence.

We may therefore recall the incantatory injunction in the book's very first poem, 'Dream, dream', which recurs in the book's penultimate poem (p. 52), and whose processes are depicted in the middle of the poetic sequence by *'first shaman song'*. The dream as an instance of the dialectical relation between different elements – the subject, the social and the spiritual – is not therefore a question of something merely interior (and consequently ineffectual) to the subject. Instead, the dream is produced as an effect of high standing in the spiritual realm (according to the Indian cultures, in which, it should be noted, spirituality resides not in a distant God but in the natural realm, in plants and animals) and as an effect of subjective discipline. The dream also obtains its *own* effects with respect to precipitating social action and arrangements, and – via the figure of the shaman – with respect to functioning as a mechanism of beneficence and restoration. Hence the appropriateness of the metaphor of *hatching* in Snyder's poem, for hatching suggests both the development of something from within which is not a willed act but a natural process (as in the hatching of an egg), yet also some kind of conscious human strategy (as in hatching a plot). Hatching is thus an activity posed somewhere between the conscious and the unconscious; it can thus be understood to be a result of meditation; and the 'new myth' is therefore analogous to the shaman's ritual song, which is partially a product of his trance-like state in which greater access than usual to the unconscious is allowed, and partially a product of his own effort, his strategy (this is why he both knows and does not know what he is doing). As Snyder wrote in his 'Lookout's Journal' on 15 August 1952 (the kind of line one can easily imagine the speaker of 'Mid-August at Sourdough Mountain Lookout' writing, given the subjective condition of that poem's speaker, even though Snyder does not reach Sourdough mountain until one summer later), 'When the mind is exhausted of images, it invents its own' (*EHH*, p. 10). The etymology of 'invent' – which is also played upon by Williams in his poem 'A Sort of a Song', discussed above – foregrounds the paradoxical element of this whole aspect of meditative dreaming, since although we usually think of *invent* as meaning 'making up', it derives from the Latin word for the verb 'to come', so that to invent is literally to come upon, to discover: to invent is thus not to produce something new but to discover something that was already there. If the mind emptied of images subsequently discovers its own images, then it is apparent that 'the mind' is not unidimensional or necessarily self-contained.

As Indian cultural practices suggest, and the poem under consideration here indicates, in order to engage the aspect of subjective mind which is differentiated from consciousness and ego – ego being the translation of Freud's German *das Ich*, literally, the 'I' – sensory alteration, especially sensory deprivation, is necessary. Hence the conventionally repellent images of eating pitch from a log, burning, stinking, fasting and absolute motionlessness. The details of the body are interspersed with details of the transitions in the landscape in order to initiate and reinforce the link between them:

> Grass smokes
> in the sun
> Logs turn in the river
> sand scorches the feet.

The images are at once *disjunctive*, metonymic, one substituting for the other without connection being specified, and yet also *connected* by the sibilant alliteration, which suggests poetic links and which therefore encourages the *readerly making of connections* as a necessary part of the meditative process of forming connection between subject and natural realm. Reading connections, we facilitate them.

The poem's imagery oscillates between figures for death and decay ('the village of the dead', 'oysters rot') and figures for birth and expansion ('rivers / are rising', 'Hatching a new myth') – images of decline and increase which are themselves synecdochic of the larger cycle of the poem. Implicit in this structure is the shamanistic (and Buddhist) notion that the diminishment of the subjective ego is prerequisite for the hatching of the 'new myth', and so access to poetic voice is not a consequence of realising the self (having a strongly defined sense of self in order to speak) but precisely the opposite. Thus unlike the Romantic poetic subject who must seek solitude in order to dramatise consciousness, the shamanistic poetic subject seeks solitude in order to dispel consciousness. The poem's last line, 'the last truck gone', which reverts to past tense locution, therefore posits solitude as absolute.[28] Utterly alone like the speaker of 'Mid-August' (note the similar elements in both poems – intense heat, smoke, and putrescent life generated by the heat, an absolutely motionless speaker), the poetic subject achieves the vision that he is not an isolated subject but rather a part of the landscape: instead of (mis)recognising the self in the Other, this subject achieves a recognition of the Other inextricable from itself.

Having achieved this recognition, the speaker gains access to a voice not of pure originality but one through which other voices can speak. Thus the characteristically Snyderian voice is one in which many different voices can be heard, a voice original in the sense of being utterly unoriginal, productive of a poetic text that is always composed of tissues of other discourses. This is not just a question of quotation, however, since quotation implies both a subject who chooses and delimits the previous text (and who is thus primary in relation to it even though speaking posterior to it), and a subject deploying a discourse that is privileged over the earlier text and in relation to which that earlier text is expected to function in some subordinate manner – as support, illustration, counter-example or suchlike. Snyder's poetic discourse appears less quotational to me than, say, Eliot's or Pound's, because there is in Snyder less of a sense that some purpose is being served by quotation: that is, the quotations (and I am including all usage of prior discourse under the rubric of quotation here for the sake of clarity at this point in the argument) cannot be seen to be serving any purpose other than that of allowing themselves to be heard *for themselves*. Hence, for instance, besides hunting poems *'for birds'*, *'for bear'*, and *'for deer'*, poem 5 in 'Hunting' details the construction of an implement in a mode resembling direct transcription of some historical or anthropological text (similar to the botanical quotation about the pine in 'Logging'). This text is not provided as a whole poem by and 'for' itself so that the reader will go out to construct the implement, but rather it consists of giving a less mediated (I do not allege *unmediated*) voice to the aboriginal inhabitants of the land, so that the American relation to the ground can be reformulated – regrounded – based on a 'new myth':

the making of the horn spoon

> The head of the mountain-goat is in the corner
>   for the making of the horn spoon,
> The black spoon. When fire's heat strikes it
>   turn the head
> Four days and hair pulls loose
>   horn twists free.
> Hand-adze, straightknife, notch the horn-base;
>   rub with rough sandstone
> Shave down smooth. Split two cedar sticks
>   when water boils plunge the horn,
> Tie mouth between sticks in the spoon shape
>   rub with dried dogfish skin.
> It will be black and smooth,
>   a spoon.

Wa, laEm gwala ts!ololaqe ka ● ts!Enaqe laxeq.

(*MT*, p. 23)

In so far as this text is offered as part of the new myth (of which Snyder's text is one vehicle), the new myth operates via the demythification strategy proposed by Barthes in *Mythologies*, in which it is adduced that the only way to combat myth is to re-mythify it. When Barthes characterises myth as speech that has been stolen and restored (myth as a sort of distortive appropriation), his subsequent solution suggests a *re*-restoration, which is not a return to the real, an orthopaedic procedure by which distortion would be eliminated in order for truth to again become visible, but rather a further twist to the elements which then make the new myth a rehabilitation.[29] So here we have a single line of Kwakiutl language denoting the procedure for spoon manufacture, which is translated – carried over – into English for the purpose of making accessible one aspect of Kwakiutl culture. Of course, any act of translation involves losses and gains, particularly when the two languages involved are as radically different as they are here. It is also certainly the case that the intention behind the translation and publication of the text has no guarantee of being effected, and that this failure is doubly provided for here – both as a general effect of language and as an effect of translation. However, what is important to remember is that such a translation is offered against *the American desire not to know*, the desire of American consciousness not to know the formations of its unconscious. Which is not to suggest that it is sufficient simply to state some fact about or feature of the unconscious to consciousness in order for it to be readily assimilated: the very notion of the desire not to know militates against any such easy assimilation or recognition. It may even be the case that Snyder underestimates the power of the desire not to know, even as he underestimates the accessibility of various mythic elements and allusions. However, if psychoanalysis is correct in characterising repression as a failure of translation, then the effects of a remedial translation may include some restoration to consciousness of what was previously unknown – a restoration which is itself productive of effects, of some reconstruction of consciousness. And whatever the success or failure of the effort, the point remains that such quotations structure the text in a way which aspires to identify and serve their own purposes rather than a more directly appropriative purpose. In the case of the horn spoon poem, an analogue exists between the spell-like, preservative content of the text and the form of its incorporation into the larger poem: it functions for the Kwakiutl (as directive text) and for the American (as new myth) to preserve an aspect of Indian culture that might otherwise be lost. It is in this sense that representation constitutes regeneration – not directly, or easily, or without loss and the possibility of failure. The production and manipulation of myth is not something over which any subject can obtain consistent control; yet the shaman-poet can manipulate myth and precipitate regenerative effects via the Other, via allowing the Other to speak and be heard.

MYTHS & TEXTS AS A REPLY TO THE WASTE LAND

The new myth which Snyder's poetry works toward constructing is elaborated in relation to many other discourses and voices. I am suggesting that the primary other voice is that which comes from the land and which is not singular or monologic but which I characterise as *a* voice in so far as it is Other to American consciousness, consisting of that articulation of alterity against which America is constituted and regarding which the desire not to know is mobilised. Snyder's choice of poetic discourse as one principal means for constructing an alternative myth means, however, that other instances of American poetic discourse which manifest and propagate the desire not to know must on some level be engaged. It is thus far from a question of the Snyderian poetic subject having to evade knowledge of poetic precursors – is not, that is, a Bloomian question – but is rather the opposite question of engaging previous evasions (of the relation to the land). Rather than avoiding, casting out, earlier poetic voice in order to create its own poetic voice, the Snyderian speaker articulates the Other in order to indicate what the earlier poetic voice is itself avoiding, casting out for the creation of its own speech.

To the extent that *Myths & Texts* is a mythic cycle in the tradition of the most famous modern American poems; in so far as it is concerned with voice and connection, with the uses of quotation and allusion, then the most powerful precursorly evasive poem with which it must engage is Eliot's *The Waste Land* (1922). It will be gathered from the account which follows that Snyder's poem not only attempts to respond to *The Waste Land*, to answer that earlier poem (the one Snyder himself has named the most important poem of the twentieth century), but also that the status of the Snyderian poetic – in which it is never a question of finding an authentic voice but rather a question of giving voice to the Other – implies a revision of the Bloomian categories of poetic analysis themselves. Further, the concern of *Myths & Texts* with quotation and allusion – the question of other voices – means that Snyder's poem revises the modernist epic tradition – revises, that is, the meaning of quotation and literary tradition – of which it is a part: it is not simply an extension of that tradition but a poem which reveals the predicative conventions of the tradition and offers an alternative to them. Three large and distinct – yet connected – claims are being made here, and they must be dealt with in turn. It is the *way* in which *Myths & Texts* responds to *The Waste Land* that necessitates both a revision of the modern poetic tradition of which *The Waste Land* is the exemplary poem and a revision of the dominant interpretive categories by which poetic tradition is understood.[30]

It is not possible to elaborate here the status of voice in *The Waste Land* or the complex terms of various voice's connections. We can only propose one fairly standard conclusion, which is that no stable enunciative position exists in the poem, and that therefore any totalisable meaning for the poem is strictly impossible.[31] What is possible here is a comparison between the final section of *The Waste Land*, *What the Thunder Said*, and the final section of *Myths & Texts*, 'Burning', particularly its closing poem, number 17. This final poem of Snyder's book exists as some kind of conclusion or coda to the whole text by comprising a section entitled '*the myth*' and a section entitled '*the text*', as if the various texts had been distilled into a single myth by the poem's end which it is the task of the final utterance to articulate. As 'conclusion', poem 17 can therefore be compared economically with the final section of *The Waste Land*. We should remember, though, that the cyclic structure of Snyder's poem problematises the notion of a final end or summary, since every end is transformed into a beginning (the poem's closing line refers the reader back to its opening). Any 'final' myth or text is therefore necessarily provisional. This provisionality differs, however, from the non-totalised, equivocal ending of *The Waste Land*, a disparity which I would suggest is ultimately a function of the different way the two poems conceive of myth and of their own relation to it. Most simply put, the vision proposed by *Myths & Texts* 'works' while that proposed by *The Waste Land* fails (it should be noted, however, that the notion of success I am using here is not one equivalent to notions of completion, totalised significance or any kind of subjective mastery of the elements involved). That is, the fragments of myths and texts invoked by *The Waste Land* are ultimately conceived by the poem as insufficient, whereas the different relation to its assorted myths and texts obtained by Snyder's poem ensures their sufficiency.

If, on a fairly general, abstract level, *The Waste Land* can be said to be concerned with connection and dislocation, then the voice which says toward the end of *The Fire Sermon* 'I can connect / Nothing with nothing' (ll. 301–2) can be read as at least a partially representative voice. This is not to say that the status of connection remains constant throughout the poem or even that it remains constant within sections of the poem, since the very motive of the text is to examine and forge various connections, which makes of its sections and fragments a dynamic struggle. However, to the extent that various modes of connection are seen to fail in various ways (this being largely an historical consequence of the cultural implications of the First World War), then the bare minimum that can be asserted is that nothing can be connected with nothing. Note that the statement is not that nothing can be connected – it does not consist of a complete renunciation of relation – but that only absence can be connected to further absence: disjunction is not absolute.

This avowal is set in the textual context of a passage whose generic label is *sermon* and which mediates on *fire* as the paradoxical source of *corruption* and disintegration – fire as libidinal lust and as destruction – but also the source of *salvation* through purification (both senses of which have their roots in biblical paradigms and images). The problematic of that section has to do with the establishing of which function of fire will predominate. The direct corollary of the struggle has to do with finding which textual references can be galvanised in the search for regeneration: whether, that is, biblical and religious references to the purificatory function of fire still hold, can still obtain significance for the present. To connect nothing with nothing is to posit a void of absence which may well image the fiery pit of hell, and it is the fiery pit of hell over which the most notable sermon in the American tradition, Jonathan Edwards's 'Sinners in the Hands of an Angry God' (1741), pictures the individual suspended at the

mercy of a righteous and indignant deity. *The Fire Sermon* ends
with reference to such an image by following the announcement of
connecting nothing with nothing thus:

> To Carthage then I came
>
> Burning burning burning burning
> O Lord thou pluckest me out
> O lord thou pluckest
>
> burning

There is allusion here to biblical images, to the images and rhetoric
of Edwards's sermon and to Augustine's *Confessions*. The image
produced by these incantatory, non-narrative fragments is that of
entering a place burning with lust (Carthage) and being plunged
into the fires of hellish damnation (either as a consequence of or as
an analogue to the situation in Carthage), from which one may be
plucked – like a 'brand', a branch – by the Hand of God, but only
fortuitously: the emphasis is on one's status as absolutely vulnerable, subject to forces utterly beyond one's control (both the fiery
pit, the city of lust and the Hand of God). Such a situation, in
which the speaker has no way of redeeming himself – the best he
can do is connect nothing with nothing – is itself a burning, a
torment. It is implied by the truncated repetition of the penultimate line that he is pleading to be – rather than being – plucked,
and that if the burning is of the purificatory dimension, there is
little evidence to suggest he will survive.

In response to these images, the mode in which they are taken
up in *What the Thunder Said*, and their implications, *Myths & Texts*
titles its final section 'Burning' and figures both fire and sexuality
in positively regenerative terms. The world is proposed as not that
from which one has to be saved and from whose desires one must
be purified but, conversely, as that which saves. Such a proposition
is made by the characteristic figuration of earth as maternal (in
'Burning', poem 7), a figural conception which responds to *The
Waste Land*'s agonies by substituting a maternal deity for the
vengeful paternal Law of Edwards and Eliot. Making God and the
earth both the same thing (mother) enables both to be sexualised,
which then allows an intimate relation with each when the speaker
is figured as a heterosexual man:

>   Face in the crook of her neck
>   felt throb of vein
>   Smooth skin, her cool breasts
>   All naked in the dawn
>   'byrdes
>   sing forth from every bough'
>   where are they now
>   And dreamt I saw the Duke of Chou
>
>   The Mother whose body is the Universe
>   Whose breasts are Sun and Moon,
>   the statue of Prajna
>   From Java: the quiet smile,
>   The naked breasts.
>
>   'Will you still love me when my
>   breasts get big?'
>   the little girl said –
>
>   'Earthly Mothers and those who suck
>   the breasts of earthly mothers are mortal –
>   but deathless are those who have fed
>   at the breast of the Mother of the Universe.'
>   (*MT*, pp. 42–3)

For this poetic subject, being with a woman recalls the source of life, which is certainly a different conception than that offered by either the Bible or *The Waste Land*, in which feminine sexuality tends to be figured as a source of corruption and death. It is thus not the case that the gender stereotype – by which the woman is aligned with matter (as opposed to mind) – is broken, but rather that its value is reversed: the feminine and the physical are not to be overcome but are to be embraced – not as a means to something other, but as the end in themselves. There is some revision in this metaphoric depiction of the traditionally gendered binary opposites, however, because instead of aligning the feminine with the moon and the masculine with the sun, the feminine is aligned with both sun and moon, which points to the primary and consequential revision of traditional gender metaphorics in so far as the structure of *opposition* via which gender tends to be thought is modified here into a structure of *reciprocity* (as distinct also from mere *complementarity*).[32] The question of gendering will be taken up later, but for now we can note the mobilisation of the feminine in the service of an alternative myth of relation between human and natural.

The history of gendered binary oppositions, of which *The Waste Land* constitutes a potent literary example, represents the most significant version of the history of metaphysics – the imperative to transcend the physical – against which *Myths & Texts* is formulated. And so in poem 13 of 'Burning', metaphysics is imaged as treachery (well before Derrida's project is known) for which poetry is offered as the antidote; and this proposition is figured in an expression which refers to Snyder's first volume and which therefore connects the two books as intertextually significant: 'Poetry a riprap on the slick rock of metaphysics' (*MT*, p. 48). This line occurs in a poem structured analogously to sections of *The Waste Land* in the sense that different voices are operative which fail to be distinguished by any consistent textual mechanism, so that the poem is dialogic, consisting of voices responding to other voices. The voice that calls poetry 'a riprap on the slick rock of metaphysics' – a *riprap* being an arrangement of stones which facilitates travel up a slippery incline – interpolates the discourse of the poem in order to distinguish between its conception of poetry and other conceptions of the mode by which progress *vis-à-vis* the natural may be achieved. Hence:

> Poetry a riprap on the slick rock of metaphysics
> 'Put a Spanish halter on that whore of a mare
> & I'll lead the bitch up any trail'
>
> (how gentle! He should have whipped her first)

The voice which designates poetry as riprap is distinct from the parenthetical voice which comments sardonically on the conventional masculine solution to natural intransigence – a voice that articulates the human and natural in terms of an elemental struggle for mastery; yet those voices are connected in their refusal of the metaphysical ideology which denigrates both the physical and the feminine ('that whore of a mare'). The reference to 'a Spanish halter' aligns the colonial settlers of the West Coast with the oppressive ideology and substitutes for that cultural imperative a poetry of the natural and the aboriginal. Toward the end of poem

13 there are references to other images and myths which connect the natural with a threatening femininity and in opposition to which unremarkable, de-metaphorised nature is stated as the privileged alternative:

> It's all vagina dentata
> (Jump!)
> 'Leap through an Eagle's snapping beak'
>
> Actaeon saw Dhyana in the Spring
>
> > it was nothing special,
> > misty rain on Mt. Baker,
> > Neah Bay at low tide.
>
> (*MT*, p. 49)

The myths of vagina dentata and of Actaeon catching Diana naked (and being consequently transformed into a stag who was then torn apart by dogs as his penalty) comprise myths from a register in which evil has a natural rather than a human source and, more specifically, in which feminine sexuality is the source of destruction. Against such myths, the voice which authorises *Myths & Texts* constructs an alternative myth, one which *mythifies by demythifying the natural of culture's negative meanings*, the meanings which make it necessary to destroy nature in order to found culture. Thus the parenthetical voice mocks the vagina dentata myth by yelling 'Jump!' and by juxtaposing the image of narrowly missing laceration from the eagle's beak. Juxtapositionally associated with that image is the allusion to Actaeon and Diana, in which seeing the woman naked eventuates in destruction by teeth, as if the dogs who tore apart the libidinous Actaeon embodied Diana's vaginal incisors. The association of the parenthetical voice with mocking humour, together with the preposterous hyperbole of the juxtaposition – its outlandish rendition of mythical teeth as savage dogs – deflates the myth and substitutes for it an image of the natural that sees mountaintops as mountaintops rather than as teeth. Although in another poem Snyder will metaphorise mountains as the bountiful breasts of Mother Earth, in this instant mountains are demetaphorised in order to substitute a myth of positive, generative nature for the dominant myth of a femininely treacherous and destructive nature.

Poem 15 ends with an image which links the sexual with fire (as in *The Waste Land*) but also with the regenerative rather than the destructive or even the purifying: 'The hot seeds steam underground / still alive' (p. 51). The vehicle of the metaphor consists of an image of lodgepole pine seeds living underground after the forest has been burned, waiting to re-emerge; the tenor of the vehicle is more explicitly sexual and consists of an image of sperm entering the vagina, unobstructed by vagina dentata. The potent metaphor-image makes burning and sexuality positive (rather than negative), to be desired rather than eschewed, and it refers forward (as well as backward) to the book's final poem, which is concerned with the effects of burning, just as *What the Thunder Said* is concerned with similar effects. What is additionally notable about the image of hot seeds underground is that although the metaphor functions as a synecdoche for both the natural cycle and the textual cycle of the poem itself, it does not index generation or regeneration in ideational terms, since neither dimension of the metaphor – neither tenor nor vehicle – consists of an abstraction: both are images of *literal* generation, forms of natural production. In this sense, metaphor does not serve metaphysics but is rather a poetic way of indicating the connections between natural phenomena, which includes the human. Rather than assimilating the human to the cultural and predicating both on the destruction of the natural, the human is assimilated to the natural and shown to be productive of interrelationships which suggest an alternative cultural formation and a different way of deriving meaning from phenomena.

In order to compare finally the conclusion of *Myths & Texts* to that of *The Waste Land*, I reproduce in full the text of poem 17 here:

the text

Sourdough mountain called a fire in:
Up Thunder Creek, high on a ridge.
Hiked eighteen hours, finally found
A snag and a hundred feet around on fire:
All afternoon and into night
Digging the fire line
Falling the burning snag
It fanned sparks down like shooting stars
Over the dry woods, starting spot-fires

Flaring in wind up Skagit valley
From the Sound.
Toward morning it rained.
We slept in mud and ashes,
Woke at dawn, the fire was out,
The sky was clear, we saw
The last glimmer of the morning star.

the myth

Fire up Thunder Creek and the mountain –
            troy's burning!
The cloud mutters
The mountains are your mind.
The woods bristle there,
Dogs barking and children shrieking
Rise from below.

Rain falls for centuries
Soaking the loose rocks in space
Sweet rain, the fire's out
The black snag glistens in the rain
& the last wisp of smoke floats up
Into the absolute cold
Into the spiral whorls of fire
The storms of the Milky Way
'Buddha incense in an empty world'
Black pit cold and light-year
Flame tongue of the dragon
Licks the sun

The sun is but a morning star

There are certain analogous conventions of ending here and in
Eliot: here, the book entitled *Myths & Texts* provides a section
entitled '*the text*' and a section entitled '*the myth*' for its final poem,
as if each were a summary of the earlier textual fragments and
mythic references in the book; while the final section of *The Waste
Land*, *What the Thunder Said*, suggests by its title that some message
is to be designated which might make the enunciative discon-

tinuities of the previous section finally interpretable and comprehensible. In both cases, we seem to be offered some compensation for the readerly effort expended in earlier sections. Although the final poem of *Myths & Texts* picks up many of the images and themes of the book as a whole, it functions as provisional summary principally by designating the way in which the text as 'sense impression' gets converted into the myth as 'symbol' – how, that is, meaning is produced from phenomena, how objects and experience are made to signify. Not only this, but the poem suggests via its allusions to *The Waste Land* that certain symbolic resonances of the landscape should be either converted into different meanings or drained of meaning. The allusion is to the beginning of *What the Thunder Said*:

> After the torchlight red on sweaty faces
> After the frosty silence in the gardens
> After the agony in stony places
> The shouting and the crying
> Prison and palace and reverberation
> Of thunder of spring over distant mountains
> He who was living is now dead
> We who were living are now dying
> With a little patience
>
> Here is no water but only rock
> Rock and no water and the sandy road
>
> (ll. 322–32)

In Eliot is elemental consternation on a cosmic scale – the anaphoric opening lines consist of repetitions with contrastive differences (heat versus cold, sweat versus frost, garden versus 'stony places', the stoicism of 'frosty silence' versus agony), which do not provide alternatives but merely various incremental dimensions of a single, inescapable narrative of torment whose biblical referent consists of Christ's final hours – the arrest by night in the Garden of Gethsemane, the throwing into prison and the confrontation with Pontius Pilate, the crucifixion, and the thunder at the moment of expiration.

Immediately subsequent to the elliptically synecdochic and metonymic rendition of these details, the Christian formula for the resurrection is inverted, 'He who was living is now dead', which eventuates a corollary inversion, 'We who were living are now dying', and whose shift of grammatical tense prolongs the agony of the speaker. By contrast, in the Snyder poem we find no myth of resurrection (or its failure), and for Eliot's apocalyptic rhetoric, the speaker of poem 17 substitutes 'Dogs barking and children shriek-ing', thereby delimiting any desire metaphorically to extend the event of fire to symbolic or apocalyptic proportions: against the exclamatory 'troy's burning!' is set dogs and children and a voice from the mountain which is neither that of the Deity instructing a prophet nor a portentously climactic pronouncement, as we find in Eliot. The desire to read in thunder a 'message', the desire to make nature and the elements signify something meaningful in relation to the human, is resisted by reading in the cloud's 'mutter' a statement which indicates the source of significance to be the human mind: 'The mountains are your mind'. This underdeter-minative utterance functions in two ways: to suggest an analogy between the human and the natural, and to prioritise the natural over the human in the analogy, which subsequently *grounds* meaning, making it resistant to extravagant symbolisation.

Signification is always a consequence of humanly derived sign systems, but that inevitability does not necessitate the over-investment of the natural with distortive symbolic meaning. The gesture is not 'against interpretation' *per se*, but rather against certain kinds of idealist interpretation which would make of a landscape the arena for a spiritual drama. The paradox of a strategy which is always converting the natural landscape into a question of spirituality and assimilating it to the human is that it eventuates a condition in which the dominant metaphor is that of a land laid waste, infertile, unsupportive. By contrast, for Snyder the land is never a wasteland, not even metaphorically.

Where in poem 17 there is an extension of the natural and the local to a cosmic scale, the image produced is the opposite of apocalyptic destruction, is instead an image of soothing relief, a salvation drained of any symbolic meaning:

> Rain falls for centuries
> Soaking the loose rocks in space
> Sweet rain, the fire's out

This is in direct contrast to the symbolic dearth of water in *The Waste Land*, an absence which is reiterated in a mode of poetic parallelism reminiscent of the lineation of biblical psalms: 'Here is no water but only rock / Rock and no water and the sandy road'. The absence of water has spiritually symbolic implications, for lines such as 'If there were water we should stop and drink' in a context brimming with religious allusions call to mind the consolatory words of Christ that advise the thirsty and weary to approach Him for sustenance that endures. The symbolic implication is therefore a corollary dearth of spiritual relief from the burdens of modern life depicted by the poem. Here is 'dry sterile thunder without rain', and the figure of sterility – a desexualised sexual figure – links both to the landscape as barren wasteland unable to provide regeneration and to the ominous sexuality apparent elsewhere in the poem which is productive of destruction rather than generation. And hence, a few lines later:

> If there were the sound of water only
> Not the cicada
> And dry grass singing
> But sound of water over a rock
>
> (ll. 352–5)

Besides the allusion we might hear to Whitman's *Leaves of Grass* – an allusion which implies the uselessness of that tradition – there is a pun audible on 'cicada', if one hears the word as Eliot or Pound would have heard it in England (Pound being the one who heavily revised Eliot's poem). 'Cicada' as *sick ardour* links – at the level of the signifier – the insect as representative sound of an unresponsive and barren landscape to the disease of love which is merely lust, the conception of the sexual as the destruction rather than the generation of life.

In poem 17, by contrast, both fire and water are regenerative, since the natural is defined as generative and as that whose desire harmonises with the human (if one allows this) rather than competing with it. When a religious symbol is allowed to overlay the text, the reference is to Eastern religion as opposed to Western Christianity, and consists of an image in which natural effects are found pleasing to the deity: the wisps of smoke rising from the extinguished fire are seen as 'Buddha incense' – an 'offering' for which, one may note, no unnecessary sacrifice has been made. What is, is sufficient.

The mythification of the event of putting out the mountain fire develops with reference to one of the earliest images from 'Logging' – that of the pine trees as dragons rising from sleep to avenge their destruction by machines: here, fire, tree and sun are not competitive but parts of a single cycle, so that the final image metaphorises the sun in order both to delimit it as centre and to return one to the beginning, to emphasise the generative, cyclic aspect of a scene of natural destruction. Metaphorically reducing the sun to 'a morning star' posits a kind of new beginning that promises expansion and optimism, and which is signified grammatically by the absence of full-stops at the end of the poem. By contrast, *The Waste Land* ends with no such optimism: the land remains 'arid', the myth of rejuvenation via the Fisher King remains unfulfilled, and the best that can be offered is a series of disjunctive fragments shored against ruin – no reconstruction, let alone regeneration, seems possible. The repetition of Sanskrit, 'Shantih shantih shantih', translates into Protestant Christian terms as 'the peace which passes understanding'; but what remains at the close of Eliot's poem is not a peace of any kind but merely pieces, and it is a condition – textual, phenomenal, epistemological and spiritual – which passes understanding. This is not provisionality but failure – which is not to suggest that as a literary artefact the poem is a failure (since it is not). It is to suggest, however, that as the production of a myth for the modern – or the recognition of the failure or impossibility of its production – Eliot's poem is answered by Snyder's construction of an alternative, affirmative, generative myth.

To argue this is to provide a textual and cultural context for Snyder's poetic beginnings. The corollary to this account, whereby Snyder modifies tradition as history or canon by positing tradition as cycle, must be argued with respect to further – and later – textual evidence below. Having pursued detailed textual analysis at some length, I now wish to indicate in more historical terms the cultural context of Snyder's poetic beginnings in the 1950s, in order to elaborate on a more general level the development of his poetics in political and philosophical terms.

HISTORIES AND POSTMODERNISMS

There are two broad ways of conceiving of poetic beginning here, the first having to do with the poetic field of American modernism which dominates the first half of twentieth century letters and in response to which a properly postmodern poetic is developed, and the second having to do with the historically determined cultural conditions of postwar America.

As the analysis offered above has suggested, Snyder begins his poetic career by responding to the most important poem of the first half of the twentieth century, the text which could be considered to exemplify a central component of modernist poetics. However, literary modernism is not homogeneous, and therefore the emergence of a postmodern poetics in the 1950s and 1960s can only be categorised under the single rubric of the postmodern rather loosely: postmodernism is necessarily heterogeneous. (The limitations of the term 'postmodern' can also be registered by speculating about the absurd inevitability of a post-postmodernism. Despite the impetus to outline a chronology of literary history here, it is therefore more useful to conceive of the postmodern in terms of a paradigm shift or in terms of a disruption of certain aesthetic formations, rather than in terms of a temporal narrative.)

Postmodern heterogeneity is also a consequence of the perceived failure of transcendental strategies; postmodernism is characterised by a refusal of any absolute and prefers instead to ground value in the non-transcendent phenomenal world. It is important to distinguish here between the postmodern as a pervasive cultural 'condition' of late twentieth-century capitalist society and the postmodern as an aesthetic category deployed critically *vis-à-vis* certain literary texts.[33] As an aesthetic category, postmodernism has tended to be theorised in relation to the genres of fiction and certain kinds of theoretical critical writing rather than in relation to older literary genres such as poetry.[34] It is difficult to say whether the theoretical differences between postmodern poetry and postmodern prose, and between postmodern writing and postmodern culture, are more significant than the similarities. Since I am concerned here with specifying the emergence and characteristics of a postmodern poetics (of which Snyder's practice is exemplary), various alternative formulations of the postmodern – formulations which, I might add, tend to constitute the dominant theoretical accounts of postmodernism – are comparatively irrelevant in so far as the critical process of characterisation and discrimination goes. However, the most significant common feature which links a postmodern poetics with theories of the postmodern pertaining to prose genres and to social organisation has to do with the resistance of postmodern phenomena to absolutes and to the transcendental. Within the broad terms of this delineative feature of postmodernism, epistemological, aesthetic and social structures are seen to be decentred: transcendent values, structures and accounts of the world are divested by postmodernity of their authority. The characteristic – and somewhat clichéd – critical terms by which this disruptive decentring has come to be known consist of formulations such as 'the crisis of legitimation' and 'the failure of master narratives'. To return to the items of my account above in the light of these definitions, we might wish to re-characterise *The Waste Land* as a postmodern epic, composed as it is of fragments for which no unifying centre or structure can be found. Such a critical possibility only serves to indicate the limitations of conventional theories of the postmodern for understanding poetry.[35]

However – and this is where theories of the postmodern converge in their understanding of the shift away from modernism – the resistance to transcendental categories – to God, to the Logos, to the centre as adequate structural principle[36] – share as their predicative feature the ethics of a response to *political* events. That is, both the disruption of social forms and the emergence of resistant, alternative aesthetics are prompted by socio-political occurrences. As Alice Jardine puts it in the best account to date of postmodern theory and fiction, 'our ways of understanding in the West have been and continue to be complicitous with our ways of oppressing'.[37] In the light of the Second World War and its legacies of atrocity, the perception of a significant link between the political and the epistemological necessitated a radical conversion of theoretical accounts of the world and of what Julia Kristeva would term 'signifying practices'.

It was thus a consciousness of the political events surrounding the Second World War – the rise of Fascism, the Holocaust, President Truman's sanction for the dropping of the atom bomb – which in large measure generated the literary response. The sense existed that the dominant forms of perceiving the world had not helped prevent the manifold atrocities of the twentieth century; it was therefore necessary to change those forms of perception, one of which consists of poetic discourse.[38] Hence Snyder in the 1960s:

> After World War II, another generation looked at Communist rhetoric with a fresh eye and saw that within the Communist

governments (and states of mind) there are too many of the same things as are wrong with 'capitalism' – too much anger and murder. The suspicion grew that perhaps the whole Western tradition, of which Marxism is but a (millenial Protestant) part, is off the track. This led many people to study other major civilizations – India and China – to see what they could learn. (*EHH*, pp. 113–14)

Although not every postmodern poet experienced complete alienation from the totality of Western values, what we might call a pervasive consensus of dissensus prevailed as a consequence of the implication of dominant American cultural and political values in circumstances that wholly ironised or inverted the meaning of the term 'civilisation'. It was thus within the values and framework of a counter-cultural movement that Snyder's postmodern poetics were produced – a fact that has contributed toward the stereotyping – and hence the marginalisation – of his work.

This brings us to the specific historical circumstances in which Snyder's literary career began – the circumstances of the Beat movement (Snyder was immortalised and rather damagingly stereotyped by his fictional characterisation as Japhy Ryder in Kerouac's *The Dharma Bums*) and the San Francisco Renaissance of the 1950s.[39] The most famous counter-cultural poem of protest in the 1950s – the one that came to exemplify the San Francisco Renaissance and the dissidence of the cultural *vis-à-vis* the national – was Allen Ginsberg's *Howl*, which Snyder has referred to as 'the most influential poem of the mid-century in America', adding that 'perhaps the only other single poem that has had that kind of impact is *The Waste Land*, in this century so far'.[40] *Howl* was first unleashed on the public at the famous Six Gallery reading in San Francisco in Autumn 1955, at which Snyder – together with many others – also read some of his early work.[41] The poem was subsequently published by Lawrence Ferlinghetti's City Lights bookstore-press and almost immediately seized for a much-publicised obscenity trial based on its content. It was thus that the counter-cultural Beats achieved notoriety in the American 'decade of consensus'.

In his long, declamatory, breath-line poem, Ginsberg bears intensely graphic witness to the multiple ways in which 'the best minds' of his generation have been destroyed by a socially enforced madness. Ginsberg emphasises his counter-cultural stance by speaking as a figure thrice marginalised from hegemonic cultural values by his ethnic, sexual and professional identities (as Jewish homosexual hippy-dropout). This is a poetic figuration of speaker as outcast, pariah, speaking not as the representative of culture (*à la* Frost), but in direct opposition to that representative function. In *Howl*, the national symbol – America – is villified via its metaphorisation as 'Moloch', the Canaanite idol to whom children were sacrificed: the speaker is thus paradigmatically imaged as victim of a predatory social order. The paradox – or, more properly, the epistemological contradiction – of such representation (and this also applies to contemporary Foucauldean accounts of the relation between social discourses and the subject they construct) is, of course, that the subject is imaged as both helpless victim and product of inordinately powerful forces of oppression and con-struction, and *simultaneously* as valiant agent of opposition, offer-ing the literary as a potent force of resistance.[42] However, as Snyder's comment correctly indicates, *Howl* was not without extremely influential *literary effects*, and it was thus within a milieu of literary protest that a postmodern poetic began to be formulated.

What is important for the purposes of my argument here is less the dimension of protest – literature of topically political protest tends to be limited to its historical moment – than the alternative poetic produced in response. The best way of characterising postmodern poetics is not in terms of 'the flourish of negativized rhetoric' that usually accompanies accounts of the postmodern,[43] but rather in the terms set out by Charles Altieri in his book *Enlarging the Temple* (1979). Altieri characterises postmodern poetics as *immanentist*, as opposed to the predominantly *symbolist* – or transcendence-oriented – poetics of modernism. Altieri does not find the model for postmodern poetics in non-Western cultures (as Snyder implies may be necessary); instead, he develops the theoretical paradigms of symbolism and immanentism in relation to English Romantic poetics, opposing Coleridge's model of the divinely creative poetic imagination (symbolism) to Wordsworth's emphasis on the poetic function as having to do with the revelation of what is already there in nature (immanentism). The develop-ment of the theory in terms of Romantic poetics can be confining, and the tendency of Altieri's argument to account for change in terms of binary oppositions (Coleridge *versus* Wordsworth, mod-ern *versus* postmodern, mind *versus* the natural) limits the possibil-ity of critical nuance with regard to historical shifts in conceptions of the literary.[44] However, it is the notion of immanence that seems to me the most useful here, not least because the etymology of the word derives from the Latin *manere*, meaning 'to dwell': immanence is but another term for the poetics of inhabitation of which I am arguing Snyder is exemplary.[45]

Immanence as 'indwelling' is strictly a theological concept which has to do with the belief in the pervasive presence of the Deity throughout the universe, including the believer as sacred container of God. To the extent that immanence implies pervasive, unlocalisable presence, its relevance for an ethical-poetical project based on knowing the *specifics of place* may seem questionable. However, the relevance of the term and its conceptual referent that I wish to emphasise is two-fold: first, the meaning of the word which allows it to stand as a metonym for inhabitation – the goal of the Snyderian project; and secondly, the implications of the concept in its anti-idealist, non-transcendental sense which provides for that metonymic status.

In a transcendent organisation, God inhabits the celestial realm of Heaven outside and beyond the Earth to which the believer must pass in order to enter His presence. The structure of immanence, by contrast, is such that God is always already present, and therefore no passing beyond is necessary in order to encounter the divine. We are not concerned with any deity here but rather with the location of value. Where symbolism – and what we might term symbolist literary criticism (which would include American deconstruction in its dimension as a legacy of New Criticism) – posits the subjective mind as the ultimate source of value, immanentism restores value to the phenomenal world, to the ordinary and everyday: immanentism thus disallows transcendental imperatives, substituting for them the impulse to find value near at hand. As in William Carlos Williams, who may be seen as a transitional poet initiating the shift from modernism to the postmodern, a red wheelbarrow represents nothing more and nothing less than a red wheelbarrow: a wheelbarrow does not have to be metaphorised as the chariot of Jehovah, for instance, to mean or to be viewed as valuable, since whatever worth it can signify is inherent, 'there', not transcendent or elsewhere. The function of the postmodern poet is simply to point to that value, to frame and reveal it (there is an analogy to be developed here between immanentist poetics and the 'found-object' art of American postmoderns such as Jeff Koons and Haim Steinbeck). As in the ambivalence between 'compose' and 'invent' in Williams's 'A Sort of a Song', the poet of immanence has both to discover what is 'there' and to put it together (compose it), to indicate the relations between its elements, and to frame it as significant.

The dimension of immanentism that is important for Snyder has to do with the identifying of and pointing to *relationships*, particularly those relationships between natural phenomena themselves, and between the natural and the human. The scientific term for the networks of relationship discovered by the Snyderian poetic is *ecology*, the politics of earth-management. 'Ecology' is the etymological derivative of the title of Snyder's first book of prose, *Earth House Hold*: 'ecology' comes from the Greek word *oikos*, meaning the economy of the house or habitat – hence the notion of household and inhabitation. As a modern science, ecology's field consists of the study of relationships between living organisms; the study, that is, of how earth manages its own household. As a version of immanentism, 'ecology' may turn out to be a characteristically postmodern term, since although the word first appeared in 1873 (as *œcology*), according to the *Oxford English Dictionary*, the unabridged edition of the *OED* published in 1933 contains no mention of the word. As *oikos* and *logos*, habitat and word, *ecology* is thus legible as a metonym for the immanentist poetic and as a synecdoche for the ethico-philosophical basis of Snyder's poetics of inhabitation.

The ecological dimension of immanentism is exemplified perhaps best by Snyder's more recent volume of poetry, *Axe Handles* (1983), since it is in this book – to my mind, Snyder's best – that non-linear models of interrelationship are imaged most cogently. In discussing *Myths & Texts* I asserted that Snyder's poetry implies a revision of the dominant model by which relationships between poets and poems are understood, which is the model of influence. Poetic influence can be conceived in relatively neutral terms – as, say, Helen Vendler imagines it; or it can be conceived in agonistic terms, as Harold Bloom theorises it; or it can be thought of in more positive terms, as Black and feminist critics have more recently sought to theorise it via the metaphor of the mother or foremother (as opposed to Bloom's notion of the poetic father who must be overcome in a violent Oedipal struggle for dominance). These alternative ways of thinking about literary influence all depend, however, upon a relatively linear notion of chronology, which makes them assimilable to conventional notions of literary history. (Gilbert and Gubar's *Norton Anthology of Literature by Women* (1985), for instance, is assimilable to the conventional *terms* of the hegemonic literary canon simply because it functions so easily as merely an *addition*, a supplement, to the pre-existing canon.)

In opposition to models of linearity and indebtedness, Snyder offers the model of the cycle (in *Myths & Texts*, as discussed), the model of the wave (in *Regarding Wave*), and the model of the loop (in *Axe Handles*). All three figures – cycle, wave and loop – are ecologically derived metaphors which emphasise process (over product), interdependence (or 'interpenetration' in 'For All', discussed earlier), reciprocity (over originality and independence), and 'influence' as a two-way flow in which no element is privileged as primary over others. It is thus never a question in Snyder of isolating cause and consequence, but rather of developing networks of connections which can only artificially be atomised and whose only primary term is the earth in which the relationships are grounded and of which in fact they consist. Inhabiting the ground is a figure for finding and learning one's place within the web of natural relationships. As an issue of structure, the project of inhabitation is therefore particularly accessible to poetic structures in which techniques of juxtaposition, elision and the metonymic arrangement of elements provide space for the insertion of the reader as active participant – although not master – in the production of sense.

AXE HANDLES

The metaphor of the axe handle – which organises the volume of that title similarly to the way in which the star and pine-cone organise *Myths & Texts* and the way the figure of the wave structures *Regarding Wave* – is both a figure for interdependence and a figure for the notion of model itself. As the first poem in *Axe Handles*, 'Axe Handles' begins the first section of the book, *Loops*, thereby advertising itself as a mode of beginning, a model of starting which always loops back to an earlier beginning. Not only does the opening poem lend the book its title, but it also features on the back of the book-jacket, printed in full, thereby functioning as both beginning and end of the book. Instead of any cover photograph of the poet, or any description of contents or critical endorsements of the book, *Axe Handles* pictures a Japanese figure on its front, painted in a modern stylised version of traditional Oriental technique by a contemporary Japanese artist, Mayumi Oda, and entitled 'Treasure Ship, Goddess of Snow'. On the back cover is reprinted 'Axe Handles': front and back cover together thus indicate by the mode of presentation – both poetic and pictographic – that the book is about modelling and about the kind of continuity provided by a certain model of modelling.

Although the book is dedicated to a place rather than any person – '*This book is for San Juan Ridge*' – there is an essential recognition and development of the notion first elaborated in *Regarding Wave* that central to the continuity afforded by models is the woman. That is, the fundamental model of the axe handle as a metaphor for model comes to be represented as inseparable from the model woman who functions generatively – through her maternal body – to provide for the continuity of the species. Thus the book's epigraph – quotation functioning as model – analogises the axe handle and the woman:

> How do you shape an axe handle?
> Without an axe it can't be done.
> How do you take a wife?
> Without a go-between you can't get one.
> Shape a handle, shape a handle,
> the pattern is not far off.
> And here's a girl I know,
> The wine and food in rows.
> From *Book of Songs* (*Shih Ching*) (Mao
> no. 158): a folk-song from the Pin area,
> 5th c. BC.

The model of the axe handle thus begins to look unpleasantly familiar to readers of Lévi-Strauss, or Irigaray, or Eve Sedgwick – those theorists who have analysed the way in which women function as a medium of exchange between men, women coming to be defined as objects exchanged by men, their substitutable- and object-status representing the guarantee of male masculinity, which masculinity in turn is defined as the participation in and maintenance of that exchange.

Within the terms of this social arrangement of gender, it is also therefore not accidental that 'Axe Handles' images continuity in patrilineal terms, the axe handle coming to represent the model for the patrimonial training in masculinity which passes from father to son – the implication being, of course, that the boy learns how to be a man from his father. And patrilinearity is certainly not an alternative model of influence or tradition; instead it represents the very embodiment of tradition traditionally conceived. It is insufficient here to argue that we cannot expect any different from the epigraph considering its historical setting, since although the text originates at a time when a wife was more overtly an object to be procured by or for the man, that structural relation between the sexes survives today in the symbolic function of the Law and its institutions – the Name of the Father, the marriage ceremony in which the bride is 'given' to the husband by her father, and suchlike. The structure has indeed been reinforced rather than dissolved by its transformation from a relatively literal structural arrangement into a more symbolic one. Neither is it acceptable to suggest that modelling and continuity is bound to be figured in terms of patrilineal masculinity as a consequence of the poet's family structure in which there are two sons but no daughters. The question has rather to do with the place of the woman in the structure of continuity and with the function of a certain *image* of woman as that structure's security. Ultimately, this gender question extends to issues such as the figuration of American land as feminine, to the figuration of the natural cycle via the metaphor of the female cycle of fertility, and consequently, to the place of the woman who wishes to write. If the feminine – as land, cycle, Muse or voice[46] – functions as enabling metaphor for the man who writes, then what is the woman's relation to those metaphors, and how is the project of inhabitation gender-biased and heterosexist? These questions require extensive examination which is not possible here. However, I wish to indicate at this point the inextricability of the gender question from the terms and objects of analysis, so that in the space remaining such questions can be brought to the foreground, and in this way the issue of poetic beginning, the issue of writing as a man in the American West – together with the implications and stakes of these contextual issues for my argument – can be considered more fully.

The place to begin – the place at which the textual paraphernalia I have been describing directs us to begin – is the poem 'Axe Handles', which I cite in full below.

Axe Handles

One afternoon the last week in April
Showing Kai how to throw a hatchet
One-half turn and it sticks in a stump.
He recalls the hatchet-head
Without a handle, in the shop
And go gets it, and wants it for his own.
A broken-off axe handle behind the door
Is long enough for a hatchet,
We cut it to length and take it
With the hatchet head
And working hatchet, to the wood block.
There I begin to shape the old handle
With the hatchet, and the phrase
First learned from Ezra Pound
Rings in my ears!
'When making an axe handle
    the pattern is not far off.'
And I say this to Kai
'Look: We'll shape the handle
By checking the handle
Of the axe we cut with —'
And he sees. And I hear it again:
It's in Lu Ji's *Wên Fu*, fourth century
A.D. 'Essay on Literature' — in the
Preface: 'In making the handle
Of an axe
By cutting wood with an axe
The model is indeed near at hand.'
My teacher Shih-hsiang Chen
Translated that and taught it years ago
And I see: Pound was an axe,
Chen was an axe, I am an axe
And my son a handle, soon
To be shaping again, model
And tool, craft of culture,
How we go on.

Unlike the majority of the poems I have analysed in detail so far,
'Axe Handles' is more overtly a narrative poem (as opposed to the

shorter descriptive, reflective lyrics which characterise what is best
– as far as I am concerned – about the earlier work). The poem is
also more directly autobiographical, referring as it does to the
proper name of Snyder's elder son, and comprising a consistent
narrative voice from which other voices are clearly distinguished
by the foregrounding of quotation. The narrative moves from a
specifically defined locale and event – an afternoon near the end of
April, throwing and making an axe with the son – to a generalised
statement regarding the continuity of community and culture. This
narrative movement of the poem, in which both the son and the
father are seen to learn something new, provides a structural
analogy between the tropic form and the reflective content of the
utterance: in each instance there exists the movement from the
particular to the general, and the generalisation – the making
general – has to do precisely with realising oneself as a general
instance rather than as a specific individual. That is, it is not only
the *statement* which is made general, part of a larger whole, it is also
the *speaker* who is made general, part of a process of which he is but
an element. In this way, the text functions analogously at both the
constative and performative levels, and both the subject of the
enunciation and the subject of the statement become subjectively
dissolved or generalised. The process of generalisation, of the
dissolution of specificity, is achieved by beginning with alliterative
details and with identifiable, distinctive voices. Thus, for instance, I
think we can detect the indirect discourse of either father or son in
the phrase, 'And go gets it' (this is not just a single narrative voice,
whose grammar would be 'And goes to get it'). The sense of
process, of narrative re-enacted rather than reported, is also
produced by the present tense, which then contrasts with the
past-tense reporting of memory, quoted in the present tense to
indicate its resonance for the present process, yet shown as
anterior to the discoveries made in the poem.

The importance of memory for continuity is made apparent
early, since the child first 'recalls the hatchet-head', which then
prompts the speaker's first recollection – 'A broken-off axe handle
behind the door / Is long enough for a hatchet' – and subsequently
prompts further remembered analogies. What is significant is that
the speaker remembers his own models – Pound, Chen – as he
himself *becomes* a model for his son in the act of *making* a model.
And what are remembered are words, words which 'ring' in the
ear like axe-blows, and which are seen to be analogous to the axe

handle as model by their intermediate status: just as the epigraph claims that one can no more make an axe handle without an axe handle than one can get a wife without a go-between, so the transmission of culture and its laws is seen to be dependent on linguistic mediation.

It is tempting to compare the avowal of 'the phrase / First learned from Ezra Pound' with the avowal 'I cannot remember things I once read' at the centre of the earlier poem, and to suggest that it is only once one is sufficiently established to become a model for others that the relation to one's own models can be articulated. Such an argument is tempting to elaborate principally because Snyder's poetics often seem so Poundian. However, I think it is less a case of uncovering a poetic repression than it is of perceiving another way in which the Other speaks through the subject, a perception which the poem's speaker clearly achieves: just as the son 'sees' what his father shows him, so too the speaker 'see[s]' his own sonship *vis-à-vis* Pound, Lu Ji and Shih-hsiang Chen (biographically, we might note that the mentor Chen is the 'father' for whom the 'son's' literal second son is named). In this way the speaker recognises himself as the *tool* of earlier speakers: once again, rather than recognising the self in the Other, he recognises the Other in the self.

To the extent that the model relation is associated with an 'Essay on Literature', it is possible to interpret this poem placed at the head of the book as an implicit statement of poetics; if this interpretive extension is correct, then the poetics is a traditional one of mimesis, in which continuity between representation and its referent is assured because 'The model is indeed near at hand'. Although the mimetic relation appears to involve no loss, it is still the case that it is a cultural relation which must be *learned*: it must be translated and taught to the next generation so that its transmission is assured. One mode of that transmission is, of course, poetry. Thus although figuring transmission in patrimonial terms makes the relation a linear one, it is the interdependence of cyclical relation which the volume wishes to stress.

The acknowledgement of necessary mediation constitutes a recognition of the voice of the Other – whether that Other be linguistic, paternal, the landscape, the teacher or the woman. In allowing the Other to speak – indeed, by making it the function of poetic discourse to articulate the Other's voice – a relation of interdependence is seen to exist. It is in this sense that the notion of a mediated relation between the sexes (which is proffered as analogy for the model of model-making by the epigraph) – that is, the idea of the impossibility of even *bodily* immediacy in a sexual relation – in fact constitutes a Lacanian notion, a notion of impossibility which is held as a consequence of recognising the linguistic alterity whose very intervention makes relation possible.[47] The paradox of the Other is that it both enables relation and disables relation, rendering communication always imperfect and effectively disharmonising connection. That is, the necessary routing of desire through the Other of symbolisation – through language, the Symbolic – precipitates an opacity which alienates the subject from any direct relation to its own desire. It is for this reason that Lacan can say that 'man's desire is the desire of the Other' – which does not translate as implying me desiring what you want, but rather signifies the way in which the Other, the function of alterity, commandeers desire, making its fulfilment strictly impossible. Hence the much-vaunted Lacanian pronouncement upon the impossibility of the sexual relation – a pronouncement whose emphasis is not on the impossibility of the sexual but on the impossibility of *relation*.

There is in Snyder both a recognition and a refusal of such mediacy. The recognition occurs in the form of identifying and acknowledging structures of interdependence – in which, for instance, one is not just a father but also *at the same time* a son. The disavowal of mediacy occurs principally *vis-à-vis* language, when the notion of mediacy makes of language a mediate function analogous to the *tool* (say, an axe handle). As Heidegger discusses it in 'The Origin of the Work of Art', the tool occupies a curiously indeterminate – because intermediate – relation between the worker and the object.[48] The inner jacket-cover of *Axe Handles* quotes David Lattimore quoting Jakobson in an appropriately displaced assertion about language's mediacy: 'Language is chief among tools that make tools. Poetry as language is a tool to make tools – a tool, but also a model, like the axe handle.' This is drastically incorrect. Language is not a tool, since language speaks the subject rather than the reverse (we note in passing the diametrically opposed interpretations derived from Jakobsonian linguistics by Lattimore and Lacan). No one can master language in the way that somebody like Snyder can master the craft of tool-making and tool-use. The unconscious as an effect of language – an effect, that is, of the disjunction between signifier and signified – means that language is constantly evading our grasp, failing to effect our intent. Unlike the axe or the saw, language is always doing rather more or rather less than we either desire or know.

It is for just this reason that the Other cannot ever be directly spoken *for*. The Other can speak *through* the subject – this is Snyder's shamanist poetics – and can indeed speak the subject (in which case it is the subject who tends to be spoken for), but the recognition of the Other in the self implies the impossibility of self-mastery, let alone any control over the Other. This provision is imaged in the second poem of *Axe Handles*, a poem which connectively loops back to 'Axe Handles' in its specification of what the children should be taught. 'For/From Lew' images the lesson learned in 'Axe Handles' as the message of the Other:

For/From Lew

> Lew Welch just turned up one day,
> live as you and me. 'Damn, Lew' I said,
> 'you didn't shoot yourself after all.'
> 'Yes I did' he said,
> and even then I felt the tingling down my back.
> 'Yes you did, too' I said – 'I can feel it now.'
> 'Yeah' he said,
> 'There's a basic fear between your world and
> mine. I don't know why.
> What I came to say was,
> teach the children about the cycles.
> The life cycles. All the other cycles.
> That's what it's all about, and it's all forgot.'

To contextualise the poem's topic: Lew Welch was a Nevadan poet (associated with the Beats) who graduated from Reed College like Snyder, and who was a close friend. In a 1988 radio interview, Snyder tells of how Welch disappeared in May 1973, leaving a suicide note in his truck – which was not found until the following morning – and departing with a gun and Snyder's trousers and work-jacket that he had borrowed. Friends and neighbours came to search for the body, scanning the sky for vultures which might indicate the whereabouts of the corpse, but after five days searching an area they themselves knew well, no body – not even vultures – could be found. Snyder adds that the people concluded that if Welch wanted so much to disappear, then it would be disrespectful to pursue the search. Four or five years later, Snyder fell into a kind of hallucinatory trance in the sauna in which he had the vision described in the poem.[49]

It is thus as an Other and an Other's discourse that the unconscious appears to apprehension. The discourse of the Other is framed in the colloquial diction that repeats the important fact – 'the cycles' – and which speaks without textbook grammar – 'it's all forgot'. This poem images in a different way the unconscious lesson which has to do with the articulation of cycles; in connecting backwards both to a figure whom Snyder says has 'become one of the spirits of the place' and to the memories of what others have taught in the previous poem, 'For/From Lew' forms a loop which begins a cycle. The doubling of the title indicates by its grammatical infelicity the way in which the poetic utterance is apprehended as produced by the subject ('For Lew') and simultaneously as produced by the Other ('From Lew'). It is the way in which the Snyderian subject allows for the Other's voice to be heard that constitutes the ethical strength of Snyderian poetics. The *unreliability* of this mode of discourse – in which it can only ever be an illusion that the speaker can speak *for* the Other, can control the discourse of the Other – represents the criterion by which Snyder's poetic utterances must be measured, since the commitment to such a poetics can always tend toward the desire to appropriate the Other in the sense of *making* it speak, directing its speech – which tendency obtains as the corollary of conceiving of language as the speaker's tool. It is indeed precisely the *continuity* of culture – which 'Axe Handles' images – that necessitates the ways in which language and symbolisation must always exceed the subject as a consequence of their bearing the meaning of the Other.

There is another source of continuity and relation to be found in *Axe Handles* whose lineaments are crucial for Snyder's conception of poetry's social function. It is the body. In making the body connect both poetry and work as well as poetry and world, Snyder's conception of the poetic is indeed Whitmanian. Snyder has said that physical labour is such an important element in his poetry because poetry derives – according to Whitman – from body and soul together.[50] For Whitman, one dimension of the 'soul' was the body's breath, the means by which outside and inside are related. In substituting for conventional metrics a poetry based on the breath-line (which has been taken up most notably in the twentieth century not by Snyder, but by Ginsberg), Whitman sought to link poetry both to the body and to the real, the American world. The breath-line materialises poetry.

Snyder emphasises the body and its labour in his poetry for reasons linked to Whitman's reasons and in order to achieve additional effects. To begin an elaboration of the desired effects of representing the body, I turn here to 'Look Back', another poem in *Axe Handles*, to observe how the body provides an image for continuity – a continuity both of subjective history (the subject's relation to himself) and of the landscape's history (the subject's relation to the territory). Returning to Piute mountain, Snyder returns to a geographical source of his subjectivity, much as Wordsworth does when he returns to the Wye Valley five years after his initial visit and composes 'Tintern Abbey' (1798):

Look Back

> Twice one summer
> I walked up Piute mountain,
> our trailcrew was camped at Bear Valley.
> I first had chainsaw practice
> cutting wood there for the cook.
> Piute mountain. And scanned the crest
> of the Sawtooths, to the east.
> A Whitebark pine relict stand
> cut off from friends
> by miles of air and granite – me
> running out ridges.
> Jimmy Jones the cook said 'I
> used to do that, run the ridges
> all day long – just like a coyote.'
> When I built a little sweatlodge
> one Sunday by the creek
> he told me to be careful,
> and almost came in too.

Today at Slide Peak in the Sawtooths
I look back at that mountain
twenty-five years. Those days
when I lived and thought all alone.

I was studying Chinese
preparing for Asia
every night after trail crew work
                                        from a book.
Jimmy Jones was a Mariposa Indian.
One night by the campfire
drinking that coffee black
he stood there looking down at my
H. G. Creel, 'Those letters Chinese?'
'Yes', I said. He said, 'Hmmmmm.
My grandpa they say was Chinese.'

And that year I quit early,
told the foreman I was headed for Japan.
He looked like he knew, and said 'Bechtel.'
I couldn't tell him something strange as Zen.

Jimmy Jones, and these mountains and creeks.
The up and down of it
stays in my feet.
            VII, '78, The Sawtooths.   (*AH*, pp. 28–9)

The body may bear the traces of memory as well as the mind (this
is what psychoanalysis teaches about the symptom), but the
memory can only signify when translated into language (which is
how psychoanalysis proposes to cure the symptom). Memory
characterises the precipitation of the subject within a history
whose meaning determines the subject and which is determined
prior to the subject's existence. Identity consists of finding one's
place in this history, of advancing subjectivity by casting backward
into the flow of meaning to locate determinate moments. Significantly for the speaker who would have us believe that memory's
form is located in the body and that memory's *content* consists of
the body's labour, the backward gaze of the poem begins by

looking back to *poetic* beginnings – specifically three lyrics of *Riprap*: 'Piute Creek', 'Milton by Firelight', and 'Above Pate Valley'. Beginning thus acquires meaning and subsequently forms memory only in so far as it is inseparable from *linguistic* events and effects. Hence the poetic repetition of name, the savouring of the signifier charged with meaning: 'Piute mountain'.

Yet Piute mountain only bears resonance because it had a meaning which preceded the speaker and to which he learned to accommodate himself – so much so, in fact, that it now appears as if he was in possession of its meaning, as if that signification formed a part of his corporeal frame. Thus the summer in which he scaled the mountain twice – the opening line foregrounding the thematic of repetition – was his summer of initiation: his first chainsaw practice, his pacing the ridge, repeating his Indian teacher, Jimmy Jones. There is a structure of repetition built into the speaker's developing knowledge of the ground, because Jimmy Jones had used to run along the ridges 'just like a coyote', and then the speaker traces the same path, just like the Indian: from coyote – wild creature thought of as half-human by Indian cultures – to Indian – thought of as half-animal, instinctual and at home in the wild – to white man, learning the landscape and his body's relation to both the terrain and its inhabitants. This substitutive structure is one which does not consist of the violent ousting of the Indian by the White, but rather one in which the White learns how to inhabit the ground like an Indian, becoming part of the meaning of the landscape. For this reason, a metonymic image is juxtaposed to the elliptical depiction of this process in the poem: the 'Whitebark pine relict', which as 'relict' represents a plant species surviving from an earlier environment. The implication of this juxtaposed image is double: suggesting first, that species does not have to overwhelm and exterminate species in order to inhabit the ground; and secondly, that the substitution of species for species can occur as part of the natural cycle, part of the landscape's development. Crucially, however, this is not a question of extermination but rather of learning to live in different arrangements.

The 'relict' tree 'cut off from friends' is analogous to the young man who writes around that time, 'A few friends but they are in cities', and who remembers the time twenty-three years earlier as 'Those days / when I lived and thought all alone'. The point, however, is less that he was alone than that when one is far from friends one makes new friends, establishes new arrangements of sociality: one's relations depend upon one's place, one's situation, and are determined by that place. In this sense, in the wilderness one can never be alone. However, to remember oneself as alone is to reconstruct events such that one's subjectivity starts to look like the product of one's own labour – one's running the ridges, reading in books, learning Zen and writing poems. That is, subjectivity is remembered as one's own, partially a consequence of the place, but never a consequence of another subjectivity.

It may seem attractive as one reconstructs the literary history of one's own subjective trajectory to imagine one's past self as a Thoreauvian character – as like Thoreau, but then, by virtue of that likeness, not like 'other men' (Thoreau's insistent drive toward self-differentiation), and therefore absolutely independent of other people, if not of the land. But 'Those days / when I lived and thought all alone' are in fact peopled by the likes of Jimmy Jones, who was not only a friend, 'the chainsaw boy' of 'Milton by Firelight' (*RR*, p. 7), but who is also revealed by 'Look Back' to have been another model for the speaker in various ways. Not only did the Indian teach the younger self about the terrain and warn him about the sweatlodge, but he is retroactively understood by the poem, by the narrativising function of memory, to have been more than a partial *mentor* for the speaker: he is also *metaphor* for the speaker – and not just because the young man runs around the land like the Indian used to do. The Indian is able to function as metaphor because he is also part Chinese – or so 'they say': as both Indian intimate with the land and part Asian, Jimmy Jones can function in memory as an ideal ego in so far as the subject of the poem is both getting to know the American land and preparing to get to know Asian land. Metaphorically combining Indian and Zen, Jones prefigures – or rather, *post*figures, achieves meaning in retrospect (by *Nachträglichkeit*, as Freud called such mental operations) – Snyder. The Indian who is described as 'boy' in the earlier poem is thus in a sense the child who is father of the man, the doubly inscrutable Other in relation to which the poetic speaker's subjectivity is constructed and reconstructed, narrativised. Yet the Indian seems to have been incorporated by the Snyderian subject in a curious way, since it is not that the Indian is merely remembered, but that he is in the speaker's body, a part of his feet. For in making the Indian a metaphor for his own subjectivity, the radical alterity of the Other is declined, since as metaphor the Snyderian subject substitutes for the Indian subject (metaphor being defined as substitution by resemblance). When the other man is deprived of a subjectivity, the illusion is fostered that the subject which has come to take his place 'lived and thought all alone'. The crucial respect by which Snyder in 'Look Back' differs from Wordsworth in 'Tintern Abbey' has to do not with their relationship to other people and other subjectivities but with their relationship to the landscape, which Snyder can acknowledge as constitutive Other in a way that Wordsworth cannot.[51]

By this line of argument, it is not just the Indian character – with his name which signifies so little in the early 1950s (the summer to which the first part of the poem looks back), but which by late 1978 will sound so uncanny to West-Coast American ears, thereby achieving meaning in retrospect analogously to the utterance and its events – who combines the aboriginal and the Asian, since Snyder's very own first book exhibits exactly the same cultural combination.[52] 'Look Back' contains multiple half-hidden allusions to the images and themes of *Riprap*; and in addition, it would seem that 'Piute Mountain' has become for the Snyderian speaker a version of Han-shan's 'Cold Mountain', the translation of whose poems Snyder publishes with a re-issue of *Riprap* in 1965. And as Snyder commented in his introduction to *Cold Mountain Poems*, 'Cold Mountain' designates the eccentric Chinese poet-hermit Han-shan himself, as well as his mountain home and 'his state of mind' (*RR*, p. 33). The name is made to signify both the landscape and the subject of that landscape; it thus also signifies their relation, which we can come to understand as a relation between a subject and a landscape devoid of other human subjects. 'Piute Mountain' operates similarly in 'Look Back' to the way in which 'Cold Mountain' functions for Han-shan, and it is therefore not only the case that Snyder substitutes himself for Han-shan and Jimmy Jones – or even that he remembers himself half a lifetime later by remaking himself in those earlier images – but that he looks back in 'Look Back' to a *poetic* version of the self, the version imaged in the poems of *Riprap*. The 'up and down' of the mountain is thus never only in the body, but crucially also in the word, in discourse. The loop-back of the poem is therefore to earlier poems, and so the cycle constructed by the various loops is not just referential (referring, that is, to experiences, relations and objects in the world), but intertextual. If one prepares to inhabit Japan by reading in a book authored by H. G. Creel, then one prepares to re-inhabit American land by reading a book entitled *Riprap*, even if

– indeed, *especially* if – one's name is on that book's cover.

If the poetic construction of a cycle (or series of loops or intertextual links) comprises a form of narrative, then the loop-back to a book of verse endorses Roland Barthes's pronouncement about narrative in *S/Z* when he says that 'What is told is always the telling'.[53] That is, narrative tends always to tell the story of that special event which is the work of its own making. In this case, the story of a subject's construction, imaged as a memory of work but also reading, is the story on some level of his earlier writing. So that when the enigmatic colloquialism 'Bechtel' is exclaimed by the foreman, the wager that ultimate motives will be expressed – 'Bet you'll tell' – is in the process of being confirmed by the *form* of the poetic utterance itself. Snyder responds to the foreman's question-pronouncement with a denial, 'I couldn't tell him something strange as Zen', because to tell him about Zen and one's reading might risk one's incorporation by another subject. One can tell an unlocalised, generalised addressee, however, and so that 'something strange as' finds its narrative images in the best lyrics of *Riprap*.

Another name for some instances of Zen-like conditions and attitudes as they get figured in *Riprap* and elsewhere is the *sublime* – that which is so strange that it always to some extent exceeds representation, yet which is nevertheless crucial as a means of subjective reinforcement.

AMERICAN SUBLIMITY

Besides bearing a long history and an extensive iconography, the sublime has been the object of a recent explosion in critical theorisation.[54] Although aesthetic treatises on the sublime stretch back to Longinus's third-century work, *Peri Hypsous* (whose title is variously translated as *On the Sublime*, or *On Great Writing*),[55] it is as the central category of eighteenth-century European aesthetics that the sublime receives its most influential theorisation. Where Longinus sees sublimity as an essentially *rhetorical* effect produced by magisterially elevated writing, Edmund Burke's *Philosophical Enquiry into the Origin of our Ideas of the Sublime and Beautiful* of 1757 seeks to ground sublimity in natural objects. Influenced by Lockean empiricism and assuming a sensationalist theory of uniform sense-responses, Burke argued that sublime affect could only be an effect of objects in the world, natural properties. However, it is with Immanuel Kant's third critique, *Critique of Judgement* (1790), that aesthetic theory receives its eighteenth-century summation. Against Burkean *empiricism*, Kant argues that the sublime can only ever exist as an effect of the *subject*: the sublime does not inhere either in objects or linguistic events but in the subject; it is therefore historically unverifiable and immune to property relations (because unexchangeable).

Kant distinguishes between the *dynamical* sublime of nature and the *mathematical* sublime which consists of the mind's ability to think a measure or series unavailable to sense. Since both forms – dynamical and mathematical – will be pertinent to my analysis, I include portions of Kant's exposition on both versions. Of the dynamical sublime – and in opposition to Burke – Kant says:

> Sublimity, therefore, does not reside in anything of nature, but only in our mind, in so far as we can become conscious that we are superior to nature within, and therefore also to nature without us (so far as it influences us). Everything that excites that feeling in us, e.g. the *might* of nature which calls forth our forces, is called then (although improperly) sublime. Only by supposing this idea in ourselves and in reference to it are we capable of attaining to the idea of the sublimity of that Being which produces respect in us, not merely by the might that it displays in nature, but rather by means of the faculty which resides in us of judging fearlessly and of regarding our destination as sublime in respect of it.[56]

The subjective faculty which provides for our judging an object in nature as sublime is the faculty which means sublimity is subjective, since our ability to *think* the sublime eventuates a judgement on the part of the reflective faculty whose conclusion is that *we* are sublime. The sublime is therefore a means by which subjecthood is reinforced; it can thus make subjects in a way that objects cannot, and is therefore crucially a *non-social* means of effecting subjecthood. Hence the drive toward solitude – the absence of other persons or other consciousnesses – as a precondition for sublime experience.

As non-phenomenal and non-sensual, the sublime can be experienced without being in nature, and it is the *mathematical* sublime which obtains when the subjective mind finds itself able to grasp infinity:

> The faculty of being able to think the infinite of supersensible intuition as given (in its intelligible substrate) surpasses every standard of sensibility and is great beyond all comparison even with the faculty of mathematical estimation, not, of course in a theoretical point of view and on behalf of the cognitive faculty, but as an extension of the mind which feels itself able in another (practical) point of view to go beyond the limits of sensibility.
>
> ... As this, however, is great beyond all standards of sense, it makes us judge as *sublime*, not so much the object, as our own state of mind in the estimation of it.[57]

The mind's capacity to imaginatively totalise that which exceeds both cognition and any guess or rational procedure reflects less on the greatness or number of the objects of perception than back on itself. In this way, the sublime exalts the subject, provoking exultation in its own powers.

In a more recent meditation on Kant's mathematical sublime, Neil Hertz has provided a useful emphasis on the moment of blockage, the moment prior to sublime elevation when the mind's capacities are temporarily stymied by the object.[58] Hertz's argument suggests that the mind's confusion at the point of blockage depends upon the plurality of the object, its seeming inability to be synthesised, which thus confirms subjective unity (the one unable to grasp the many precisely because of its unicity). By identifying with the agent of blockage itself – which is achieved via the formation of a specular structure in which the mind *reads* rather than thinks its face-to-face identification – a totalised subjective unity is registered whose consequence is sublime exaltation, the leap of overcoming the inability to think something which cannot be measured. Hertz's persuasive account is important for several reasons: first, because of its foregrounding of the essential function of the blockage; secondly, because it reorients the process to one of vision and legibility – the interpretation of something seen; thirdly (and subsequent to the second), because it emphasises the necessary totalisation and imposition of form which obtains as the precondition of legibility; and finally, because it enhances psychoanalytic accounts of the formation of subjectivity (Hertz's account must be read alongside Lacan's 'mirror stage' theory in which the infant achieves a totalised sense of self by perceptually misrecognising itself in the Other).

It should thus be apparent that perhaps the paramount significance of the sublime is its provision for the making of selfhood. To anticipate what follows, we may suggest that if the sublime makes subjects then theorising the sublime may make theorists. And in relation to Snyder, writing the sublime in the opening pages of *Riprap* is one way of establishing a poetic subject. Recalling those pages when gazing at the landscape in 'Look Back' is a way of making poethood the determinant of subjectivity rather than the reverse, for instead of trying to make the subject into a poet, subjectivity comes to be understood via the myth of a poem like 'Look Back' as an effect of poetic writing. In this way, one identifies oneself – by the identification with a former self – as *always already a poet*.

As a way into examining the Snyderian sublime in more detail, and by way of acknowledging Hertz's foregrounding of the visual, I want to discuss sublimity as it emerges as the focus of American painting. The image I put on my book's jacket (and which I reproduce as Plate 6 for readers of copies without a book-jacket) represents an exemplary pictographic representation of the American sublime. Although Frederic Church was the most influential painter of the sublime in mid-nineteenth-century America (after the Romanticist sublime of Thomas Cole earlier in the century), Albert Bierstadt comes a close second and can be considered as the primary painter of sublime *Western* landscapes. Bierstadt is also interesting for his combination of more traditionally sublime modes – say Church after Cole – with mid-century American luminism. Bierstadt's *The Sierra Nevada in California* (1868) is multiply significant for my purposes, and only initially because the scene it claims to depict is that portion of the American landscape – the Sierra Nevada – in which Snyder currently makes his home.[59]

I say '*claims* to depict', thereby casting doubt on its mimetic veracity, because the painting was made when Bierstadt was in Rome as part of a European tour; it is thus not painted directly 'from nature', but rather represents the imaginative composition of the Western landscape which Bierstadt had visited and sketched in the early 1860s. There is historical and epistemological significance in these details of its imaginative composition. Historically, the landscape of the American West was practically unknown to a large proportion of United States citizens at the middle of the nineteenth century (most of whom were settled either on the Eastern seaboard or in the South), so Bierstadt's enormously popular representation provided a model image facilitative of a general conception of the meaning of the Western landscape. The gradual encroachment of 'civilisation' upon the West, however, meant that tracts of 'unspoiled' nature were rapidly being taken over by settlement, the railroads and suchlike; there was therefore some desire to 'capture' the West in its Romantic wildness, as a primordial and ahistorical vision. It is partly for this reason that no human figures can be found in the canvas.

In epistemological terms, the painting as composition is significant for the desire it manifests regarding the landscape. When it was exhibited in Boston in 1869, a newspaperman for the *Boston Post* reported of the painting, 'It is a perfect type of the American idea of what our scenery ought to be, if it is not so in reality. . . . We advise all our readers to inspect the painting.'[60] Educated Easterners were exhorted – in a journalistic version of the Puritan discourse of typology – to peruse the canvas not for a real representation of the furthermost parts of their country's spectacular landscape, but rather for what it could signify about the ultimate *meaning* of the landscape, as if the land constituted a text which had been suitably interpreted by the painter (much in the manner of a sermon's exegesis of the biblical text). We might interpret the ideology behind the newspaperman's directive as revelatory of the American *desire vis-à-vis* the landscape – a desire not to discover, but to *invent* its signification. In this sense the painting functions as a national ideal, an image of the land to which one might aspire. The irony, of course, is that this ideal is not one of harmonious social organisation or of a non-exploitatively settled land, but rather an ideal of a landscape devoid of the human and so overwhelming as to suggest uninhabitability.

The graphic alterity of the terrain – disallowing any sense of homeliness – is suggested by the very dimensions of the representation, which exceed any human subject: six by ten feet, the range of the scene is such that its elements cannot be apprehended by the eye simultaneously. The materiality of the painting thus exemplifies a potential for the Kantian mathematical sublime described above. Unable to fix the image, the gaze must travel around the canvas, from the lucid details of the foreground to the darkened vertical frames, and up from the slice of bright white at the centre of the visual field (the waterfall) to the celestial realms of snow-capped mountains and heavenly clouds. The visual elements comprise various conventional features of sublime landscapes: mountains were considered sublime as a consequence of their identification with the lofty deity,[61] and the storm – shown in Bierstadt's painting at the upper left, having just passed – always constituted an indicator of sublimity because of its threat to any subject (it was an example of a natural object which could emerge from nowhere to overwhelm the vulnerable human). The painting is also characterised by chiaroscuro, the interplay of starkly contrasting areas of light and dark, which visually metaphorise the oscillation between certainty and confusion whose tropic negotiation – as Hertz emphasises – is necessary for the production of sublime affect.

I refer to Bierstadt's painting as related to luminism in response to the depiction of the lake, which is imaged as calmly tranquil after the passing of the storm, and which thereby functions as a mirror, laterally and glassily reflective. Luminism, exemplified by four American painters – Fitz Hugh Lane, John Frederick Kensett, Martin Johnson Heade and Sanford Gifford – is characterised (superficially) by the play of light on calm surfaces of water.[62] The luminist dimension in Bierstadt's sublime canvas is significant because, as one commentator has noted, 'In luminist painting the viewer does not experience nature from outside the picture but from within as an intuited phenomenon: the plane of a luminist canvas extends toward the viewer to encompass his presence in the conceptualized space of the landscape itself.'[63] Although 'intuited' is hardly the best term for the process of identification, it is certainly the case that the reflective surface of the lake, which in Bierstadt extends from the base of craggy cliffs toward the beholder, functions as some kind of mirror drawing in the viewer's subjectivity to participate in the elements of the scene. In this respect, an initial point of partial identification may be the deer of the foreground who are lured to the lake with the storm's cessation: we approach the narrative of sublime identification as the deer approach the mirroring surface of water.[64]

Taking in the dimensions of the image thus, it is as if the viewer is inserted into the landscape, having to look around in order to establish co-ordinates for orientation. The visual text can function in the service of a national and international audience as a consequence of its compositional co-ordination, the way in which the image – enormously expansive though it is – is framed and organised by its perceptual origin. That is, its levels of detail and abstraction, its structured points of clarity against background areas of opacity (the bright sluice of the fall framed by a block of dark stone and focused beneath a hazily indistinct and indeterminate play of muted insubstantiality) effect a rudimentary narrativisation of the scene. Its natural elements are composed such that it is possible to projectively imagine co-ordinating one's subjectivity with the landscape via an orientation of gaze. In this sense, the landscape becomes legible as personified, as representing a subjective state of mind in which the agitation of a storm is receding and is replaced by a reflective tranquillity whose reflection points one up to sublime heavenly raptures. The landscape is therefore presented as absolutely wild and uninhabited, yet simultaneously as a coherent natural scape amenable to a subject: one may thus begin to inhabit the ground by first inhabiting the painting. The scene's importance and attraction is as a sublime space in which an American subjectivity may be dramatised.

That dramatisation requires a legible narrative whose points we amplify here. Drawn into the visual space by the sandy path which moves from slightly right of centre of the lower frame (and along which the deer have implicitly passed), the subjective gaze encounters the reflective surface of the lake whose shimmering light directs one to the vertical slash of bright white water (which itself contrasts with the horizontal white limit of the reflective surface). The dark vertical borders of the image – cliffs and forest – serve to push the gaze inward and upward, and the dark blocks of stone which frame the waterfall in the middle distance operate analogously: it is as if the canvas comprises two roughly V-shaped blocks, one within the other, so that the dark outer V frames the light in the centre of the painting, while within that luminous space exists the smaller V whose centre-space comprises the bright waterfall. Both Vs push the gaze upward, and I would suggest that the hazier opacity above and behind the fall constitutes the visual area equivalent to the 'blockage' which must be surmounted in order to experience the sublimity of the irridescent peaks and heavens above. Overcoming the blockage requires that *form* be imposed upon indeterminacy, and although this specular process must operate differently in a painting by comparison with a literary text (since the painting presents an image more directly than a text), I think the necessary leap of totalising form is graphically provided for by the shapes of the darker peaks in the upper right-hand area of the frame, since their shapes analogise and magnify the shape of the cliff over which the waterfall pours. The shift of gaze from fall to these cliffs eventuates a transformation of white fall into snowy peaks pointing to the sublime white light of heaven, which irradiates the whole sublime central plane (Bierstadt's lake may be luminist but his billowing clouds are not). Partaking of that directed visual narrative, the beholder dramatises and insures an American subjectivity in the Western wilderness. The process of identification produces a sense of subject in place wholly different to the earlier sublime landscapes of Cole, which relied on the illusion of the pioneer mastering the Eastern terrain.[65] The gazing subject of Bierstadt's canvas is assured of a Western inhabitability which makes of the landscape a magnificent arena exceeded only by its subject. The structure of inhabitation is therefore made inseparable by the sublime from idealist transcendence. And the interpretation of the topos, the transcendent imperative, is imaged – in the mode of the United States's earliest political documents – as blessed by God: the Deity's light shines on the subject of the American sublime.

Thus it becomes clear – even without considering those critics who assert the luminist sublime as the equivalent visual paradigm of Emersonian transcendentalism (via their shared root in Kantian idealism)[66] – that this American sublime operates in contradistinction to any notion of the postmodern immanentism within whose terms I have been discussing Snyder's poetry. In order to theorise this contradiction – for which the oppositional relation between Altieri's paradigms is unable to account – I turn now to one of those early sublime poems of *Riprap* to which I have been alluding: 'Piute Creek'. From the details given in 'Look Back', we may see that 'Piute Creek' speaks of that summer in 1955 when Snyder 'lived and thought alone'. 'Piute Creek' images that solitude, but its importance and aesthetic significance derive not from informational purposes – the biographical or contextual details we can glean intertextually – but rather from the poetic relation between subject and landscape. That is, we do not need to know the subject's proper name or the landscape and the historical moment and conditions of his sojourn there to read the subjective stakes of Western sublimity.

Piute Creek

One granite ridge
A tree, would be enough
Or even a rock, a small creek,
A bark shred in a pool.
Hill beyond hill, folded and twisted
Tough trees crammed
In thin stone fractures
A huge moon on it all, is too much.
The mind wanders. A million
Summers, night air still and the rocks
Warm. Sky over endless mountains.
All the junk that goes with being human
Drops away, hard rock wavers
Even the heavy present seems to fail
This bubble of a heart.
Words and books
Like a small creek off a high ledge
Gone in the dry air.

A clear, attentive mind
Has no meaning but that
Which sees is truly seen.
No one loves rock, yet we are here.
Night chills. A flick
In the moonlight
Slips into Juniper shadow:
Back there unseen
Cold proud eyes
Of Cougar or Coyote
Watch me rise and go.

(*RR*, p. 6)

Although the trace of anthropomorphism at the poem's end – in which the beast is attributed some hauteur (without being observed) and reified by the capital letter – weakens the effect, this is a quite brilliant and complex poem. The mind's initial quailing in the face of the landscape's almost featureless infinity, together with the abstract summation of 'A million / Summers' and the ascetic transformation of subjectivity, combine to make this text look at first glance like an instance of Kant's mathematical sublime. The state of rarefied perception, which seems to have been achieved within the interstice of the stanza break, is problematised, however, by the sense that the subject of perception is no longer the speaker – who becomes instead an object of the gaze of the Other – but is rather the unseen, merely imagined, wild beast.

Yet the subject and object of vision are problematic in the first part of the poem, since the avowed unassimilability of the scene to visualisation is rendered via an intensity of imagery which calls to mind the Western visual representations of Ansel Adams and Georgia O'Keeffe. The 'folded and twisted' successive fabric of hilly rock could well describe the paintings made by O'Keeffe in New Mexico in the 1930s and 1940s (such as *Black Place No. 1* or *From the White Place*),[67] in which no human figure or detail provides relief for the beholder's vision.

The imagery of Snyder's poem also brings to mind some of Ansel Adams's photographic images – Adams (1902–84) representing the major twentieth-century inheritor of Bierstadt's nineteenth-century Western American sublime.[68] One of Adams's later and more famous images is *Moon and Half Dome*, taken in Yosemite National Park in 1960 – precisely the location of Piute creek and mountain. Indeed, as maker of the twentieth-century American version of a natural sublime, Adams's first photographs were of the Sierra Nevada, and throughout his career he returned countless times to Yosemite to photograph the rock known as Half Dome. The sheer chiaroscuro cliffs which overwhelm the visual field of Adams's 1960 image (Plate 7) are relieved only by a three-quarter moon toward which the gaze inevitably tends and which necessarily provides perspective for the perceptual space. This moon is not the 'huge moon' denotative of excess that we find in Snyder's poem, but the *effects of infinity* in each image are analogous. A tradition of imaging the Western landscape as inhumanly sublime thus becomes legible in its extension to photography as the supremely American and twentieth-century artform (Adams as a pioneer of that artform). The question consistently posed by these scapes – by Snyder's poetic text and the visual texts of O'Keeffe and Adams – is how any subject can find a space for itself in such landscapes. The question, that is, posed at its starkest extreme, is how to inhabit the ground.

In 'Piute Creek' I think we can see processes of inhabitation forming, being formulated, by the speaker's recourse to traditions of sublimity. First, the opening images are offered as projected images, details which would enable a subject to anchor itself in the scene by some kind of identification with an object of manageable dimensions. Initially, the sublime of infinity is eschewed as 'too much', as excessive of the subject. With no thing on which to focus, 'The mind wanders', away from any confrontation with stark inhumanity. It appears, however, that the mind's desultory idling enables totalisation, the synthesis of 'endless mountains' into the unity of 'A million / Summers' with which a unitary subject can then effect some provisional identification. If the promise of the sublime is, as Thomas Weiskel has characterised it, that the human can transcend the human,[69] then that movement of transcendence is imaged as the effect of the subjective identification with 'A million / Summers' (as the blockage) by the metaphors of stripping away and dissolution, so that the rock of 'endless mountains' itself 'wavers' when confronted with the mind's capacity for projective totalisation. Here, the sublime is manifested definitively as the subject in excess of anything else that could possibly count, including the human heart and language itself:

> Words and books
> Like a small creek off a high ledge
> Gone in the dry air.

The sublime thus consists in a reversal of a condition in which the landscape is absolutely excessive of the subject to a condition in which the subject exceeds the landscape. In the imagery of this reversal, the air is 'dry', and the image for the disappearance of signs and their codification is formed as an analogy ('Like a small creek'), because there is no creek: beginning the poem with a desire for the sufficiency of (among other things) 'a small creek' gets transformed into the creek's imagined disappearance as linguistic representation fails the experience and the poem temporarily ceases. There is a sense in which the sublime must always exceed representation since it accords the subject an experience of aggrandised self-presence to which representation (as *re*-presentation) is definitively immune. What remains is the mind, transparently available to the full range of perceptual signification:

> A clear, attentive mind
> Has no meaning but that
> Which sees is truly seen.

Such transcendence obtains the ambivalent status of Emerson's transparent eyeball, which, nothing itself, registers the light-waves of all. Snyder also sounds here like the Emerson of 'The Poet', who writes, 'The sublime vision comes to the pure and simple soul in a clean and chaste body.'[70] It is certainly within this paradigm of sublime asceticism that the Snyderian speaker is operating here, for he continues, echoing Eliot in the final section of *The Waste Land*, 'No one loves rock, yet we are here.' The incantory desire in Eliot for some water to relieve the monotony of rock (quoted above) is reinforced by Snyder's admission that the rock cannot be loved but only endured for the sublime experience its solitary contemplation may afford. In this sense, the impulse is toward the land only in so far as it may be transcended and a new mode of perception achieved. The transcendent moment dissolves, however, when the subject becomes aware of itself as object of another's watchful gaze: the 'me' enters the poem as object rather than subject of the look. The antidote to transcendence is offered in those slightly weaker lines, which close the poem and in which subjective consciousness is shown its limits, by acknowledging not the consciousness of another person but of an animal, a consciousness which can count in the realm of nature. It is in this respect that the subject is not excessive of the natural. Yet the qualification is only achieved by attributing to nature a consciousness which has been revealed as excruciatingly lacking by the poem's opening lines. The problem is thus not whether or not nature can have a consciousness that can count in relation to human consciousness, but rather whether consciousness can possibly be conceived in other than human terms.

This is the point at which the critical account requires not just an opposed valuation of immanentism to counter sublime transcendence, but requires instead an alternative account of subjectivity that might relativise the Kantian idealist account. It is notable that the major recent theoretical analyses of sublimity have been predominantly psychoanalytic (Freud, Bloom, Weiskel, Hertz) as a consequence of Kant's insistence on sublimity as dependent upon subjective interiority rather than natural exteriority.[71] However, within the general designation of psychoanalytically oriented accounts, it is equally notable that the arguments about identification have followed a classical Freudian model with an emphasis on the Oedipus. I therefore offer Lacan as a psychoanalytic corrective to these accounts in so far as the question of identification in Lacan is asserted to be infallibly founded on precisely fallibility, the subject's error.[72] Although Bloom can charge that every reading is a misreading, his argument never makes a connection between this paradox and the Lacanian dictum that every recognition by the subject comprises a misrecognition, a *méconnaissance*, an always-missed encounter. Lacan's theory of the mirror stage, which is often misguidedly over-emphasised,[73] posits the infant's first sense of itself as a self, its accession to a totalised body-image, as based on a misrecognition – crucially a misrecognition of the self in the Other – which forms the basis for all subsequent identifications. Identification, 'trapped' within the Imaginary register of binary images, is therefore condemned to repeat its illusory certainties across the trajectory of the subject's history of self-recognition – one part of which must be sublime experience (as an experience, that is, of specular identification). What I am suggesting is that the identifications precipitative of sublime affect as I have described them in Snyder's poem and Bierstadt's painting are something like mistakes – mis-takes, images improperly taken to represent something other than that which they are. Such identifications depend on precisely the recognition of the self in the Other (as opposed to the recognition of the Other in the self which I have attributed above to Snyder's work as an effect of inhabitationist poetics), and hence the disavowal of the Other. The American sublime functions by denying the Other as Other – that Other which consists of a relation to the land as the unconscious support of an American subject. The American sublime thus also can be written under the sign of S (Ø).

It is the Other as resistant to meaning that is resisted. That is, I would suggest that it is less the prospect of infinity which threatens the speaker of 'Piute Creek' than it is the possibility that the landscape will fail to signify, will in fact be meaningless, semiologically redundant. A granite ridge, or a tree, a rock or 'a small creek' would suffice because any of these would provide a point around which significance could be centred and from which some meaning could flow – much like Stevens's jar in Tennessee, whose placement instantly provides significance and coherence for the landscape. Thus although I think it constitutes a beautiful poem – a poem which can be desired because it manifests desire (the desire for meaning) – 'Piute Creek' shows that Snyder is not wholly resistant to the resistance to the Other as resistant to meaning. When the landscape threatens to be unavailable to sense, it must be made to mean. That is not immanentism.

I would suggest further that in the visual image, it is not opacity which threatens signification but the bright white light of heavenly sublimity itself, since as reflective of all light, whiteness is visually significant of nothing. Whiteness as representing nothing can image the sublime as the ineffable or as radiant purity, but its blinding risk is the risk of absence, the failure – rather than the transcendable limit – of representation itself. It is those white areas of the visual field of Bierstadt's canvas that threaten to substitute for identification and self-confirmation an Otherness of non-signification which is disruptive of the subject, for such would substitute for a subject that exceeds all barriers of sense an Other that exceeds the subject precisely as both predicate and successor of the subject – that which determines meaning (and the impossibility or failure of meaning) for the subject, rather than betokening the expanded limits of the subject's production of sense. As soon as the landscape has something like what counts as a consciousness, its prerogatives obtain at the cost of those of an American subject, whose capacity for sublime extension is consequently proportionally diminished if not thoroughly eradicated – for as Lacan says, 'There is no Other of the Other' (this distinguishes Lacan's Other as the function of alterity from Sartre's personified Other, for the latter of which there can and always will be an Other).

The image of whiteness for the Other operates perhaps most significantly in the visual arts, but it can also be found in another sublime poetic meditation of Snyder's, a poem which brings to the fore the related and intransigent question of gender. The disjunction between this poem's title and its main text – which, in a reversal of the usual structure, manifests itself by a title that is longer than the text – indicates that two orders of representation are involved. As excessive of representation, the sublime body of the text is resisted by the subject of its title, which tries to recuperate the experience for representational, denotative purposes:

24:IV:40075, 3:30 PM,
n. of Coaldale, Nevada,
A Glimpse through a Break
in the Storm of the Summit
of the White Mountains

> O Mother Gaia
> sky   cloud   gate   milk   snow
> wind-void-word
> I bow in roadside gravel
>
> (AH, p. 71)

Although the sublime experience is avowed by the body of the poem to induce in the speaker reverence in respect of the sacred (and is thus figured as a *beneficent* experience), the title suggests the psychoanalytic defence against a *traumatic* experience which is known as *isolation* – the splitting of the experience from subjective history by an excessive detailing of its spatial and temporal locale (we are given the date, the time, the geographical location and a discursive descriptive summary of the event): the experience is minutely *framed* and thereby separated from what preceded and what succeeded it; its significance is thus delimited.[74] Paradoxically, the detail serves only to indicate the event's importance for its speaker, an importance which the body of the poem declares to be of a sacramental nature. If the sublime is characterised by terror[75] – the fear of being overwhelmed, the insupportable dimension of excess – then the body of the poem represents a disavowal and conversion of the terror whose enormity is signalled by the title.

That a question of opposition (between the subject and the landscape, and disavowed as such) is at stake may be seen by referring to the nominalised opposition between black and white encoded within the title: 'Coaldale' versus 'the White Mountains'. The storm is, of course, a classic image for sublime terror, since – as I have mentioned – it represents the force of nature as it threatens to overwhelm the subject. In this instance, the storm breaks momentarily to reveal an object of sublimity (improperly so called) beyond its own sublime plane. It is as if the break in the storm represents the paradoxical blockage which facilitates a momentary identification productive of the sublime; this being the case, it is again not opacity but rather opacity's discontinuity which effects the sublime movement. The moment can therefore be compared with Bierstadt's imagery, in which the passing storm reveals the summits of snowy mountains. And the analogy strengthens the sense that sublimity is always the product of narrative or of a tropic movement, the substitution of one agent of the sublime (the storm) for another agent (the mountains), in which the subject must find its way and its identificatory place. The sublime thus starts to look more like a *structure* (of substitution or oscillation) than a *content* (storm, mountains and suchlike).

Analogies for Snyder's poem also extend back beyond nineteenth-century American painting to English Romantic poetry, in which – for more conventionally generic reasons than Snyder – Wordsworth titles *Tintern Abbey* prior to 1804, *Lines Written a Few Miles Above Tintern Abbey, on Revisiting the Banks of the Wye during a Tour, July 13, 1798*; – and in which Shelley's sublime is paradigmatically figured *vis-à-vis* the white mountain in 'Mont Blanc'. Like Snyder apostrophising the mountain as sublime, Shelley addresses the 'Ravine of Arve':

> Thou art pervaded with that ceaseless motion,
> Thou art the path of that unresting sound –
> Dizzy Ravine! and when I gaze on thee
> I seem as in a trance sublime . . .

The opposition in the Shelleyan sublime is between a vertiginously perpetual specular motion, which is attributed to the mountain, and an elevatedly motionless consciousness, which is attributed to the subject. What is notable in both instances is the rhetorical technique of apostrophe which allows the subject to address the landscape as if it were a single, personifiable entity with a consciousness capable of receiving speech. The personification converts the sublime opposition into a case of one-on-one in which a measure of subjective identification can be achieved. However, when it is a question of identifying with the Deity – as it is in Snyder's poem – identification can only ever be partial; as in Judaism, no mortal can look upon the divine visage. Instead of looking, the Snyderian speaker bows to the majesty of the sublime spectacle of Mother Earth (Gaia was the name the Greeks gave to their Earth goddess) and attempts to represent the encounter in a starkly metonymic form.

Unlike the title, in which relations and conditions are specified by grammatical connectives, the body of the poem elides such connectives as an indicator and effect of the disruption of subjective relation and the discontinuity which characterises any sublime narrative. Thus from the initial apostrophe, which designates the poem's addressee (a different addressee than the poem's title), we move to a metonymic chain of associative substitutions, followed by a meta-metonymic chain of connection, which precipitates the concluding gesture of the speaker: the act of reverence. The subjective discontinuity of the sublime – the moment of blockage, for Hertz – is rendered by the graphic spacing of the poem on the page (the black against white of 'Coaldale' versus 'White Mountains' made into black writing and white space), and the metonymic arrangement of images and words. The insertion of an interpreting subject makes the second line legible as a narrative of the whole event: the visual field of *sky* features the 'block' of *cloud* which gives way to, and is identified with, the *gate*, the break in the storm as a means of transcendental access, which opens for the subject an image of the Deity as good mother, giving *milk*, which is then highlighted as metaphor, as the subject's rhetorical substitution, by *snow*. The sublime consists here in the ability to perceive, beyond the raging storm, the mountain-top as the mother's breast – to perceive, that is, nurturant nature beyond and within destructive nature.

The associative chain of significance – which is *structurally* sublime in so far as it makes of the subject the producer rather than the product of natural meaning – is then metaphorised one level further by an image of connection in discontinuity: 'wind-void-word'. The discontinuity of the storm (wind) which breaks (void) gives rise to the 'word' not as the Word of God but as the subjective word which allows the subject to conceive of itself as sublime as a consequence of its ability to project – via a synthesising totalisation – a word, a representation, for that which is allegedly beyond representation as such. Since the rhetorical strategy can only derive from the subject, it is that subject which must ultimately be conceived of as sublime (although the speaker of the poem will structurally disavow this by imaging the conclusion as homage to the mountain rather than to his own interpretive facility).

This condition – and its corollary, transcendence – are far from the immanentist position which acknowledges the land as a necessary Other in the self and which seeks to elaborate that relation. What might be described as a 'failure' of the immanentist poetic with respect to the Snyderian speaker simply testifies to the representational power and influence of earlier rhetorical strategies *vis-à-vis* the American ground, which make of the landscape by the twentieth century the field of the 'already said'. Although the poem immediately subsequent to 'Piute Creek' in *Riprap*, 'Milton by Firelight', will declare:

No paradise, no fall,
Only the weathering land
The wheeling sky

(*RR*, p. 8)

the legacy of those earlier biblically derived paradigms for interpreting and relating to the land can be seen to be less easily
escapable than Snyder perhaps would wish. This fact, together
with the 'failures' discussed, does not impugn the project of
inhabitation in any way. It rather indicates the difficulty of the task
and the effective power of representation as mediator of the real,
which Snyderian poetics choose to evade. By way of returning to
Snyder's emphasis on the body and on work as those features of a
poetic which secure the best, least mediated relation to the real, I
want to focus on the way in which the question of gender erupts at
the heart of, and *as*, the difficulty – the problem of transcendence
(the Deity figured as maternal) and the problem of the poet's
manhood (which is inextricable from the problem of poetry's
relation to the real).

CHERCHEZ LA FEMME

The question of gender has been emerging with increasing fre-
quency throughout this analysis (it will not be repressed) – a feature
which is not least a consequence of the fact that my psychoanalytic
approach has been learned from feminist readings of Lacan. By
positing the phallus as the determining signifier ('the signifier
intended to designate as a whole the effects of the signified'[76]),
Lacan has argued that the accession to subjectivity and language is
inseparable from the question of sexual difference. That is, there
does not exist a gender-neutral subject position: despite fantasies
to the contrary, every subject is gendered. This means that (as
Jacqueline Rose has noted) any account of Lacan which attempts to
split the unconscious and sexuality cannot make sense; it can
instead only ever constitute at best a partial account.[77] However, as
Rose has also more recently indicated, the dominant accounts of
postmodernity – both fictional and theoretical – tend to discuss the
social via the metaphor of the psyche (and hence the unconscious)
while persistently foreclosing or disavowing the question of sexual
difference.[78] Rose concludes her essay on fantasies of the modern

and postmodern by asserting that: 'If the psychic is to be evoked as a model of the social (as diagnosis and/or metaphor) – sexual difference must be seen as centrally part of that account, or else the fantasy of the woman will merely reduplicate itself, whether as squalor or as one of the interchangeable trappings of everyday life.'[79]

My own account – and indeed Snyder's own conception of the social at various points – has conceived of cultural organisation in terms of psychic metaphorisation by the identification of an unconscious structure which supports American consciousness. The place of sexual difference in that structure therefore no longer can be ignored. In this respect, my position differs from Snyder's and therefore constitutes an outright critique of his position on the matter (which is basically that it doesn't matter). As my book draws toward a close, the critical question is thus pushed from the issue of how an American consciousness is formed on the trace of its unconscious (and what a poet does in relation to that) toward the issue of the place of the woman in the structure, and of what, therefore, it means for American masculinity to be engaged in literary pursuits.

American literature has long been recognised as consisting of affairs between men (I use the term advisedly),[80] and although feminist literary critics have sought to redress the balance by recuperating women writers and a female literary tradition, the best feminist work is that which addresses the way in which the American literary tradition is *founded* on its suppression of the woman, its disavowal of the question of sexual difference. In 1981 Nina Baym provided an excellent introductory analysis of how what has historically come to count as 'American literature' (the canonical textual corpus) is based largely on a procedure which would be highly suspect in the political arena (after McCarthyism) – namely, that of establishing how 'American' something is.[81] The most American texts then count as canonical literature (this strategy follows the earliest demands for a national literature by figures like Whitman, for whom *American* literature would count as that literature adequate to the national landscape and democratic politics). The problem is then what counts as American. And historically the answer has been that what counts as American is the pioneer against the wilderness, the individual against the claims of the social – and in both instances, women or the feminine have represented the social and the landscape (figured as feminine, virgin land), while the individual has tended to be male or to represent traditionally masculine values of dominance and mastery. The oppositional struggle of America and the American, its propensity for self-definition via negation, is thus always gender marked and indeed gender polarised. The woman then enters American literature as the enemy, according to Baym, and American literature can thus be characterised by the feminist as the historical representation of 'melodramas of beset manhood' – not humanity beset by the trials of the wilderness or of an inhospitable society, but the masculine beset by the claims of femininity. It is particularly the case for American culture that its society is founded not on the primal murder of the father (Freud's account) but rather on the primal repression of the mother (Irigaray's account[82]) – this being a consequence of the history of the frontier (its representational history[83]) and its mythic requirement of masculine virtues. The ambivalence toward the mother is manifested in those passages quoted earlier from Turner, in which nature tends to be maternal (or neuter: never paternal), and in relation to which the American pioneer-hero is either figured as a child receiving nurturance (this is Nature as the good mother, Mother Gaia, allied with the Indian as Noble Savage), or as the aggressor having to dominate and master wild nature (Nature as untrustworthy, seductive, corruptive, possessed of 'feminine wiles' [Lawrence], and featuring the devilish Indian who, as cannibal, will incorporate the innocent American hero – the fantasy of intra-uterine existence). There is inescapable ambivalence toward the natural realm, as my argument has demonstrated, yet what remains constant is the gendering of the natural as feminine and the gendering of the American as masculine, so that cultural ambivalence operates within stereotypical dichotomies of the feminine as either virgin or whore, mother or temptress – indeed, operates within stereotypical dichotomies of the sexual *per se* (male versus female).

In Snyder, the land as maternal is both the holy mother and the feminine Muse; the emphasis of his poetic is thus on the idealised rather than the denigrated pole of the dichotomy. As indicated earlier, however, the value accorded the woman by the Snyderian poetic revises the traditional value-opposition by assigning virtue and privilege to the feminine and the earth; yet it fails to question the fundamental structure which aligns the woman with the land, with matter, and with the body. If it would not be found so laughable in some quarters, we should have to say (with Patrick

Murphy) that the strategy of gendering the land as female – and thence valorising it – simply perpetuates the oppressive patriarchal ideology it is trying to subvert.[84] Ultimately, we shall have to conclude that Snyderian poetics and ethics are no help to any feminist project. We shall also have to register the masculine fantasy which disavows sexual difference in Snyder's politics and political statements. Thus, for instance, in an epistolary response in 1983 to Sherman Paul's critical analysis of his work, the question of the woman appears as a point of difficulty, the sticking point, and Snyder responds: 'I'd rephrase it slightly: "To serve the matrifocal values by (not patriarchal but) solitary transcendence." Remove the question of gender. As above, the unit is a band, a family, a village, a watershed.'[85] The desire to 'remove the question of gender' is a persistent one, a nostalgic fantasy which yearns for the pre-feminist days when 'man' meant everybody and taking the masculine as representative was not seen as a problem, when sexual difference made no significant political difference. The 'unit', a totalised entity, is then seen as immune to sexual differentiation, simply because it gets silently re-gendered as masculine (the man always at the head, the family representative, the one who counts in the 'village', the one who has the most say), which then blindly is taken to be gender-neutral, thereby securing the historical dominance and privilege of the masculine.

In relation to the poetic project of ground-inhabitation, we thus have to question the way in which the project – although radically progressive in relation to certain structural elements of the dominant culture – simply repeats other patriarchal values and structures of inequity exemplified by that dominant culture. We may point to the insistence on metaphors – and literal instances – of the traditional (although non-nuclear) family as guarantees that woman's place within the proposed alternative structure remains unimproved. We may indicate the ways in which the valorisation of the maternal enjoins upon women the most traditional of roles, defining them in terms of body, fertility, reproductive sexuality and compulsory heterosexuality *per se*. We may look to biography (although I have no wish to psychoanalyse any historical subject) and see Snyder's mother as an example of the woman who used to write until the demands of family disallowed that, leaving the son to take up the literary vocation, a son supported by a traditional family structure in which he occupies the traditional role (as head and support). We can then gauge the constraints imposed by taking the earth as maternal and the muse as feminine in the poetry, the traditional inequitous gender paradigms centrally involved in the positing of alternative cultural models (the patrilinearity at the heart of 'Axe Handles', for instance). My point is therefore that a refusal of sexual difference (a refusal, that is, of its potential significance, its potential *for* meaning) – and a concomitant reinscription of the most conservative patriarchal gender biases – *is inextricable from* the new myth of ground inhabitation proposed by Snyder's poetry.

One way to analyse this further is by examining the relation between vocational identity – what it means to consider oneself a poet – and sex-gender identity – what it means to consider oneself a heterosexual man. When I wrote to Snyder about this, he replied:

> (Why does everybody have to call everything a 'problematic' these days, and make everything into a 'project'?) There is no problem in being what you are. As Dogen says, water studies water, water is the teacher of water studying water. . . . – So, I am a man, writing poetry in the west. It happens that this is the post-frontier west, that I am a native of Turtle Island, and my work is on the far side of the post-white-guilt watershed, we are deconstructing the US and planning a millenium ahead. This is not just transcending patriarchy, it is going beyond the national state & civilization itself.

One does not need to read Lacan to know that there is every problem in 'being what you are'. Psychoanalysis points to the category of the unconscious as that which consistently undermines any stable identity, as that which marks the failure and limits of secure selfhood. Such is not a function of neurosis but rather a structural function of subjectivity *per se*. The notion of 'no problem in being what you are', wherever it originates, does not harmonise with any notion of social change or any political project – which are, after all, central to Snyder's life and work. The naturalisation of identity perversely separates the personal from the political and implies that although national identity and its effects may obtain paramount political importance and complexity, sexual or gender identity are not part of that problem, are instead simply *there*. The irony by which the naturalisation of gender – nothing less than gender essentialism – mirrors the naturalisation of an exploitative national relation to the ground against which the whole Snyderian project is arraigned constitutes an irony to which these sentences are blind. We might add that the disavowal of gender as part of the problem is historically typical of Left politics, in which political radicalism – and indeed literary radicalism (say, canonical American modernism) – has been combined with the most reactionary gender attitudes and stereotypes. The characteristic nostalgia of sexual conservatism is manifested in the passage quoted by the parenthetical query which expresses rhetorical indignance over the problematisation of gender identity 'these days'. The fact that such problematisation is an historical product of the Women's Movement and feminism, that 'these days' are days in which one of feminism's political effects has been to disallow the unreflexive, natural ease of gender oppression, represents a fact and an historical condition from which the traditionally masculine man would rather retreat (the questioning of naturalised power is always apprehended as threatening). We might also recall here Snyder's comment in a radio interview: when asked to characterise his beliefs, he responded that his commitment was to 'old-fashioned', very Asian beliefs and value-systems. Whatever the merits of the Asian relation to the ground, it is very clear that the Asian relation to the woman is trenchantly chauvinistic and anti-feminist.

The texture of the passage quoted above is significant: following the exhibition of masculine nostalgia and the disavowal of sexuality and gender as any kind of difficulty, there is the naturalisation of the literary identity along with the sexual: 'So, I am a man writing poetry in the west. It happens that this is the post-frontier west. . . . This is not just transcending patriarchy, it is going beyond the national state & civilization itself.' It is not possible to transcend patriarchy. Patriarchy can be resisted and struggled against (this is the feminist project), but to do so requires at the very least the acknowledgement of gender's centrality to patriarchy's structure and operation. Patriarchy here is seen as a system not based on gender but on a certain gender-neutral, exploitative capitalist social organisation. The national state is seen as a larger, more intransigent force than patriarchy, which from the feminist viewpoint is not only preposterously absurd, it is also the kind of masculine political evasion which *reinforces* patriarchy while seeking political change. Patriarchy, the rule and law of the father, functions most successfully when its ideology of male universality remains intact, an ideology which makes the father's maleness invisible, not subject to question (this is what one gets by disavowing the question of gender). My point is thus not merely that the Snyderian project as it is articulated here misses the question of gender, but that the project cannot succeed in its 'deconstruction' of the United States while the intimate link between the national and the masculine remains unnoticed or ignored. One cannot deconstruct a nation, but one can deconstruct a notion, a *concept* of the national. However, in order to do so, it is necessary to analyse – as the first part of this book tries to do – the sets of binary oppositions which constitute the concept. In the case of a concept of the United States, the value of masterful masculinity is never far from the political definition of the national.[86]

The 'post-frontier west' may allow work 'on the far side of the post-white-guilt watershed',[87] but 'post-frontier' does not eventuate the elimination of the frontier's ideological effects (since these are constitutive of the West itself). As the analysis of Turner and others has shown, the frontier and the West depend upon ideas of mastery and masculine action and aggression. Writing poetry does not fit that model of masculinity and action, since poetry has tended to be associated historically in the United States with femininity, while literary writing in general has also been associated with the woman, with the mediate (non-self presence) – and hence divorced from action and the real.[88] As suggested, there are both historical and metaphysical reasons for these associations, and their net result has been that heterosexual masculinity is called urgently into question when a literary vocation – particularly the vocation of poetry as the pinnacle of the literary – is adopted by any American man.

In his most recent book, Frank Lentricchia provides an extended account of Wallace Stevens's struggle with his conflict between gender and vocational identity – between, that is, his sense of himself as a middle-class heterosexual American man, and his sense of himself as a poet. Lentricchia quotes from one of Stevens's earliest letters to the woman who was to become his wife in which he expresses his anxiety about his practice of verse-writing by referring to 'my habits' as 'positively lady-like'.[89] Although his relation to feminist discourse is as anxiously fraught with masculine paranoia as Stevens's relation to the feminised literary marketplace,[90] Lentricchia has identified and begun to elaborate an important issue. If his argument ultimately founders, it is precisely because in making it his heterosexual masculine sense deems it necessary to overthrow the feminist 'mothers' of American literary criticism in a classic structure of masculine self-assertion in the face of the strong woman: in the literary academy perceived by Lentricchia as not merely feminised but also 'feminist-ised', it appears necessary both to partake of the feminism (and its institutional power) yet simultaneously to disavow any connection with the feminine in order to save one's moustached critical face (if this textual strategy were not so offensively typical, the whole procedure would be quite comic). Critical anxieties aside, the issue Lentricchia identifies is important, and half-way through his essay it is characterised thus: 'The issue of Stevens' sexual identity as a writer – his effort to phallicize poetic discourse – is not just related to but just *is* the canonical modernist issue of poetic authority: the cultural powerlessness of poetry in a society that masculinized the economic while feminizing the literary' (p. 168).

If the issue of sexual identity as tied to vocational identity comprises *the* issue of authority of American modernism (which seems to me a fair assessment, whether or not one takes Stevens as paradigmatic, and whether or not one pursues the issue in the way Lentricchia does), then the terms of that issue may be altered by the postmoderns, but the fact remains that the postmoderns – the poets like Snyder starting out as poets half a century after the moderns – inherit the problem intact. Although they may provide different answers, postmodern poets in America must therefore begin with the same question. Thus we find record of Snyder retrospectively expressing similar anxieties to those of the early Stevens in an interview with one James McKenzie in 1974. Speaking of his decision in the mid-1950s to terminate his graduate studies at Indiana University and therefore to relinquish the prospect of a professional career in anthropology and/or linguistics in favour of poetic vocation, Snyder said:

> It was a very chancy feeling at the time, you know, like I had the kind of question that I was asking myself, the very prosaic question of like how am I going to make my living. So my answer to that was, I'll be a working man. So I worked for several years after that, logging, and I worked on the docks in San Francisco; I did just all kinds of things for a few years.[91]

The question of how to make a living is, of course, a wholly legitimate one; but what is significant here is the term by which the question is designated: the essential question of making a living is a 'prosaic' question, a very ordinary, unimaginative, *unpoetical* question – prosaic as unpoetical reality, that is, in the way that prose is unpoetical language. The answer to the question of how to make a living thus seems to definitively exclude the business of poetry as a possible solution – indeed, to exist in direct opposition to it. The only possible solution is 'I'll be a working man'.

Being a regular working guy (how Snyder images himself – hence the book-cover photographs) seems opposed to being a poet, and so when the interviewer presses Snyder with 'But you were also a poet', the hesitant response sounds like an admission of deviancy, an embarrassing failure of the masculine role: 'Well yeah, sure. Yeah, that was a part of it. That kind of choice, that was my own personal, and sort of scary at that time.' The anxiety has to do not just with the legitimate way in which starting out as a poet from a background far less economically privileged than, say, Wallace Stevens's, represents an economic threat, a jeopardisation of the means of making a viable living; it has also to do with the gender incompatibility of the poetic domain with that of the Western working man, the man of action and physical labour whose masculinity crucially depends upon physical prowess and economic self-sufficiency (the latter following as a consequence of the former in the Western myth). The generic development of poetry – as opposed to literary prose forms – means that the poetic has always obtained a more distant relation to phenomenal experience and physical labour than the novel (poetry in America inheriting a long tradition steeped in the classics, the novel emerging in close connection to the work of journalism).[92] Snyder attempts to overcome these inherited historical and cultural contradictions between literary vocation and heterosexual masculinity by designating poetry as 'the real work', as something which has intimate relation to the real, to physical labour, and which can function analogously to the way in which a tool of manly labour – say, an axe – functions. Besides the various metaphors of physical work and tools used to describe the poetic project, the principal strategy for trying to accomplish this feat has been the mythic restoration to language of experiential worldly immediacy – making words operate as if they had no problematic relation to their referents.

THE POETICS OF NOMINALISATION

The archaeology within which words become separated from the things they designate (a separation located historically just prior to the Renaissance) has been outlined by Foucault in *The Order of Things*. Referring to a prelapsarian linguistic order (which may or may not have been mythic), Foucault writes – in a discourse which could well have come from either an Emersonian or Snyderian journal – of the time when *verba* remained inseparable from, an integral part of, *res*:

> language is not an arbitrary system: it has been set down in the world and forms a part of it, both because things themselves hide and manifest their own enigma like a language and because words offer themselves to men as things to be deciphered. The great metaphor of the book that one opens, that one pores over and reads in order to know nature, is merely the reverse and visible side of another transference, and a much deeper one, which forces language to reside in the world, among the plants, the herbs, the stones, and the animals.[93]

Compare this with the closing poem of *Riprap*, the last poem of the first book, which functions as a distilled poetic summation of the Snyderian aesthetic:

Riprap

Lay down these words
Before your mind like rocks.
    placed solid, by hands
In choice of place, set
Before the body of the mind
    in space and time:
Solidity of bark, leaf, or wall
    riprap of things:
Cobble of milky way,
    straying planets,
These poems, people,
    lost ponies with
Dragging saddles –
    and rocky sure-foot trails.

> The worlds like an endless
>   four-dimensional
> Game of *Go*.
>   ants and pebbles
> In the thin loam, each rock a word
>   a creek-washed stone
> Granite: ingrained
>   with torment of fire and weight
> Crystal and sediment linked hot
>   all change, in thoughts,
> As well as things.

(RR, p. 30)

Change is in thoughts as well as things because thoughts are figured *as* things, having an equal status with rocks and with people. Such a notion represents a development of Williams's demand for poetry, 'No ideas but in things', since ideas, natural phenomena and linguistic units are spoken of by 'Riprap' as evidencing the same ontological status. A riprap is 'a cobble of stone laid on steep slick rock to make a trail for horses in the mountains', according to a note on the title-page of *Riprap*; the onomatopoeic term and its referent thus appear homologous by the juxtapositional placing of similar-sounding syllables to form a word which describes the juxtapositional placing of similar-looking units of stone to form a means of access. The analogy – which the poem would have us believe constitutes an identity – extends from the poem to the book to which it lends its title and for which it is the summation: the poems in the volume function like stones leading across difficult territory toward the understanding of relation as it is figured in this final poem, and the visual patterned spacing of the words on the page mimics the arrangement of the riprap of stone in the world. The syllabic unit 'rap' as slang for speech serves to strengthen the analogy between word and rock-in-relation, thereby pointing to the analogy between poetic structures and social structures. If 'Riprap' is seen as an aesthetic statement or declaration of poetic *method*, then a further analogy can be read from the etymology of 'method', which stems from the word for path-cutting or trail-making. The critical bipartite feature of such an aesthetic or method – the characteristically Snyderian method – consists of the emphasis on structure as predicative of access.

It is important here to distinguish both the means and object (the aim, the what-is-to-be-attained) of access, since the prominence of rock as a theme of the declaration of poetics recalls the classic Formalist tenet that 'art exists to make the stone *stony*'.[94] Although both aesthetics may appear superficially similar, they are in fact counterposed to one another, since formalism declares, 'Art is a way of experiencing the artfulness of an object; the object is not important' (ibid.); while Snyder's poem always privileges the object over its representation: the poem exists not to make the stone stony, but to make the stone *real*. And as I have already indicated, this real consists in the homologising of word, idea and object to the same level of referentiality – a level of reality which renders each dimension available to use, amenable to manual work. Thus in the riprap of the poem, anything can be used to construct the path, and the imagery expands metonymically outward, casting from the minute details of 'Solidity of bark, leaf, or wall' to include the entire universe, the Milky Way and 'straying planets'. Riprap as a metaphor for poeticity suggests that the business of poetry is the discovery of relations between all elements and dimensions of the cosmos.

It is not only the largest and smallest natural phenomena which must be found to be related; also the world of the text and language in its reflexive – besides its referential – capacity can count in the construction: the referentially reflexive 'rocky sure-foot trails' can be included, and even 'These poems', the parts of the book itself (the textually reflexive), form an element in the structure. Thus it is not merely the three-dimensional phenomenal world of 'space and time' which comprises the field of the structural arrangement, but rather whole 'worlds like an endless / four-dimensional / Game of Go' (*Go* consisting of a Japanese game of unit-structure and relation similar to draughts – in England – and checkers – in the United States). The simile images the hopping over and strategic positioning of elements which is achieved with words in the poem, with things in the world (properly done), and with worlds in the Milky Way.

To elaborate on the structural arrangement of terms in the poem (the textual riprap), we may assert that if riprapping constitutes a metaphor for poem-making, then the method or technique of that making is resolutely metonymic, consisting of the substitution by term rather than by resemblance. The indented third line of the poem – which elaborates the opening, two-line sentence – begins the imitative form of presenting words as objects, elements for construction and apprehension. The arrangement of these object-words follows in the following twelve lines, in which the metony-mic placing of elements juxtapositionally both resists the hierarchic structure of metaphoric meaning and symbolisation (dependent as these latter are upon a literal vehicle or image and an abstract, non-phenomenal tenor or idea), and functions in the radically metonymic mode of the *list*, in which relations are implied rather than directly indicated. The second part of the poem, beginning a new sentence with 'The worlds like', links by its syntactical structure the *words like rocks* which begin the poem (and which the intervening lines have elaborated or produced) with the *worlds like a game of Go*: poetic structure thus relates words, things and worlds in a single plane, a metonymic, non-hierarchic, non-symbolic chain of relations.

From this overarching perspective – the meta-perspective of the poem-maker who can see and order relations – the attention shrinks back to a focus on the minute constitutive details of 'ants and pebbles / in the thin loam', as if presenting another natural image for the visual arrangement of the riprap, and, crucially, in order to avoid any tendency toward transcendence. The reminder that value inheres in the smallest, apparently insignificant ele-ments represents both a tacit endorsement of immanentism and a kind of Emersonian gesture of finding an essential relation be-tween the tiny (the ant) and the sublime (the endless 'four-dimensional / Game of *Go*' in Snyder, and the endless, sleepless labour of Herculean proportions in Emerson). The difference between the Snyderian system of relations and the Emersonian Transcendentalist system is that no 'seeing beyond' is necessary in Snyder: where for Emerson 'the visible world is the dialplate of the invisible', for Snyder the visible world is the dialplate of the world of natural relations. Transcendent vision is not necessary for Snyder; rather, the requirement is for a kind of vision – named here by 'Riprap' as poetic – which consists in the finding within relations a non-disruptive place for the human – a 'finding' imaged here as a journey, a making way which is the partial effect of poetic utterance properly deemed work.

In this poetic scheme, the figural is literalised, the image literally concretised. That is, in its conclusion, 'Riprap' focuses attention on the rock as that figure of substantiality which may ground the word. Rather than the avowal of word as rock, we read:

each rock a word
a creek-washed stone
Granite: ingrained

The rock represents both the fundamental element of the riprap and the fundamental element of the cosmological system within which the riprap functions. The simile which begins the poem – words like rocks – has solidified into a metaphor – each rock a word – as an effect not of language but of, precisely, rock: 'Granite: ingrained' indexes and *is* that metaphor, since granite is both rock and word (a type of rock and a particular linguistic unit); etymologically, 'granite' derives from the word for 'ingrained' (Latin *granum* means grain). Granite forms by the action of volcanic heat on rock, compressing different elements (chiefly feldspar and quartz), so that the geology of each element is implicated in the other. Granite as the effect of this 'torment of fire and weight' bears the physical force of its history locked into both its substance and its name (an analogy is found in the gentler, alliterative 'creek-washed stone', whose shape is the product of an opposite natural action). Hence the link between etymology and natural processes – 'all change, in thoughts, / as well as things'. This allusion to Williams's 'A Sort of a Song' (1944) makes thoughts into things by using the rocks broken by flowers (the metaphor) in Williams's poem to construct the riprap of Snyder's poem.

This materialising of language – of which 'Riprap' is Snyder's best early example – represents the effort to link poetry to the body, to work, and thus to what is taken as the immediacy of the real. Poetry is thereby accorded a continuity with the world and can be seen as effective in socio-political terms. Snyder is indeed correct to emphasise the materiality of language and its potential for effects. However, language's material dimension – the dimension of the signifier – is precisely that which renders it resistant to the manipulation of human intention.[95] It is thus less a question of Snyder's conception of poetic language operating in opposition to the Lacanian account of language with which we ally ourselves here, than it is a question of emphasis: both conceptions of the linguistic properly highlight the realm of linguistic effects; the difference resides in the conception of how linguistic effects are obtained. This question – the one with which I conclude – is nowhere more prominent than at the site of nominalisation, the locus of poetic naming.

And you could maybe travel to a place that you'd never been, steering only by songs you had learned.[96]

The function of naming is both the oldest and the most mythic function ascribed to language. The relation between language and power can be most clearly seen in the image of Adamic nomination – an inaugural act which not only *denominates* (names what exists, naming as attaching a linguistic label to an object), but also *generates* by orienting language's user to the object in a certain way. From the very beginning, then, language has been productive of effects somewhat in excess of a purely denominative function (initially as a consequence of the separability which exists between sign and referent).

That a name not only indexes an object in a purely objective fashion but also orients us to that object in one way or another is an effect of language's power to nominate that is amply recognised by Snyder. In the 'Introductory Note' to *Turtle Island*, his Pulitzer Prize-winning volume of 1974, Snyder writes:

> Turtle Island – the old/new name for the continent, based on the many creation myths of the people who have been living here for millenia, and reapplied by some of them to 'North America' in recent years. Also, an idea found world-wide, of the earth, or cosmos even, sustained by a great turtle or serpent-of-eternity.
>
> A name: that we may see ourselves more accurately on this continent of watersheds and life-communities – plant zones, physiographic provinces, culture areas; following natural boundaries. The 'U.S.A.' and its states and counties are arbitrary and inaccurate impositions on what is really here.

We can immediately notice the double pull of Snyder's aesthetic: the pull toward recognising the power of naming as a form of representation (representation as determinative of effects in the world), and the pull toward a material reality to which we can obtain access without the problem of representational mediacy (representation as simple transparency, naming what is 'really here').

As I have indicated, the renominalisation 'makes it new' by

making it as old as possible – by reviving an original name, that is, which has reference to ancient Indian myths.[97] This version of naming relates to the name charged with meaning in 'Look Back' – the name 'Piute Mountain' – by the shared implication that repetition of name delivers the term to significance and thereby alters subjective orientation; it relates also to the naming of the house for a plant ('kitkitdizze') and the naming of the first part of *Turtle Island* for another plant ('Manzanita'), the plant which rehabilitates land analogously to the Snyderian poetic. In each of these instances, the name achieves effects in excess of mere denomination, accruing additional meaning at both the denotative and connotative level in ways that are not always controlled by the namer.

This aspect of naming constitutes another dimension of Snyder's poetics of metonymy. The naming of Turtle Island consists of the most radical form of poetic metonymy, since metonymy as a substitution by term or by name (literally, the transfer of name) is generally taken to be the condition of possibility for metaphor – and even the basis of narrative (substitution by word or term – by, that is, denotative unit) – yet metonymy is rarely considered to be so radically determinative of effects as it is in Snyder. Another way of putting this would be to say that Snyder's metonymic poetics evidence most strongly Lacan's claim (for the determining effects of the signifier for the subject) that rather than conceiving of metonymy as an impoverished version of metaphor we should instead understand metonymy as that crucial linguistic function which enables metaphor as such.[98]

In this conception of linguistic relations and their effects, a single unit (which is only and always in relation – is, in fact, the product of its position in the field of relations) can become a whole poem. Emerson understood that 'Every word was once a poem', and – as if anticipating a poetics of metonymy such as we find in Snyder – Emerson added, 'Bare lists of words are found suggestive to an imaginative and excited mind.'[99] We find a striking example of such practice in Whitman's late poem 'Yonnondio', in which, like Snyder, the name is poetically charged with meaning in relation to the Indian. 'Yonnondio', the poem's title, names both the text, its form (a dirge or lament), the object of the lament (the Iroquois Indian from whom the term, meaning lament, is derived and for whom it could also take the place of a proper name), and the onomatopoeic wail generated within the poem as a response to 'the vanishing American':

(Race of the woods, the landscapes free, and the falls!
No picture, poem, statement, passing them to the future:)
Yonnondio! Yonnondio! – unlimn'd they disappear;

Cultural continuity is seen as a product of representation, and the apparent absence of representations of Indian life is equated with the evanescence of the race itself. The name 'Yonnondio' becomes the sign for that loss; yet, simultaneously, becomes – like the name in Snyder – the means of beginning to make good the loss: 'unlimn'd they disappear' means that the Indian's disappearance is a consequence of not being represented in poetry or pictures; yet the link between 'limn' and line – the delineation of the Indian not only in the form of a line drawing but also in the form of poetic 'lines' – means that the poetics of name is serving here the ancient preservative function of lyric (what the Greeks named *kléos*). The name becomes both the potential for and the sign of this preservative effect.

If in Whitman the name becomes a poem, in Snyder it becomes a heuristic device, a means toward the effort of knowing.[100] With reference to his own gloss on the naming of 'Turtle Island', the motive adduced for renominalisation is that of corrective perception – 'that we may see ourselves more accurately'. As in Emerson and American Romanticism generally, perception is but a figure for knowledge, and so here Snyder recognises a disjunction between, on the one hand, what is mapped and named as extant, and on the other hand, what is 'really here' (the deixical 'here' functioning to provide the illusion of contiguous, perceptual immediacy). The disjunction between the arbitrary name 'U.S.A.' and the land it names is the effect of a series of ideological operations (analogous to the original misnomer 'Indian') which this book has sought to analyse. Beyond the fact than any name must be more or less arbitrary, Snyder still deserves credit for developing a mythology attaching to the *less* arbitrary name, Turtle Island.

If the United States is renamed Turtle Island, then our disciplinary practice perhaps ought to be named Turtle Island Studies – or at the very least United States Studies, since 'America' only denominates the United States synecdochially, the most powerful part coming to stand for the extensive whole. Just as the official name, the USA, obscures the other Americas, including those within its territorial boundaries, so the austere cartographical grid obscures the natural contours of the landscape, making the ground conform to a certain political definition of the national. The American unconscious consists in the effect of this misfit. Snyder's shamanistic poetry of metonymy provides a means toward recognising the different America, the American Other; his poetic lineation helps us read beneath the map lines, and thus helps us read *between* the lines, reading palimpsestically to discover the traces of another, repressed culture which supports the American subject as its effect. Reading between the lines is a mode of reading attentive to that which cannot be spoken directly in what is actually getting said. Another name for such activity is psychoanalysis.

Notes

Notes to the Introduction

1. Sigmund Freud, *Civilization and its Discontents*, trs. James Strachey (New York: Norton, 1961) pp. 91 and 63.
2. See Sigmund Freud, 'A Note upon the "Mystic Writing-Pad"' (1925), in *Standard Edition of the Complete Psychological Works of Sigmund Freud*, ed. James Strachey (London: Hogarth Press, 1953–74), vol. 19, pp. 225–32, and Derrida's classic reading of it in Jacques Derrida, 'Freud and the Scene of Writing', in *Writing and Difference*, trs. Alan Bass (Chicago, Ill.: University of Chicago Press, 1978) pp. 196–231.
3. Quoted by Snyder in a radio interview with Roberta Berke, 'The Cool Around the Fire', BBC Radio 3, Spring 1988. I am grateful to Tony Austin for bringing this broadcast to my attention and for recording a copy for me.
4. I am thinking here specifically of Harold Bloom, since the other critics associated with deconstruction at Yale – Paul de Man, Shoshana Felman, Geoffrey Hartman and J. Hillis Miller – do not provide accounts of American poetry. Bloom does provide such an account which consists of a lineage he traces to the present, but Snyder forms no part of that tradition.

Notes to Part 1: The American Unconscious

1. A catalogue of typical objections to and suspicions of psychoanalysis has been voiced recently by Françoise Meltzer in her editor's introduction to a special issue of *Critical Inquiry*: Meltzer, 'Editor's Introduction: Partitive Plays, Pipe Dreams', *The Trial(s) of Psychoanalysis*, *Critical Inquiry*, vol. 13, no. 2 (Winter 1987) pp. 215–21. (This special issue was published in book form by University of Chicago Press under the same title in 1988.) The occasion of Meltzer's collection is in some sense a response to – and is, in fact, proleptically responded to by – a similar collection edited a decade earlier by Shoshana Felman whose own editor's introduction is not exhausted by Meltzer's objections: see Felman, 'To Open the Question', *Literature and Psychoanalysis – The Question of Reading: Otherwise* (Baltimore, Md: Johns Hopkins University Press, 1982) pp. 5–10 (originally published as a special double issue of *Yale French Studies*, vols 55/56, in 1977). What intervenes between and occasions both the opening of the question in 1977 and its being brought to trial in 1987 is the influence of Lacan. My own analysis of the relation between literature and psychoanalysis (and between these two collections and their respective claims) is too long to reproduce here; it is available in manuscript and should be forthcoming.

2. Joan Copjec, one of Lacan's best American readers, makes this point and elaborates some of its implications in her editor's introduction to a special issue of *October* devoted to psychoanalysis: see Copjec, 'Discipleship', *October*, 28 (Spring 1984) pp. 4–6. Copjec's essay in that volume, 'Transference: Letters and the Unknown Woman' (pp. 61–90), both informs my own understanding of Lacan and transference, and is essential reading for those wishing to follow up what my introduction to Lacan merely outlines.

3. Jacques Lacan, 'Intervention on Transference', in Juliet Mitchell and Jacqueline Rose (eds), *Feminine Sexuality: Jacques Lacan and the école freudienne*, trs. Jacqueline Rose (New York: Norton, 1982) pp. 61–73. Subsequent references to this essay give pagination in main text. Rose's introduction to this volume is the single best account of Lacan's meaning for feminism.

4. Unlike Barthes, Foucault and Derrida, Lacan was not an academic. The exception now would be Julia Kristeva, who is both a professor of linguistics and a full-time psychoanalyst.

5. Jacques Lacan, 'Intervention sur le transfert', *Écrits* (Paris: Seuil, 1966) p. 216.

6. Jacques Lacan in his Seminar of 16 June 1954: 'That is it – the grunt is entirely analysable in terms of mechanics. But, as soon as it wants to have something believed and demands recognition, speech exists.' See Jacques-Alain Miller (ed.), *The Seminar of Jacques Lacan. Book I: Freud's Papers on Technique, 1953–1954*, trs. John Forrester (Cambridge: Cambridge University Press, 1988) p. 240.

7. Joan Copjec makes clear the status of the Other in relation to language and the unconscious:

    We can only read the unconscious Other as it emerges, or becomes caught, in the interstices of the symbolic (the language of the) Other. . . . Although in Lacanian terminology, the unconscious and the symbolic structure of language are both designated by the same term and it is important to recall that they are closely related – the unconscious being the effect of language – they are nevertheless neither identical nor homologous. There is between them a constant nonconformity. It is just this fact which forbids a finalism to the theory of psychoanalysis and makes it impossible for the subject ever to master the Other. ('Transference', p. 73)

8. See Mitchell and Rose (eds), *Feminine Sexuality*, for Lacan's writings on 'what Freud expressly left aside, the *Was will das Weib?* the *What does the woman want?*' (p. 151). Lacan's 'return to Freud' was thus both a return to the radical discovery of the unconscious and its effects (a discovery which Lacan claimed had been lost), and a return to Freud's unfinished business, the question of feminine sexuality: neither of these elements – the unconscious, feminine sexuality – achieves its full conceptual meaning without the other.

Lacanian psychoanalysis has proven very productive for feminism in Britain, France and the United States, so that although the
conjunction of the two discourses is still an area of intense debate,
a recent critique levelled by David Macey in his *Lacan in Contexts*
(London: Verso, 1988) that Lacan has nothing positive to contribute
to feminism simply misses the massive contribution that *has already
been made* (or extorted): see Jacqueline Rose, *Sexuality in the Field of
Vision* (London: Verso, 1986) and Jane Gallop, *The Daughter's
Seduction: Feminism and Psychoanalysis* (Ithaca, N.Y.: Cornell University Press, 1982), to cite just two of the best-known instances.

9.   See Louis Althusser *et al.*, *Reading Capital*, trs. Ben Brewster
     (London: New Left Books, 1970) and Althusser, *Lenin and Philoso-
     phy*, trs. Ben Brewster (London: New Left Books, 1971). See also the
     work of Stephen Heath, Christian Metz, Laura Mulvey and Jac-
     queline Rose in 1970s issues of *Screen*.

10. For an eloquent refutation of this objection, see Joan Copjec,
     'Dossier on the Institutional Debate: an Introduction', *October*, 40
     (Spring 1987) pp. 51–4.

11. See Lacan, 'The insistence of the letter in the unconscious', trs. Jan
     Miel, *Yale French Studies: Structuralism* (special issue, ed. Jacques
     Ehrmann), nos 36/37 (1966) pp. 112–47. This essay was subsequent-
     ly translated by Alan Sheridan and included in the English edition
     of the *Écrits* ('The agency of the letter in the unconscious or reason
     since Freud', in Jacques Lacan, *Écrits: A Selection*, trs. Alan Sheridan
     (New York: Norton, 1977) pp. 146–78).

     See also Jacques Lacan, 'Of Structure as an Inmixing of an
     Otherness Prerequisite to Any Subject Whatever', in Richard
     Macksey and Eugenio Donato (eds), *The Structuralist Controversy:
     The Languages of Criticism and the Sciences of Man*, 2nd edn (Balti-
     more, Md: Johns Hopkins University Press, 1972) pp. 186–200. Part
     of the comedy of Lacan's lecture derived from the fact that it was
     delivered in a mixture of French and English, thereby demonstrat-
     ing the linguistic 'otherness' he deemed prerequisite to his occupy-
     ing the place of the speaking subject on the occasion of his first
     intervention 'in person' in the United States.

12. Both Jacques-Alain Miller and Slavoj Zizek have recently marked
     the significance of Lacan's distance from academic structuralism:
     see Miller, 'How Psychoanalysis Cures According to Lacan', and
     Zizek, 'Why Lacan is not a "Post-structuralist"', *Newsletter of the
     Freudian Field*, vol. 1, no. 2 (Autumn 1987) pp. 4–30 and 31–9
     respectively.

13. Besides *Newsletter of the Freudian Field* in the United States, relevant
     journals which include material devoted to Lacanian psychoanaly-
     sis are: the art-theory journal *October* and the film-theory journal
     Camera Obscura. English-speaking critics whose work leads the field
     in the development of Lacanian theory are: Joan Copjec, Mary Ann
     Doane, Shoshana Felman, John Forrester, Jane Gallop, Stephen
     Heath, Ellie Ragland-Sullivan, Jacqueline Rose, Kaja Silverman and
     Stuart Schneiderman.

14. 'Editorial', *Newletter of the Freudian Field*, vol. 2, no. 1 (Spring 1988) p. 3.

15. See Jacques Derrida, *Dissemination*, trs. Barbara Johnson (Chicago, Ill.: University of Chicago Press, 1981).

16. See Mikkel Borch-Jacobsen, *The Freudian Subject* (1982), trs. Catherine Porter (Stanford, Cal.: Stanford University Press, 1988).

17. Mikkel Borch-Jacobsen, 'The Freudian Subject: From Politics to Ethics', trs. Richard Miller, *October*, 39 (Winter 1986) pp. 109–27. Compare Borch-Jacobsen's assimilation of the subject to the Other with Stephen Heath, 'Notes on Suture', *Screen*, vol. 18, no. 4 (Winter 1977–8) pp. 48–76: 'As active break, the unconscious is finally not so much a position as an *edge*, the junction of division between subject and Other, a process interminably closing' (p. 49). See also Parveen Adams's development of Borch-Jacobsen's work on identification in Freud: Adams, 'Per Os(cillation)', *Camera Obscura*, no. 17 (May 1988) pp. 7–29.

18. See Ferdinand de Saussure, *Course in General Linguistics* (1915), trs. Wade Baskin (New York: McGraw Hill, 1966); Roman Jakobson, 'Two Aspects of Language and Two Types of Aphasic Disturbances', in his *Selected Writings, II: Word and Language* (The Hague: Mouton, 1971) pp. 239–59; Claude Lévi-Strauss, *Structural Anthropology*, vol. 1, trs. Claire Jacobson and Brooke Grundfest Schoepf (New York: Basic Books, 1963). Lacan refers to and develops for his own purposes Saussure's compositional analysis of the sign and Jakobson's distinction between metaphor and metonymy most famously in 'The insistence of the letter'.

19. See, for examples of such confusion in what are otherwise useful analyses: Russel J. Reising, *The Unusable Past: Theory and the Study of American Literature* (London: Methuen, 1986); and Charles H. Hinnant, *Samuel Johnson: An Analysis* (London: Macmillan, 1988) esp. pp. 66–83.

20. Jacques Lacan, 'The agency of the letter', in *Écrits*, p. 149.

21. Jacques Lacan, 'The signification of the phallus', in ibid., p. 284.

22. Jacques Lacan, 'The subversion of the subject and the dialectic of desire in the Freudian unconscious', in ibid., p. 316. This definition of the signifier recurs throughout Lacan's work: together with the aphoristic definitions, 'the unconscious is structured like a language', and 'the unconscious is the discourse of the Other', it constitutes a kind of poetic motif, accreting meaning to itself by repetition and providing a cognitive anchor-point for the reader in more difficult texts.

23. Jacques Lacan, Seminar of 9 February 1955, in Jacques-Alain Miller (ed.), *The Seminar of Jacques Lacan, Book II: The Ego in Freud's Theory and in the Technique of Psychoanalysis, 1954–1955*, trs. Sylvana Tomaselli (Cambridge: Cambridge University Press, 1988) p. 122.

24. Jacques Lacan, *Television*, trs. Denis Hollier, Rosalind Krauss and Annette Michelson, *October*, 40 (Spring 1987) p. 9.

25. On 22 June 1955, Lacan gave a specially prepared lecture, 'Psychoanalysis and Cybernetics, or, On the Nature of Language',

at the conclusion of a lecture series entitled 'Psychoanalysis and the Human Sciences' at the Clinique de la Faculté de Médicine in Paris, in which he meditates on the meaning of asserting the determinative occurrence of chance: 'What do we mean when we say that something happens *by chance*? We may mean one of two things, which may be very different – either that there is no intention, or that there is a law' (in Miller (ed.), *The Seminar of Jacques Lacan, Book II*, pp. 294–308). I draw attention to this lecture-essay as an antidotal response to the recent emergence of various 'new pragmatisms' (associated with names like Stanley Fish, Steven Knapp and Walter Benn Michaels), which more or less seek the restoration of intentionality at the expense of the Freudian discovery – in response, that is, to the ideology of *intentionalism*, no less, which reduces the unconscious to a question of mere mechanics. See the essays collected in W. J. T. Mitchell (ed.), *Against Theory: Literary Studies and the New Pragmatism* (Chicago, Ill.: University of Chicago Press, 1985).

26. See Julia Kristeva, *Revolution in Poetic Language*, trs. Margaret Waller (New York: Columbia University Press, 1984) esp. Part I, 'The Semiotic and the Symbolic', pp. 19–106. For an overview of this theorisation of the speaking subject, see Kristeva, 'The System and the Speaking Subject' (1973), in Toril Moi (ed.), *The Kristeva Reader* (Oxford: Basil Blackwell, 1986) pp. 24–33.

With reference to the Lacanian subject as a subject in process, the following gloss by Stephen Heath is useful:

The psychoanalytic subject for Lacan is not the subject of the enunciation, *is* not any *thing*, is defined topologically and not punctually, is the action of a structure. Freud's description of the *fort/da* game in *Beyond the Pleasure Principle* is luminous in this respect: what it finds as subject is not the baby boy but the circulation of a series of elements (hand, cot, voice, reel, string . . . a whole space), the subject constituted – constituting – across those elements in the process of the repetition. ('*Anata mo*', *Screen*, vol. 17, no. 4 (Winter 1976–7) pp. 49–66; extract from p. 50)

27. Lacan, Seminar of 23 June 1954, in Miller (ed.), *The Seminar of Jacques Lacan, Book I*, p. 248.

28. See Claude Lévi-Strauss, 'The Effectiveness of Symbols', in his *Structural Anthropology*, vol. 1, pp. 186–205 – an important essay to which Lacan refers in his early paper, 'The Mirror Stage', in *Écrits*, pp. 2–7, and to which I shall return.

29. See in this regard the accounts of Lacan and his work provided by Catherine Clément, *The Lives and Legends of Jacques Lacan*, trs. Arthur Goldhammer (New York: Columbia University Press, 1983); and Stuart Schneiderman, *Jacques Lacan: The Death of an Intellectual Hero* (Cambridge, Mass.: Harvard University Press, 1983). These books are good places to begin for the reader new to Lacan. Both Clément (pp. 5, 19, 35) and Schneiderman (p. v) compare Lacan's style to

poetry; and Clément characterises Lacan as a shaman (pp. 5, 49, 56, 202), while Schneiderman sees him operating like a Zen master (p. 81). The significance of these characterisations for our purposes does not have to do with any biographical interest in Lacan himself but depends instead upon their depiction of Lacan's pedagogic and therapeutic use of language, a use which recognises 'the effectiveness of symbols' and thereby makes the function of the Lacanian text analogous (although not identical) to that of the Snyderian poetic text.

30. In a preface to the first academic book on his work, Lacan said, 'My *Écrits* are unsuitable for a thesis, particularly an academic thesis: they are antithetical by nature' ('Preface by Jacques Lacan', in Anika Lemaire, *Jacques Lacan* (1970), trs. David Macey (London: Routledge and Kegan Paul, 1977) p. vii). Elsewhere (Postface to *Les quatre concepts fondamentaux de la psychanalyse*, p. 251, which is not included in the English translation), Lacan has said that his *Écrits* are 'made not to be read' (*'un écrit à mon sens est fait pour ne pas se lire'*), which paradoxically means two related things: first, that as distillations of the voice, of speech, they are meant, ideally, to be *heard* (and misheard), to be open to the play of signification in speech which is productive of a significant portion and dimension of their 'meaning'; and secondly, that they are not meant to be read discursively, as one might read, say, a nineteenth-century novel, to gain a totalised, accessible meaning. Meaning is derived differently from the *Écrits* than by this conventional kind of reading: the Lacanian text functions more as an object for meditation, so that readerly attention shifts from the signified (what the text 'means' conceptually, logically) to the signifier (what of significance might be 'getting through' at a different level). That is, reading Lacan instructs us in a new mode of reading, one analogous to that reserved for the iconic religious or poetic text.

31. Forthcoming is my essay on Samuel Johnson which outlines both a poetics of lexicography and the beginning of a Lacanian poetics: '"Dictionary Johnson": a Lacanian Psychopoetics of Lexicography'.

32. Lacan, Seminar of 9 March 1955, in Miller (ed.), *The Seminar of Jacques Lacan, Book II*, p. 153.

33. Juliet Flower MacCannell, *Figuring Lacan: Criticism and the Cultural Unconscious* (London: Croom Helm, 1986), pp. 5 and 19 respectively. Despite the similarities between MacCannell's title and my own, and between both titles and Frederic Jameson's *The Political Unconscious: Narrative as a Socially Symbolic Act* (Ithaca, N.Y.: Cornell University Press, 1981), my account and use of Lacan differs considerably from both MacCannell's and Jameson's.

34. The algorithm S(Ø) appears in the margin on the first page of *Television* (*October*, 40, p. 7); and as part of a graph which is subject to extended discussion in 'The subversion of the subject' (Lacan, *Écrits*, esp. pp. 314–18).

The graphs and diagrams in Lacan's work, together with the

representation of concepts in algebraic formulae, appear as both the most difficult part of Lacan's *oeuvre* to comprehend and that part which generates most resistance. Clément, for one, thinks the mathematical portion of his thought not the most important (*Lives and Legends*, p. 27), and I think it is necessary to remember that the algebraic signs and formulae do not obtain the precision they tend more toward in mathematics: that is, it is not a question – as it generally seems to be in mathematics – of 'decoding' a correct 'answer', of establishing a stable, unequivocal unit or feature from the algorithm. This difference (between mathematical usage of algorithms and Lacan's usage) is not only a consequence of the difference between language and numerical units; it is also, conversely, the case that what the algorithms obtain – namely, scientific precision – occasions the employment of the mathematical paraphernalia from the beginning (the drive to obtain for psychoanalysis the credibility of science in the way that semiology, say, can be considered a science). I had once (incorrectly) assumed that the algorithms were used so that Lacan's concepts would not be subject to 'the play of the signifier' in quite the same way that they would if they consisted merely of names and words. As algebraic formulae they are indeed *not* subject to this 'play' in *the same way*; but, crucially, it is also *not* the case that they are not subject to signifying movement. In other words, it seems that far from stabilising the concepts as directly translatable signs, the use of algebraic formulae *increases* the possibility of meaning accruing to – rather than inhering in – the sign:

> I have introduced [a concept] in the form of an algorithm; and it is no accident that it breaks the phonematic element constituted by the signifying unity right down to its literal atom. For it is created to allow a hundred and one different readings, a multiplicity that is admissible as long as the spoken remains caught in its algebra. ('Subversion of the subject', in *Écrits*, p. 313)

It would be somewhat hasty to announce that what Lacan 'intends' for one specific algorithm applies to them all. However, the fact that such an unmathematical logic can apply to one means that the *possibility* that it could apply to more than one is open: that is, the algorithms are not to be read *exclusively* in mathematical terms. This possibility also accounts for Lacan's refusal to provide – or allow – a translation for the concept termed '*objet petit a*'. Jane Gallop provides a stimulating account of Lacan's algorithms for metaphor and metonymy in 'The Agency of the Letter' in Chapter 5 of her *Reading Lacan* (Ithaca, N.Y.: Cornell University Press, 1985) pp. 114–32, in which she reads (for feminism) the algorithms analogously to the way in which Freud taught that the most resistant elements of the dream should be read.

35.   Jacques Lacan, *The Four Fundamental Concepts of Psycho-Analysis*, ed. Jacques-Alain Miller, trs. Alan Sheridan (Harmondsworth, Middx: Penguin, 1977) p. 25.

36. Jacques Lacan, 'Of Structure as an Inmixing', in Macksey and Donato (eds), *The Structuralist Controversy*, p. 189.
37. Lacan, *The Four Fundamental Concepts*, p. 24.
38. Charles Olson, *Call Me Ishmael: A Study of Melville* (San Francisco, Cal.: City Lights Books, 1947) p. 11.
39. Dominick LaCapra, 'History and the Novel', in his *History and Criticism* (Ithaca, N.Y.: Cornell University Press, 1985) p. 128.
40. For representational histories of the United States, see William H. Goetzmann and William N. Goetzmann, *The West of the Imagination* (New York: Norton, 1986); Hugh Honour, *The European Vision of America* (Cleveland, Ohio: Cleveland Museum of Art, 1975); Fredi Chiappelli, Michael J. B. Allen and Robert L. Benson (eds), *First Images of America: The Impact of the New World on the Old*, 2 vols (Berkeley, Cal.: University of California Press, 1976) esp. William C. Sturtevant, 'First Visual Images of Native America', pp. 417–50.
41. John Calvin, *Institutes of the Christian Religion*, ed. John T. McNeil, trs. Ford Lewis Battles (Philadelphia, Pa: Westminster Press, 1960) p. 251 (Library of Christian Classics, vol. 20).
42. Olson, *Call Me Ishmael*, p. 14.
43. See Joseph Riddel, 'Decentering the Image: The "Project" of "American" Poetics?', in Josué V. Harari (ed.), *Textual Strategies: Perspectives in Post-Structuralist Criticism* (Ithaca, N.Y.: Cornell University Press, 1979) pp. 322–58:

> 'American literature' is an oxymoron – a notion of the belated original, of the immaculate opening of an old closure. 'American literature' has always been inscribed in such a questioning parenthesis, because its dream of 'making it new', of realizing itself originally, begins with the contradiction inherent in the notion of original or creative 'literature', of an original secondariness. What is called the modern, and 'American literature' has always been 'modern' – that is, inscribed as both an end and a beginning between two notions of history – is always an 'event' that is logically anterior yet historically posterior to that literature we call traditional or classical. 'American literature' has always played in the paradoxical margins of the 'new'. (p. 322)

44. Adrienne Rich, 'The Tensions of Anne Bradstreet' (1966), in her *On Lies, Secrets, and Silence: Selected Prose, 1966–1978* (London: Virago, 1980) p. 23.
45. The work of Perry Miller and Sacvan Bercovitch represents the canonical criticism on Puritan culture, but see also Peter White (ed.), *Puritan Poets and Poetics: Seventeenth-Century American Poetry in Theory and Practice* (Pennsylvania Park, Pa: Pennsylvania State University Press, 1985). For the best analysis of the rhetorical history of which typology is a particularly powerful instance, see Erich Auerbach, 'Figura' (1944), in Auerbach, *Scenes from the Drama of European Literature*, trs. Ralph Mannheim (Minneapolis, Minn.: University of Minnesota Press, 1984) pp. 11–60.
46. My discussion of American literary nationalism focuses on the

tradition in poetry, partly because this book is a study of poetry,
and partly because the dominant accounts of the emergence of an
American literary tradition tend to focus on fiction, which was after
all the dominant literary genre. My study may thus be read as
supplementing, to some extent, the following excellent accounts of
early American literature: Robert Clark, *History, Ideology and Myth in
American Fiction, 1823–52* (London: Macmillan, 1984); Cathy N.
Davidson, *Revolution and the Word: The Rise of the Novel in America*
(Oxford: Oxford University Press, 1986); Michael T. Gilmore,
American Romanticism and the Marketplace (Chicago, Ill.: University
of Chicago Press, 1985); Jane Tompkins, *Sensational Designs: The
Cultural Work of American Fiction, 1790–1860* (Oxford, Oxford University Press, 1985). The difference between these works and
between them and my own may be summarised thus: in terms of
content, they focus on prose while I focus on poetry; in terms of
method, they all take versions of what can loosely be termed a
Marxian approach (concerning themselves with ideology), with
Tompkins and Davidson considering feminism central to the
question of cultural ideology; while my method adds the dimension of psychoanalysis. The difference in literary genres considered
is related to the method and forms of argument because it is quite
possible to make an argument for the ideological function of fiction
in a literary culture whereas the place of poetry in culture is less
clear, its function more difficult to assess. My argument about early
American poetry assumes that it obtains some significant place
within the culture; my argument about Snyder assumes that his
poetry is at odds with, and is antidotal to, the culture in an
illuminating way, yet in a way different to that in which earlier
poetry (and fiction) illuminates the development of American
culture. This difference has not least to do with the fact that
American culture now is not literary, although it is highly semiotic,
organised around signs that require different kinds of reading: in
generic terms, American culture is now a television and video
culture. Hence the dominance of the image over the word.

47. See Harold Bloom, *Figures of Capable Imagination* (New York:
     Seabury Press, 1976), and Bloom, *Agon: Towards a Theory of Revision-
     ism* (Oxford: Oxford University Press, 1982).

48. My disagreement with Bloom has to do with his conflation of the
     national and the literary which makes it seem that the characterisa-
     tion of Emersonian expression as the pinnacle of Americanness
     and therefore Emerson as the American Orpheus (*Agon*, p. 159)
     necessarily eventuates Emerson as the origin and father of Amer-
     ican poetry. Although Bloom's notion of poetic priority is crucially
     not homologous with historical anteriority, his positing of Emerson
     as the American Orpheus, and Whitman as the American Sublime
     (ibid., p. 182), eventuates in his overlooking early poets – particu-
     larly women poets – whose poetic achievement may equal Emer-
     son's or Whitman's but whose sense of Americanness differs from
     theirs. Thus, for instance, Dickinson does not fit into Bloom's
     tradition, although in his 'Introduction' to Bloom (ed.), *Emily*

Dickinson: Modern Critical Views (New York: Chelsea House, 1985), Bloom acknowledges that her poetic originality places her on a par with Shakespeare and Freud. Bloom's inability to find just one single precursor for Dickinson leads him to characterise her as 'the American difference personified', and to claim finally that 'Dickinson at her strongest compels us to begin again in rethinking our relation to poems' (p. 6). There are three points of significance I wish to adduce here.

First, that by conflating literary priority and a version of nationalism, Bloom's critical agenda represents to a certain extent the continuation of the trend against which my book's critique is mounted. This is also evidenced by the Americanist resistance to Continental modes of reading, which leads Bloom to assert 'Deconstructing any discourse by Ralph Waldo Emerson would be a hopeless enterprise, extravagantly demonstrating why Continental modes of interpretation are unlikely to add any lustres to the most American of writers' (*Agon*, p. 156). The 'resistance to theory' is thus revealed as a nationalist resistance to any discourse which questions American specificity and originality – a kind of hermeneutic isolationism.

Secondly, that it is not only a question of 'adding' the missing pieces of the American literary tradition to Bloom's canon – that is, women poets – but of analysing how Bloom founds a tradition based not only on a certain persistent nationalist ideology but also on the exclusion of the woman writer from consideration – how, that is, the exclusion of the woman consists of the tradition's very condition of possibility. In this respect, Americanism is predicated on a specific gender bias (one which I address in more detail toward the end of Part 2).

Thirdly, and following this second point, Bloom admits that a serious consideration of Dickinson's poetry prompts a wholesale overhaul of the whole basis on which we read and understand American poetry. This is a radical claim and one whose implications Bloom himself has not developed (although it has been developed by feminist accounts of Dickinson – see Helen McNeil, *Emily Dickinson* [London: Virago, 1986]). Thus the addition of a figure like Dickinson to the existing canon, or the development of a separate 'women's tradition' of American or English literature, although useful beginnings, is just not sufficient. What is required is the fundamental redefinition of the concepts 'American', 'poetry' and 'tradition'; and the subsequent development of a new map for reading American literature. That project is not possible here, but I draw attention to its cogency as a way of contextualising the difference of my treatment of Emerson from Bloom's and my insistence on beginning with Bradstreet.

49. Ralph Waldo Emerson, *Nature*, in his *Selected Essays*, ed. Larzer Ziff (Harmondsworth, Middx: Penguin, 1982) p. 48. Unless noted otherwise, references to Emerson use this edition and give pagination in main text.

50. See Peter de Bolla. *The Discourse of the Sublime: Readings in History,*

Aesthetics and the Subject (Oxford: Basil Blackwell, 1989).

51. Bloom, *Agon*, p. 180.

52. Edward Taylor, 'Upon a Wasp Chil'd with Cold', in *The Poems of Edward Taylor*, ed. Donald E. Stanford (New Haven, Conn.: Yale University Press, 1960) pp. 465–6, date of composition unknown. The prayer for God's assistance with reading His signs in the world constituted a typical part of the devout Puritan's devotional discourse, and we can see how this tradition influences Emerson, who similarly finds a tiny insect and emphasises the significance that can be found in it by looking at it in the right way. For both Taylor and Emerson, the orderedness of the universe is utterly complete, such that no element of natural phenomena is too insignificant to be decoded as a microcosmic synecdoche of the larger, macrocosmic whole. Where Emerson substitutes Man at the centre of order for Taylor's God, Snyder decentres Emerson's Man: for Snyder, the ecosystem is ordered, complete, yet no centre holds.

53. In 'Malthus, Godwin, Wordsworth, and the Spirit of Solitude', in Elaine Scarry (ed.), *Literature and the Body: Essays on Population and Persons* (Baltimore, Md: Johns Hopkins University Press, 1988) pp. 106–24, Frances Ferguson provides a fascinating, historicised account of the necessity of solitude for the production of a Wordsworthian sense of subjectivity. See also Frances Ferguson, *Solitude and the Sublime: The Aesthetics of Individuation*, forthcoming from Methuen.

54. See Paul de Man, *The Rhetoric of Romanticism* (New York: Columbia University Press, 1984), particularly 'Autobiography as De-Facement' (pp. 67–81), 'Wordsworth and the Victorians' (pp. 83–92), and 'Shelley Disfigured' (pp. 93–123). Cynthia Chase has expertly developed the de Manian theory of disfiguration in her *Decomposing Figures: Rhetorical Readings in the Romantic Tradition* (Baltimore, Md: Johns Hopkins University Press, 1986). Ned Lukacher, another de Man student, has developed the theory of prosopopoeia in his *Primal Scenes: Literature, Philosophy, Psychoanalysis* (Ithaca, N.Y.: Cornell University Press, 1986).

55. See, for a psychoanalytic account of de Man's rhetorics – and, by implication, a meditation on the relation of psychoanalytic discourse to de Manian deconstruction – Neil Hertz, 'Lurid Figures', in Lindsay Waters and Wlad Godzich (eds), *Reading de Man Reading* (Minneapolis, Minn.: University of Minnesota Press, 1989) pp. 82–104. (Hertz has a sequel to this essay forthcoming.)

56. Although Derrida tends to 'begin' with philosophy rather than with rhetoric (working, as he does, from the position of a professional philosopher as opposed to the position of a professional literary theorist), he has analysed at some length the dependence of philosophy upon rhetoric, the way in which it is not just a question of metaphor inhabiting the text of philosophy but rather a question of the way in which *philosophy is 'in' metaphor* (as 'in' a maze). See Jacques Derrida, 'White Mythology: Metaphor in the Text of Philosophy', in his *Margins of Philosophy*, trs. Alan Bass

(Brighton, Sussex: Harvester Press, 1986) pp. 207–71.

57. See Richard L. Rapson (ed.), *Major Interpretations of the American Past* (New York: Appleton-Century-Crofts, 1971): 'The frontier thesis is America's most popular explanation of herself and it has held this place from 1893 through John F. Kennedy's call for a New Frontier and on to our explorations into space. Turner is America's historian' (p. 38).

58. Michael Kraus comments, 'If it is true that Henry Adams has had more written about him than any other American historian, Frederick Jackson Turner has probably stimulated more writing than any other – about him, surely, both praise and criticism' (in Michael Kraus and Davis D. Joyce, *The Writing of American History*, rev. edn, (Norman, Okla.: University of Oklahoma Press, 1985) p. 247). Kraus cites the work of Wilbur Jacobs, Howard Lamar, R. A. Billington and Richard Hofstadter as crucial to the assessment of Turner, and I would add the names of those whose defences and critiques of Turner appear in the text from which I shall be quoting: George Rogers Taylor (ed.), *The Turner Thesis: Concerning the Role of the Frontier in American History*, 3rd edn (Lexington, Mass.: D. C. Heath, 1972).

59. Hofstadter notes this characteristic of Turner's use of the term in his 'Introduction' to Richard Hofstadter and Seymour Martin Lipset (eds), *Turner and the Sociology of the Frontier* (New York: Basic Books, 1968).

60. Frederick Jackson Turner, 'The Significance of the Frontier in American History', in Taylor, *The Turner Thesis*, p. 3. Further references give pagination in main text.

61. Benjamin F. Wright, Jr, 'Political Institutions and the Frontier', ibid., p. 64. Serious criticism of the thesis began to appear in the 1930s, after Turner's death, and when the economic and political situation of the United States (its domestic depression and its participation in international affairs following the war) produced a climate inhospitable to the notion of American specificity and political isolationism. The economic depression of the 1930s also made it clear that the days of Jeffersonian agrarianism, upon whose image Turner's thesis so heavily relied, had indisputably given way to the capitalistic operation of the land by big business.

62. Frank J. Popper, 'The Strange Case of the Contemporary American Frontier', *The Yale Review*, vol. 76, no. 1 (Autumn 1986) pp. 101–21; quotation, p. 101. Subsequent references to this essay give pagination in main text.

63. Sigmund Freud, 'The "Uncanny"' in *Standard Edition of the Complete Psychological Works of Sigmund Freud*, ed. James Strachey (London: Hogarth Press, 1953–74) vol. 17, pp. 219–52; quotations on pp. 220 and 225, respectively.

64. In a 1973 interview with Ekbert Faas, Snyder subscribes to Turner's 'safety valve' notion and its subsequent disappearance:

> It may have been a plus in frontier times, you know, because there was always some place to go to; the individual with no

sense of cooperation would just go off by himself and do something else. That's not possible now, not even in the wildest countryside. So we have become like Europe and China. We are now at the end of our resource and space freedom and we have to learn to live within the terms of what we've got. It will be interesting to see if we can do it. (in Ekbert Faas, *Towards a New American Poetics: Essays and Interviews* (Santa Barbara, Cal.: Black Sparrow Press, 1978) p. 114.)

Snyder's comment is made in the context of a discussion of communal living modelled on social organisation in Mao's communist China, and he correctly suggests that 'run of the mill American individualism' can become a problem when space runs short. This argument would seem to coincide with Frances Ferguson's account (cited above), and just as Ferguson argues that it is less a question of too many bodies taking up space and more a question of too many *consciousnesses*, so on the American scene the persistence of the figurative dimensions of the frontier – including aggressive political expansion overseas – ensures to some extent the 'safety valve' mechanism which is apparently requisite for the formation of an individualist American subject.

In this respect, it would be interesting to compare Mark Twain's *Huckleberry Finn* (1884), the text with which Hemingway claimed American literature properly begins, and in which Huck as the American hero knows the dangers of 'sivilizing' and – famously – knows also the necessity of 'lighting out for the territory' to save his consciousness at the novel's close. The 'free' territory of the frontier, whether liberal or figurative, is thus consistently figured as the predicate of not only the American subject but also of that subject's political virtue.

65. My use of the term 'work' here to describe the ideological effect obtained within culture by an abstract or figurative notion – one which 'works' precisely in so far as it determines and is determined by cultural meanings – roughly coincides with Tompkins's use of the term (in *Sensational Designs*) and Mary Poovey's in her *Uneven Developments: The Ideological Work of Gender in Mid-Victorian England* (Chicago, Ill.: University of Chicago Press, 1988). The work of the frontier in relation to American culture is dialectical; it functions in both the dimensions of cause and effect.

66. See Richard Slotkin, *Regeneration Through Violence: The Mythology of the American Frontier, 1600–1860* (Middletown, Conn.: Wesleyan University Press, 1973) esp. ch. 8, 'A Gallery of Types: the Evolution of Literary Genres and the Image of the Indian (1755–1785)', for a useful taxonomy of images of the Indian and their historical predicates.

67. Sigmund Freud, 'Creative Writers and Day-Dreaming' (1908), *Art and Literature* (Harmondsworth, Middx: Penguin, 1985), p. 140 (Pelican Freud Library, vol. 14).

68. See Adams, 'Per Os(cillation)'; Borch-Jakobsen, *The Freudian Sub-*

ject; Jean Laplanche and Jean-Bertrand Pontalis, 'Fantasy and the Origins of Sexuality' (1968), in Victor Burgin, James Donald and Cora Kaplan (eds), *Formations of Fantasy* (London: Methuen, 1986) pp. 5–34; and see Cynthia Chase's two excellent essays on sexuality and identification which comprise readings of the same dream around which much of Adams's argument is based: 'The Witty Butcher's Wife: Freud, Lacan, and the Conversion of Resistance to Theory', *Modern Language Notes*, vol. 102 (December 1987) pp. 898–1013, and 'Desire and Identification in Lacan and Kristeva', in Richard Feldstein and Judith Roof (eds), *Feminism and Psychoanalysis* (Ithaca, N.Y.: Cornell University Press, 1989) pp. 65–83.

69. The classic refutation of Turner's account of the development of political institutions on the frontier comes from Benjamin F. Wright, Jr: see his 'Political Institutions and the Frontier', in Taylor, *The Turner Thesis*, pp. 56–69. The strongest refutation of Wright has come most recently from Michael A. Bellesiles in his prize-winning essay 'The Establishment of Legal Structures on the Frontier: the case of Revolutionary Vermont', *Journal of American History*, vol. 73, no. 4 (March 1987) pp. 895–915. The space of debate which exists between these arguments finds its mythic figuration in the contradictions of the character of Ransom Stoddard in John Ford's *The Man Who Shot Liberty Valance*, discussed on pp. 75–8 above.

70. The historical inversion by which Turner can hyperbolically figure the pioneer 'tak[ing] the scalp in orthodox Indian fashion' is characteristic of his rhetorical mode of argumentation in the thesis: scalp-taking in fact originated with the White settlers, who introduced the practice to America as the legacy of a method Cromwell had earlier found effective in controlling the Irish. Not the least of Turner's rhetorical techniques of inversion in this startling passage is the familiar political technique – mobilised against minorities – of blaming the victim (Indians as scalpers rather than scalped).

71. R. A. Burchell and R. J. Gray, 'The Frontier West', in Malcolm Bradbury and Howard Temperley (eds), *Introduction to American Studies* (London: Longman, 1981) p. 112. Apart from the way in which Burchell's and Gray's neutral terms 'replacement' and 'cultural process' naturalise the expropriation of the Indian in a way not dissimilar to Turnerian rhetoric, their account is a good summary of the topic, although they fail to consider the central role played by cinema in the formation of the meaning of the West. (This omission is characteristic of American Studies in England, in which cinema as the dominant expression of American culture tends to be overlooked.)

72. See Henry Nash Smith, *Virgin Land: The American West as Symbol and Myth* (Cambridge, Mass.: Harvard University Press, 1950) esp. the final chapter, 'The Myth of the Garden in Turner's Frontier Hypothesis', pp. 250–60.

73. Chief Standing Bear, *Land of the Spotted Eagle* (Boston, Mass.: Houghton Mifflin, 1933); quoted by C. Merton Babcock (ed.), *The American Frontier: A Social and Literary Record* (New York: Holt,

Rinehart and Winston, 1965) p. 199. I would like to make several points here. First, to avoid the *objection* that if the Indians did not own the land it is illogical to claim (as I do) that it was stolen from them, and to similarly avoid the *idealisation* of Indian relations to the land, we may adduce here that various Indian tribes did have treaties with White settlers providing for land ownership, and that these treaties were subsequently broken by Whites. See, for instance, on the White breaking of contracts with the League of the Iroquois, Clark, *History, Ideology and Myth*, esp. 79–95 and 169–70. Secondly, we may note that Indian tribes had assimilated the White concept of land ownership sufficiently by the mid-nineteenth century that disputes over land ownership erupted when the redistribution of tribal land was proposed on behalf of the United States Government by one David Dawson Mitchell. In view of the tribal origin of the author of the passage idealising Indian relations to the land in the 1930s, the following statement by Black Hawk, a leader of the Oglala Sioux in 1851, is significant: 'These lands once belonged to the Kiowas and the Crows, but we whipped these nations out of them, and in this we did what the White men do when they want the lands of the Indians' (quoted in Wilcomb E. Washburn, *The Indian in America* (New York: Harper and Row, 1975) p. 193). The survival of the Indian necessitated the adoption of some White attitudes and policies *vis-à-vis* the land at least eighty years before an Indian of the same tribe as Black Hawk described the original Indian relation to the ground.

However, a further point of significance obtrudes, which is that Standing Bear's articulation of the Indian relation to the ground in 1933 bears a striking resemblance to a certain section of Whites and their perception of their relation to Western land in the Depression. I am thinking here of the dispossession of White farmers in John Steinbeck's 1939 novel, *The Grapes of Wrath*, in which the displacement of Oklahoma farmers by Eastern business interests forces a White migration analogous to the Indian migrations a century earlier. Early in the novel, an anonymous tenant farmer, speaking in a representative voice, contrasts the farmers' sense of land ownership with that of the Eastern banks' sense: 'But it's our land. We measured it and broke it up. We were born on it, and we got killed on it, died on it. Even if it's not good, it's still ours. That's what makes it ours – being born on it, working on it, dying on it. That makes ownership, not a paper with numbers on it' (John Steinbeck, *The Grapes of Wrath*, Harmondsworth, Middx: Penguin, 1959) p. 32. Notice that, similarly to the imagery employed by Standing Bear, it is the harmony of the human cycle – birth, work, death – with the natural cycle and the intimacy of the relation that defines the farmer's notion of ownership.

74.   For the classic imagery of the Hand of God, see Jonathan Edwards, 'Sinners in the Hands of an Angry God' (1741), in Ola Elizabeth Winslow (ed.), *Jonathan Edwards: Selected Writings* (New York: Signet, 1966) pp. 150–67.

75. Bernard W. Sheehan, *Seeds of Extinction: Jeffersonian Philanthropy and the American Indian* (Chapel Hill, N.C.: University of North Carolina Press, 1973) p. 90. See also Sheehan's subsequent study: *Savagism and Civility: Indians and Englishmen in Colonial Virginia* (Cambridge: Cambridge University Press, 1980). The chapter titles of this latter text are highly indicative: 'Paradise', 'Ignoble Savagism', 'Bestiality', 'Dependence', 'Conversion', 'Massacre'.

76. The term *exploitation* appears as a positive value in the thesis, a privileged term standing for the production of every American virtue: 'The exploitation of the beasts took hunter and trader to the west, the exploitation of the grasses took the rancher west, and the exploitation of the virgin soil of the river valleys and prairies attracted the farmer' (p. 14). Since both *frontier* and *exploitation* appear as privileged terms within the thesis, we may conclude that *for Turner the frontier was synonymous with exploitation* (see note 117 below).

77. Ralph Waldo Emerson, 'At Concord'; quoted by Elémire Zolla, *The Writer and the Shaman: A Morphology of the American Indian* (New York: Harcourt Brace Jovanovich, 1973) pp. 138–9.

78. Robert F. Berkhofer, Jr, *The White Man's Indian: Images of the American Indian from Columbus to the Present* (New York: Random House, 1978). This is an oustanding book, and my argument relies heavily on Berkhofer's considerable insights.

79. D. H. Lawrence, *Studies in Classic American Literature* (Harmondsworth, Middx: Penguin, 1983) p. 55. The best account of Cooper's misrepresentations of the Indian in his Leatherstocking Tales can be found in Clark, *History, Ideology and Myth*, pp. 61–109. Clark's brilliant analysis of *The Last of the Mohicans* first appeared as 'The Last of the Iroquois: History and Myth in James Fenimore Cooper's *The Last of the Mohicans*', *Poetics Today*, vol. 3, no. 4 (Spring 1981) pp. 115–34. A version of this essay then appears at the literal centre of Clark's book: it can therefore be read as the forerunner and pivot of Clark's argument, an argument which has to do with the textual strategies – of displacement and condensation, reminiscent of the tropes of the unconscious – by which Cooper provides what he claims to be an historically accurate account of his family's appropriation of Iroquois land. The textual perversion of history – precisely its mythification – is seen to derive from two psychological forces: 'the need to repress personal knowledge of [the Iroquois's] cultural sophistication so that the conquest would seem just, and the desire to remove them from their homelands so that the patriarchal estate would appear to have been a wilderness before the arrival of the White man' (*Poetics Today*, p. 124). In this respect, Cooper's representational strategies – albeit in fiction and in the nineteenth century – are paradigmatic of the kind of cultural operations I have been detailing. Clark's account evidences a fruitful amalgamation of Marxism, Freudian psychoanalysis, close textual analysis and structuralism (early Barthes), and has indeed been inspirational for the development of my own argument, both

in terms of content and in terms of methodological possibilities.

80. On the association of women with the image, see Joan Copjec, 'Flavit et Dissipati Sunt', in Annette Michelson, Rosalind Krauss, Douglas Crimp and Joan Copjec (eds), *October: The First Decade, 1976–1986* (Cambridge: Mass.: MIT Press, 1987) pp. 296–325.

81. Jacques Lacan, 'Guiding Remarks for a Congress on Feminine Sexuality', in Mitchell and Rose (eds), *Feminine Sexuality*, p. 90; emphasised by Rose, 'Introduction – II', ibid., p. 43; see also Rose, *Sexuality in the Field of Vision*, p. 67.

82. Vine Deloria, Jr, *Custer Died For Your Sins: An Indian Manifesto* (1969) (Norman, Okla.: University of Oklahoma Press, 1988) p. 2.

83. Berkhofer, *The White Man's Indian*, p. 195.

84. It is important to distinguish what is meant by 'real' here. The Real is the third term in Lacan's configuration of Symbolic, Imaginary and Real. There is no easy or shorthand way to denote the relation between these three terms and it is not possible to say which precedes or predicates either of the others. In later texts, as Lacan sought to elaborate a topology for the unconscious and the subject, he had increasing recourse to the figure of the borromenean knot as an explanatory metaphor for the relation between the three crucial terms. The knot indicates at the very least the difficulty of naming the interrelationship between terms, as well as their inextricability (the first being a consequence of this second).

It is also important to distinguish, as Lacan does, between the Real and reality. When I speak of the subject's commitment to a real produced by the Imaginary and of the tyranny of this commitment, I am referring to a conception of reality held by the subject, which is not a question of 'false consciousness', not something that a decent dose of demystification could remedy, but rather a constructed reality (in which the subject is never agent of the construction but which rather orients the subject) that is distinguishable – at least in theory – from the Real. It is in this sense that the real (as I refer to it) can be called unreal: not the Real. There is no subjective access to the Real outside the domain of representation, outside of symbolic structures, and the impossibility of the Real for consciousness is one precondition of intersubjectivity. It is in this respect that I find Clark's analysis weak, in that it more or less gestures toward a reality – whose name is history – which could be known beyond the veils of ideology and narrative myth-making. This is not the case as far as my account is concerned.

When Lacan defines the Real as that which always returns to the same place, he means that the Real is not subject to the signifying chain, is not something endlessly displaced by language as the subject and its desire are. The Real tends to be experienced as a resistance. Frederic Jameson's account, 'Imaginary and Symbolic in Lacan: Marxism, Psychoanalytic Criticism, and the Problem of the Subject' (in Felman (ed.), *Literature and Psychoanalysis*, pp. 338–95), fails to get anywhere near the Lacanian concept of the Real.

However, a useful, discriminatory account, which also considers the relation of the Real to cinema, can be found in Heath, '*Anata mo*'.

85.   In *The White Man's Indian*, Berkhofer comments:

> Whites overwhelmingly measured the Indian as a general category against those beliefs, values, or institutions they most cherished in themselves at the time. For this reason, many commentators on the history of White Indian imagery see Europeans and Americans as using *counterimages* of themselves to describe Indians and the *counterimages* of Indians to describe themselves. (p. 27; emphases mine)

86.   If the term 'dialectics' appears here as startling or inappropriate, looking like the importation into a psychoanalytic account of a properly Hegelian or Marxian diction, then one should recall the development of Lacan's career from a strong Hegelian influence and remember the claim that his theory of the unconscious is materialist in the sense that the term is understood by politically oriented theory. One should also refer to 'Intervention on Transference' (in Mitchell and Rose (eds), *Feminine Sexuality*, pp. 62–73), in which the dramatisation of the subject is discussed explicitly in dialectical terms.

87.   Berkhofer, *The White Man's Indian*, p. 26.

88.   Hayden White, 'The Noble Savage Theme as Fetish', in Chiappelli *et al.* (eds), *First Images of America*, p. 125.

89.   This horror may be defined more specifically in psychoanalytic terms as *abject*. See Julia Kristeva, *Powers of Horror: An Essay on Abjection*, trs. Leon S. Roudiez (New York: Columbia University Press, 1982): 'It follows that jouissance alone causes the abject to exist as such. One does not know it, one does not desire it, one joys in it [*on en jouit*]. Violently and painfully' (p. 9); and, 'I experience abjection only if an Other has settled in place and stead of what will be "me"' (p. 10). For early European discoverers, the Indian was the occasion of abjection.

90.   Leslie Fiedler, *The Return of the Vanishing American* (New York: Stein and Day, 1968) p. 42. After the bulk of my manuscript had been completed I came across the work of Michael Rogin, whose accounts of American political strategies *vis-à-vis* the land and the Indian, and with respect to cinema, are very close to my own. Although Rogin's methods are less psychoanalytic than mine, his concept of *demonology* is very close to what I am describing in terms of splitting and projection. See Michael Paul Rogin, *Fathers and Children: Andrew Jackson and the Subjugation of the American Indian* (New York: Random House, 1975), and his *Ronald Reagan, the Movie and Other Episodes in Political Demonology* (Berkeley, Cal.: University of California Press, 1987) esp. ch. 1 on the recent political effects of cinema; ch. 5 on the Indian; and ch. 6 on Nature.

91.   See Honour, *The European Vision of America*, p. 1.

92. See Leo Marx, *The Machine in the Garden: Technology and the Pastoral Ideal in America* (Oxford: Oxford University Press, 1967).

93. See Berkhofer, *The White Man's Indian*, pp. 34–8.

94. Fiedler, *Return of the Vanishing American*, p. 23.

95. The persistence of the American desire to abandon history and 'start afresh' has been charted by Frances Fitzgerald in her fascinating account of American sub-cultures whose power and prominence radically call into question the relation between the categories of culture and its subsets. See Frances Fitzgerald, *Cities on a Hill: A Journey Through Contemporary American Cultures* (London: Picador, 1987).

96. White, 'Noble Savage Theme as Fetish', Chiappelli *et al.* (ed.), *First Images*, p. 130.

97. See Berkhofer, *The White Man's Indian*, p. 47; Marx, *The Machine in the Garden*; Smith, *Virgin Land*; Zolla, *The Writer and the Shaman*; and Guy Davenport, 'The Indian and His Image', in his *The Geography of the Imagination: Forty Essays* (London: Picador, 1984) pp. 353–8.

98. Sheehan, *Seeds of Extinction*, p. 278.

99. Michael Fried, *Absorption and Theatricality: Painting and Beholder in the Age of Diderot* (Chicago, Ill.: University of Chicago Press, 1980).

100. For the implications of cinema as the most Imaginary of representational apparatuses, see Christian Metz, *Psychoanalysis and Cinema: The Imaginary Signifier*, trs. Celia Britton, Annwyl Williams, Ben Brewster and Alfred Guzzetti (London: Macmillan, 1982); and Jacqueline Rose's indispensable essay 'The Imaginary' (1975), in her *Sexuality in the Field of Vision*, pp. 166–97 (together with the other essays in Part 2 of Rose's book).

101. For theories of the star in cinema, see Richard Dyer, *Stars* (London: British Film Institute, 1979), and Richard Dyer, *Heavenly Bodies: Film Stars and Society* (London: Macmillan, 1987).

102. See Rogin, *Ronald Reagan, the Movie*, ch. 1.

103. Burchell and Gray, 'The Frontier West', p. 105.

104. If Fenimore Cooper's Leatherstocking Tales count as the first instance of the American Western, then Clark's summary is pertinent: 'The total effect of Cooper's novels is to displace the Iroquois from their original homelands, convert them into French Indians, and turn New York State into a wilderness that the Cooper family can appropriate without guilt' (Clark, 'The Last of the Iroquois', *Poetics Today*, p. 128).

105. Thomas Schatz, *Hollywood Genres: Formulas, Filmmaking, and the Studio System* (Philadelphia, Pa: Temple University Press, 1981) p. 46. Schatz's account is remarkable for trying to have its theoretical cake and eat it – and for managing neither: although the book's jacket claims its contents 'steer away from élitist critical attitudes' and that the book concerns itself instead with popular culture and the commercial side of film production, there is persistent allusion throughout to élite critical discourses, principally various versions of Continental structuralism and post-structuralism. The main problem – besides the indeterminate status of the text and the

consequential confusion regarding its implied audience – is that certain critical discourses and theories are impoverished by their muddled appropriation. Most seriously, Schatz speaks about the Hollywood film system as the site of American myth production (pp. 261–7), and he uses the early Barthes (of *Mythologies*) to 'theorize' this part of the account, while completely missing the meaning of myth – specifically, its political meaning, its loadedness – for Barthes. Rather than going anyway toward demystification – which constitutes the whole of Barthes's political project in *Mythologies* – Schatz uses Barthesian terminology while *valorising* the social function of myth as something that helps us live our lives. Un-selfconsciously deploying a classic American ideology of *adaptation*, Schatz counsels the understanding of myth as that which innocently and beneficently structures our lives: the impetus of his account therefore consists in the kind of American ideologising – like Turnerianism, like adaptive ego-psychology – against which my critique is mounted.

106. On 'train-brain' and the link between the railroad and early cinema, see Lynne Kirby's excellent essay 'Male Hysteria and Early Cinema', *Camera Obscura*, no. 17 (May 1988) pp. 113–31.

107. In *The White Man's Indian*, Berkhofer notes (p. 99) that the nineteenth-century American publishing house of Beadle and Adams was the first to standardise the genre of the Western dime novel, and that its first number, published in 1860, consisted of a story by Mrs Ann Sophia Wintherbotham Stephens, entitled *Malaeska; The Indian Wife of the White Hunter*, which, significantly for my purposes here, took the question of miscegenation and its penalties as its central theme. It would thus seem that the socio-sexual question of miscegenation has been central to the Western genre from its inception.

108. In this respect, it would be interesting to compare another American narrative which centres the combined thematics of land acquisition, empire-building and the escape from history around the figured nemesis of a miscegenation that has already occurred. I am thinking here of Faulkner's *Absalom! Absalom!*.

For an interesting account of the unreliability of skin colour as racial determinant, and for an argument that American culture is inseparable from – is indeed predicated on – the aesthetics of American racism, see Walter Benn Michaels, 'The Souls of White Folk', in Scarry (ed.), *Literature and the Body*, pp. 185–209.

109. The term (and its concept), 'between men', has gained currency mainly via Eve Kosofsky Sedgwick's *Between Men: English Literature and Male Homosocial Desire* (New York: Columbia University Press, 1985); but see also René Girard, *Deceit, Desire, and the Novel: Self and Other in Literary Structure*, trs. Yvonne Freccero (Baltimore, Md: Johns Hopkins University Press, 1965), and Luce Irigaray, *This Sex Which Is Not One*, trs., Catherine Porter (Ithaca, N.Y.: Cornell University Press, 1985), pp. 192–7. These theories all derive from – and develop in different ways – those put forward by Claude

Lévi-Strauss in *The Elementary Structures of Kinship* (Boston, Mass.: Beacon Press, 1969).

110. Reference to the *apparatus* of cinema here should be understood to denote not just the technical machinery by which the image is projected, but also the social ideologies which determine its meanings' and the modes of those meanings subjective inscription, their psychological import: see Teresa de Lauretis and Stephen Heath (eds), *The Cinematic Apparatus* (London: Macmillan, 1980).

111. Jane Tompkins, 'West of Everything', *South Atlantic Quarterly*, vol. 86, no. 4 (Autumn 1987) p. 377.

112. Ibid., p. 359.

113. Roland Barthes, *Mythologies*, trs. Annette Lavers (London: Granada, 1973) p. 144. And see note 105 above.

114. Richard Slotkin, 'Myth and the Production of History', in Sacvan Bercovitch and Myra Jehlen (eds), *Ideology and Classic American Literature* (Cambridge: Cambridge University Press, 1986) p. 70.

115. Berkhofer notes in *The White Man's Indian*:

> What the captivity narrative started the Western novel and movie continued to finish long past the actual events of conquest – as if the American conscience still needed to be reassured about the rightness of past actions and the resulting present times. That the basic conflict over land and lifestyles should be so indelibly engraved upon the White mind so long after the actual events took place would seem to suggest the destruction of Native American cultures and the expropriation of Native American lands still demand justification in White American eyes. (p. 104)

> Berkhofer is, of course, right; but I call attention to this useful summary here in conjunction with Snyder's comment about the Indian as ghost 'lurking in the back of the troubled American mind' in order to emphasise the common metaphors both writers use – that is, metaphors of the psyche. Berkhofer refers to the American 'conscience', 'mind' and 'eyes' – the sense of national consciousness and perception. It is precisely the aptness of these metaphors – pointing to the predication of an American subject upon the repression of knowledge of the land and the Indian – that makes the discourse of psychoanalysis so critically useful: how else account for the modes of displacement by which knowledge of the Indian is evaded, or for the *excess* of political response generated when the repressed returns? Thus psychoanalysis can be seen to provide not only a theory and vocabulary to account for certain cultural and political phenomena, but also an account of how the repression of this historical knowledge is 'primary' – that is, constitutive of a subject: American culture is *founded* on this repression, on its unconscious (the unconscious as *support* of the subject). We are therefore dealing with fundamental – not marginal – questions.

116.   One of Frost's most influential recent critics, Richard Poirier, in *The Renewal of Literature: Emersonian Reflections* (New York: Random House, 1987) (for example, p. 192), evidences considerable participation in and support of the kind of nationalism fostered by the Frostian ideology: which is to say, there is in Poirier's book a renewed polemic against European critical influences – principally deconstruction – that counsels the remedy of a kind of critical isolationism, a turning toward and valorisation of our 'most American' writers, such as Emerson and Frost. This is nothing less than the propagation of critical nationalism whose effects are especially troubling when they seem analogous to the Reaganite revivification of political nationalism and when they seem to continue the kind of Americanist history I am critiquing. The repudiation of Continental theories and the turn inwards to what we might call Americography also characteristically manifest a tendency toward anti-intellectualism, of which there is a strong tradition in the United States, but which is particularly dismaying when it emerges in the academy.

117.   Howard Lamar, 'Frederick Jackson Turner', in Marcus Cunliffe and Robin Winks (eds), *Pastmasters: Some Essays on American Historians* (New York: Harper and Row, 1969) p. 85. Regarding the cultural stakes of *The Turner Thesis*, Michael Kraus's analysis of Turner's career is illuminating.

   First, regarding the vexing question of exploitation (see note 76 above), Kraus, writing approvingly in *The Writing of American History* (op. cit.) of Turner as a Progressive historian, notes Turner's apparent concern with Indian exploitation: Turner's first publication – his doctoral dissertation which consisted of his reworked master's thesis – was *The Character and Influence of Indian Trade in Wisconsin*, which set the question Kraus claims was to dog Turner throughout his whole career:

   > 'The exploitation of the Indian is generally dismissed,' [Turner] observed, 'with the convenient explanatory phrase, "the march of civilization".' Then came his troubling question: 'But how did it march?' Confining his research to America to illustrate this social process, Turner foreshadowed his own late approach when he wrote of the effects of the trading post upon the white man: 'In every country the exploitation of the wild beasts, and of the raw-products generally, causes the entry of the disintegrating and transforming influence of a higher civilization.'   (p. 243)

   Despite his manifest intention, Kraus's prose works to highlight Turner's bias: 'The exploitation of the Indian is generally dismissed', writes Turner in a formulation which replicates that very same dismissal by focusing on 'the march of civilization' and by transforming the exploitation of the Indian into a question of 'the exploitation of the wild beasts, and of the raw-products generally'.

   Further significance regarding the historian's unconscious defence of Turner – Kraus's disavowal of his predecessor's own disavowal of the Indian – and with respect to the cultural investment in Turner's infallibility can be adduced when we read Kraus's remarkably revelatory chapter, which continues three pages after the passage cited above with the following gem: 'Sadly, both of Turner's volumes to win the Pulitzer Prize (this one and a collection of essays published in 1932 entitled *The Significance of Sections in American History*) did so after his death in 1932' (p. 246). It is especially difficult to read the error here, but in a university press book with next to no typographical errors, this one is especially instructive. In *The Psychopathology of Everyday Life* (1901), Freud suggests that typographical errors by copyists and compositors (such as this one) are psychologically motivated – which is to say, interpretable. It is not only in 'Freudian slips' of the tongue and the pen, but also in slips of this kind that something of the unconscious is trying to get through: an Other discourse is speaking besides the conscious, rational one. The error in this instance, apart from the misplaced bracket, is the omission of the word 'failed' preceding the diction of winning. In the very act of admitting a failure on Turner's part the word slips, as if it were quite literally unspeakable that Turner should be noted to fail – as if it were better, in fact, for the failure to be transferred to whichever typesetter or proof-reader were responsible for the 'typo', rather than for the record of 'America's historian' to be compromised. This, then, is another index of – another way of reading (made possible by psychoanalysis) – the general American investment in Turner as the national historian. It suggests that the psychic operations which seek to maintain the American subject, to guard it from its own unconscious, are operative at a multiplicity of levels.

Notes to Part 2: The Real Work

1. See Harold Bloom, 'Editor's Note' to Bloom (ed.), *Contemporary Poets: Modern Critical Views* (New York: Chelsea House, 1986):

    > Wordsworth, in relation to the European tradition from Homer through Goethe, was a true original. No one since Wordsworth, in any language, has been able to achieve such discontinuity again. Himself shadowed by Shakespeare and Milton, Wordsworth nevertheless triumphantly made it new.... As the discoverer of a poetry that had no subject but subjectivity, Wordsworth permanently both saved and ruined poetry. (p. x)

2. See Alice Walker, *In Search of our Mothers' Gardens: Womanist Prose* (London: Women's Press, 1984) esp. pp. 231–43; and the enabling early work of Elaine Showalter in *A Literature of Their Own: British Women Novelists from Brontë to Lessing* (London: Virago, 1978). The work of Gilbert and Gubar conceptualises itself in similar terms, seeking to reconstruct a hidden 'women's tradition' in explicit

opposition to Bloom's masculinist lineage of influence. Thus, for instance, in Walker as well as in Sandra Gilbert and Susan Gubar's *The Madwoman in the Attic: The Woman Writer and the Nineteenth-Century Literary Imagination* (New Haven, Conn.: Yale University Press, 1979) – and in opposition to Bloom – the dominant metaphor of literary influence is that of the mother. The feminist paradigm posits an apparent dearth (only apparent because occluded by patriarchal operations) of 'foremothers' in contrast with the excess of poetic forefathers which predicates the Bloomian model. One interesting question to consider is the ways in which the feminist model may require revision as the poetic field 'fills up' and dearth is converted into excess (will influence operate so generously at that future point?). A subsequent question – within the terms of these competing models – must be that of the contemporary male poet for whom (thanks largely to the effects of feminist work) the field of literary history comprises formidable mothers *as well as* fathers.

3. In terms of scholarship on Snyder's work, bibliographical information can be found in: David Kherdian, *Six Poets of the San Francisco Renaissance: Portraits and Checklists* (Fresno, Cal.: Giligia Press, 1965) pp. 47–70; in Katherine McNeil, *Gary Snyder: A Bibliography* (New York: Phoenix Bookshop, 1983); and in Patrick D. Murphy (ed.), *Critical Essays on Gary Snyder* (forthcoming from G. K. Hall). Snyder's papers are located in the library of the University of California at Davis, where Snyder has held a professorship in the English Department since 1985. There are two full-length critical studies of Snyder's work extant: Bob Steuding, *Gary Snyder* (Boston, Mass.: Twayne, 1976); and Charles Molesworth, *Gary Snyder's Vision: Poetry and the Real Work* (Columbia, Mo.: University of Missouri Press, 1983).

Although my analysis of Snyder's work is made within the context of the extant and varied critical discourse on that work, my argument is also made *against* the main trends and paradigmatic terms – Beat, Zen counterculturalist, ethnopoetics, Romanticism – of that discourse. The shape of my argument makes it impractical to set every reading and interpretation within its complete critical context; what is outlined here instead are the main interpretive categories by which Snyder's work has been received to date – what I am calling critical stereotypes as a shorthand way of designating their inadequacy to identify and articulate what I see as most radical and important in the poetry.

In *In Search of the Primitive: Rereading David Antin, Jerome Rothenberg, and Gary Snyder* (Baton Rouge, La: Louisiana State University Press, 1986), Sherman Paul reads Snyder within the context of Beat counterculturalism. Paul's meditative analysis is useful (as is his earlier essay on Snyder's work in his *Repossessing and Renewing: Essays in the Green American Tradition* (Baton Rouge, La: Louisiana State University Press, 1976) pp. 195–235), but it tends toward a misleading emphasis on the Beat aspect in the sense of reading

Snyder's work through the lens of Kerouac's fictional character, Japhy Ryder, in his Beat novel, *The Dharma Bums*. A similar emphasis can be found in Vimala C. Rao, 'Oriental Influence on the Writings of Jack Kerouac, Allen Ginsberg, and Gary Snyder' (PhD dissertation, 1975). By contrast, Molesworth's book treats Snyder in resolutely counterculturalist terms, but without the Beat dimension, so that Snyder's work is read as synthesising values derived from Buddhism and American Indian lore. While Molesworth's characterisation is undoubtedly correct, the emphasis on Buddhism (and the East) obscures the central importance of Snyder's work for mainstream American culture (and the West).

The paradigm of Zen is one within whose terms many critics persistently read Snyder, thereby effectively ensuring his critical marginalisation and the apparent irrelevance of his work for American Studies and theoretical literary criticism. See Julian Gitzen, 'Gary Snyder and the Poetry of Compassion', *Critical Quarterly*, vol. 15, no. 4 (Winter 1973) pp. 341–57; Rudolph L. Nelson, '"Riprap on the Slick Rock of Metaphysics"': Religious Dimensions in the Poetry of Gary Snyder', *Soundings*, vol. 62, no. 2 (Summer 1974) pp. 206–21; Roy Kazuaki Okada, 'Zen and the Poetry of Gary Snyder' (PhD dissertation, University of Wisconsin, 1974); Bert Almon, 'Buddhism and Energy in the Recent Poetry of Gary Snyder', *Mosaic*, vol. 11, no. 1 (1977) pp. 117–25, and *Gary Snyder* (Boise, Ida.: Boise State University Press, 1979).

A more recent article discusses Snyder much more intelligently in terms of Zen and the haiku form: Jody Norton, 'The Importance of Nothing: Absence and its Origins in the Poetry of Gary Snyder', *Contemporary Literature*, vol. 28, no. 1 (Spring 1987) pp. 41–66. Although Norton discusses Snyder's use of the haiku in relation to Pound's use of that poetic form, there is no effort to see the usage within the framework of an American poetic tradition. I think Snyder's use of haiku is influenced by both Pound and the Eastern tradition, but Pound's haiku (and haiku-derived poetic forms) are significantly westernised and distinguishable from their origins in Oriental translations by the way in which, in Pound, there is always an *implied* subject ('subject' in the philosophical sense), whereas in haiku of the Eastern tradition the subject is deliberately absent – this indeed being part of the traditional meaning of haiku (compare Pound's famous 'In a Station of the Metro' with 'Ts'ai Chi'h', a haiku he translated from the Chinese, both written in 1916). We find this Poundian, Western influence in Snyder most especially in the various forms of technical elision and compression in the poetry, the characteristic use his poetics make of the rhetorical device of asyndenton – particularly the elision of the first-person pronoun, 'I'.

Steuding's book also discusses Snyder in terms of Pound as a central influence, but one of the principal problems with Steuding is that so many influences for Snyder are found without being properly differentiated that it is unclear whether or not he belongs in one 'tradition', in them all, or in none at all. Steuding discusses Snyder as the inheritor of a Pound–Williams line in American poetry, but then also reads him as the inheritor of English and American Romanticism (Steuding, *Gary Snyder*, p. 37). Thus obtrudes another familiar critical stereotype for Snyder: that of seeing him as a twentieth-century version of Thoreau. See, for example, Linden Peach, '*Earth House Hold*: a Twentieth-Century *Walden*?', *Anglo-Welsh Review*, vol. 25, no. 4 (1975) pp. 108–14. In an early essay, 'Gary Snyder's Lyric Poetry: Dialectic as Ecology' (*The Far Point*, vol. 4 (1970) pp. 55–65), Charles Altieri sets Snyder squarely within the tradition of American Romanticism: 'Snyder with his innocence, pragmatism, vitality and perpetual wandering Eastward or into the wilderness belongs in the tradition of American Romanticism' (p. 65); while in his later book, *Enlarging the Temple: New Directions In American Poetry during the 1960s* (Lewisburg, Pa: Bucknell University Press, 1979), Snyder is discussed by Altieri in terms of English Romanticism (my analysis of Altieri's critical paradigm in *Enlarging the Temple* follows later, see pp. 142–5). For another version of Snyder in relation to English Romanticism, see Laurence Goldstein, 'Wordsworth and Snyder: the Primitivist and his Problem of Self-Definition', *Centennial Review*, vol. 21, no. 1 (Winter 1977) pp. 75–86.

Altieri's article, 'Dialectic as Ecology', also discusses Snyder within the terms of the fourth critical stereotype I designate – that of ethnopoetics. On this aspect, see also Thomas J. Lyon, 'The Ecological Vision of Gary Snyder', *Kansas Quarterly*, vol. 2, no. 2 (1970) pp. 117–24; and Patrick D. Murphy, 'Sex-Typing the Planet: Gaia Imagery and the Problem of Subverting Patriarchy', *Environmental Ethics*, vol. 10, no. 2 (Summer 1988) pp. 155–68.

To conclude this general characterisation of Snyder scholarship, I should note that although the extant criticism is broadly inadequate for the reasons I outline here (and which I develop in more detail in the course of my argument), the critics whose work I have found most useful as places to begin are: Altieri, Paul, and Robert Kern's 'Clearing the Ground: Gary Snyder and the Modernist Imperative', *Criticism*, vol. 19, no. 2 (Spring 1977) pp. 158–77.

4.   See, for example, the frontispiece daguerreotypes of Emerson and Thoreau used in the following popular editions of their texts: Ralph Waldo Emerson, *Selected Essays*, ed. Larzer Ziff (Harmondsworth, Middx: Penguin, 1982); and Henry David Thoreau, *Walden and Civil Disobedience* (Harmondsworth, Middx: Penguin, 1983). An extended analysis of the critical uses and meanings of the famous Dickinson daguerreotype can be found in my 'Dickinson in the Field of Vision', forthcoming.

5.   Donald Allen (ed.), *On Bread & Poetry: A Panel Discussion with Gary Snyder, Lew Welch & Philip Whalen* (Bolinas, Cal.: Grey Fox Press, 1977) p. 16. Whitman's self-representational strategies were so successful that D. H. Lawrence referred to him in *Studies in Classic American Literature* (Harmondsworth, Middx: Penguin, 1983) as the

first truly American poet – significantly, as a consequence of Whitman's relation to the ground: 'This was Whitman. And the true rhythm of the American continent speaking out in him. He is the first white aboriginal' (pp. 181–2). Whitman's Americanness is so intensely authentic that he looks like an aborigine: successful Americanisation can thus be seen to depend upon the absolute and irrevocable displacement of the Indian.

6.   Compare here Plate 5, the frontispiece photograph to Gary Snyder, *A Range of Poems* (London: Fulcrum Press, 1966). Snyder is presented to the British reader of the 1960s as nothing less than an Indian – and thus as a native poet of America, as traditionally 'unliterary', and as irremediably foreign, Other. Presenting an American poet to British reading culture in this way thus looks like a version of literary export as cultural exoticism.

7.   On the epistemological status of the frame, see Jacques Derrida, *The Truth in Painting*, trs. Geoff Bennington and Ian McLeod (Chicago, Ill.: University of Chicago Press, 1987) esp. Part 1, 'Paregon'.

8.   See Harold Bloom, *Poetry and Repression: Revisionism from Blake to Stevens* (New Haven, Conn.: Yale University Press, 1976): 'in poetry memory is always the most important mode of thought' (p. 30).

9.   See, for instance, Charles Altieri, 'Gary Snyder's *Turtle Island*: the Problem of Reconciling the Roles of Seer and Prophet', *boundary 2*, no 4 (1976) pp. 761–77, in which the critic comments upon his critical perspective:

> And, more important, I am satisfied to approach his poems as one possible mode for contemplating experience. I treat them as acts of mind which formulate a particular way of viewing experience, and I ignore any possible consequences his vision might have for guiding my moral and political actions. I return Snyder's work to the aesthetic mode he seeks to transcend.   (p. 768)

I draw attention to Altieri's critical self-reflection here not simply as a demonstration of the currency of the aestheticising paradigm, but rather because the essay includes some intelligent discussion of the problems of that paradigm *vis-à-vis* Snyder – the ways in which his poetry both invites and resists such an approach.

10.   Bloom's revisionist theory of poetic influence was put forth most cogently in the 1970s in a series of five books: *The Anxiety of Influence: A Theory of Poetry* (New York: Oxford University Press, 1973), *A Map of Misreading* (New York: Oxford University Press, 1975), *Kabbalah and Criticism* (New York: Seabury Press, 1975), *Figures of Capable Imagination* (New York: Seabury Press, 1976), and *Poetry and Repression* (op. cit.). It is worthy of note that *Figures of Capable Imagination*, the book most concerned with the tradition of American poetry (as opposed to the British tradition), is the book least often referred to by those discussing Bloomian theory (the

Bloomian poetics of 'influence' is described as having been adv-
anced in a critical 'tetralogy', of which *Figures of Capable Imagination*
forms no part). One reason for this might be that the figure of
Dickinson renders Bloom's father–son Oedipal model weakest
when it comes to any discussion of the American poetic tradition.

There is no doubt that, within his own critical terms, Bloom is
one of the 'strongest' contemporary readers of poetry. However,
Bloom is not without his own critical precursors, the most significant of which would be the Eliot of 'Tradition and the Individual
Talent' (1919). Although Bloom writes *against* the Eliot who placed
little importance on the English Romantics, the continuities between the institutionalised orthodoxy of New Criticism (as Eliot's
legacy) and the Bloomian poetics of influence is important to
recognise since it helps account for the indifference of a critic like
Bloom to the work of a poet like Snyder. By this I mean that just as
Snyder's poetry does not fare well by the terms of the New
Criticism which dominated the academy from the 1930s to the
1960s – the New Critical terms which privilege categories of irony,
density, paradox and allusion – so also does his poetry seem of
little interest to a criticism concerned with poetic 'acts of mind'
vis-à-vis the poetic tradition (a criticism which assumes, that is, that
poetry's primary concern is itself, the means and mode of its own
production and transmission). Thus it is that Bloom's central
critical aphorism as it is elaborated in *The Anxiety of Influence* – that
'The meaning of a poem can only be another poem' (p. 94) –
sounds very much like the central tenet put forth by Eliot over half
a century earlier:

> if we approach a poet without this prejudice [the tendency to
> insist, when we praise a poet, upon those aspects of his work in
> which he least resembles anyone else], we shall often find that
> not only the best, but the most individual parts of his work may
> be those in which the dead poets, his ancestors, assert their
> immortality most rigorously.
> ... I have tried to point out the importance of the relation of
> the poem to other poems by other authors, and suggested the
> conception of poetry as a living whole of all the poetry that has
> ever been written.   (T. S. Eliot, *Selected Prose*, ed. Frank Kermode
> (New York: Harcourt Brace Jovanovich, 1975) pp. 38–40)

When Bloom is understood not as absolutely original (although his
criticism *is* nevertheless highly idiosyncratic) but rather as a
contemporary version of New Criticism, then the aestheticising
tendency of New Criticism, of the Bloomian poetics of influence
and of Fried's criticism all become comprehensible as modes of
critical formalism (despite the distance both Bloom and Fried
would wish to draw between their own work and anything labelled
formalist), which we might then trace back to the aesthetics of
Kantian idealism. Such a characterisation does not mean to elide

the differences between the critical works mentioned; rather, it seeks to explain the overall terms of their inadequacy for reading a poetry such as Snyder's – an inadequacy which my argument is suggesting is not limited to the possibility of reading one set of local poetic texts.

11. See J. Hillis Miller, *The Linguistic Moment: From Wordsworth to Stevens* (Princeton, N.J.: Princeton University Press, 1985).

12. The opposite version of aestheticising criticism – that is, overtly self-identified 'political' criticism – also manages to overlook or deem irrelevant Snyder's work. See, for instance, Robert von Hallberg, *American Poetry and Culture, 1945–1980* (Cambridge, Mass.: Harvard University Press, 1985) whose survey manages to miss completely Snyder's contribution to postwar American culture. What one might call the more conventional critical 'middle ground', as exemplified by a more traditional Americanist such as Alfred Kazin, is also blind to Snyder, despite the pertinence of Snyder for the topic of Kazin's most recent book: see Alfred Kazin, *A Writer's America: Landscape in Literature* (New York: Alfred A. Knopf, 1988).

13. It is not that other persons are not important for, or do not figure in, *Riprap* (see 'For a Far-out Friend', p. 11, and 'Migration of Birds', p. 17), but rather that the relation to the land tends to take precedence over the relation to other humans. In *Regarding Wave* (1970), the relation to the lover, the woman, and the relation to the ground are figured as interdependent, which makes of *Regarding Wave* for a poetic-critic such as Allen Grossman Snyder's best and most interesting volume of poetry. That is, when poetry's function is held to be homologous with that ancient preservative function accorded lyric by the Greeks – as it is for Grossman – then the majority of Snyder's poetry is again found to be of little interest: see Allen Grossman, *Against Our Vanishing: Winter Conversations on the Theory and Practice of Poetry*, ed. Mark Halliday (Boston, Mass.: Rowan Tree Press, 1981). My point here is simply that Snyder conceives of the function of poetry in wholly different terms.

14. For the critical consensus regarding the 1950s as a decade of consensus, see: Arthur M. Schlesinger, *The Vital Center: The Politics of Freedom* (Boston, Mass.: Houghton Mifflin, 1949); Daniel Bell, *The End of Ideology: On the Exhaustion of Political Ideas in the Fifties* (New York: Free Press, 1962); David M. Potter, *People of Plenty: Economic Abundance and the American Character* (Chicago, Ill.: University of Chicago Press, 1954); Henry Steele Commager, *The American Mind* (New Haven, Conn.: Yale University Press, 1950).

15. Although Eliot and Pound may be judged the most influential of American moderns and HD perhaps the least influential, HD is to my mind the best and most interesting modern American poet (and she was indeed not just personally, but – more importantly – *poetically* a great influence on Pound – a point which is often missed or underestimated). Snyder's *Myths & Texts* has been compared both to *The Waste Land* (Gitzen, 'Gary Snyder and the Poetry of

Compassion', p. 346) and to *The Cantos* (Paul, *In Search of the Primitive*, p. 225).

16. Since the completion of *Myths & Texts*, Snyder has been working on another epic poem, *Mountains and Rivers Without End*, which yet remains incomplete thirty years later (although parts of it have been published as *Six Sections from Mountains and Rivers Without End, Plus One* (San Francisco, Cal.: Four Seasons Foundation, 1970) and, more recently, 'Haida Gwai North Coast, Naikoon Beach, Hiellen River Raven Croaks', in H. Daniel Peck, *The Green American Tradition: Essays and Poems for Sherman Paul* (Baton Rouge, La: Louisiana State University Press, 1989) pp. 284–5.

   For help with the mythic references in *Myths & Texts*, see: Howard McCord, *Some Notes to Gary Snyder's* Myths & Texts (Berkeley, Cal.: Sand Dollar Press, 1971); William J. Jungels, 'The Use of Native American Mythologies in the Poetry of Gary Snyder' (PhD dissertation, State University of New York, Buffalo, 1973); and Patrick D. Murphy, 'Alternation and Interpenetration: the Structure of Gary Snyder's *Myths & Texts*', forthcoming in Patrick D. Murphy (ed.), *Critical Essays on Gary Snyder*, I believe.

17. When Derrida says 'There is nothing outside the text', he is not claiming – as is often mistakenly asserted by his opponents – that all we have are words and books or that language is all that counts; rather, he is indicating the textual status of phenomenal experience itself, the ineradicable meaning of its spatially and temporally differential structure which is continuous with the differential operation of semiological significance in written texts (this he names *différance*). See, for instance, 'Différance', in Jacques Derrida, *Margins of Philosophy*, trs. Alan Bass (Brighton: Harvester Press, 1982) pp. 1–27.

18. Ekbert Faas, *Towards a New American Poetics: Essays & Interviews* (Santa Barbara, Cal.: Black Sparrow Press, 1978) pp. 139–40.

19. In *Sacred Discontent: The Bible and Western Tradition* (Baton Rouge, La: Louisiana State University Press, 1976) Herbert Schneidau discusses the relation between the Bible and other mythic texts in order to demonstrate how the absolute separation between God and His creation posited by the Judaeo-Christian tradition makes provision for the human destruction of that creation as a consequence of the perception of the natural world as non-sacred – this logic operating in direct contrast to the sense of sacred continuity between creator and created as it is apprehended by Eastern religions and American Indian beliefs.

20. An alternative literary-mythological version of the sexualising of trees as feminine can be found in HD's 1927 novel, *Her* (London: Virago, 1984; first published as *HERmione* in the United States by New Directions, 1981), in which subjective feminine identity in crisis is partially expressed and explored via the complex identification of the self as dryad ('Dryad' being Pound's pet name for HD) with the landscape and the state (the spirit of the tree – sylvan – as the root of the placename Pennsylvania). The happy assignment of

femininity to the landscape in Snyder is seen from the other side – as problematic – by the female narrator of *Her*.

21. See Joseph Riddel, 'Decentering the Image: the "Project" of "American" Poetics?', in Josué V. Harari (ed.), *Textual Strategies: Perspectives in Post-Structuralist Criticism* (Ithaca, N.Y.: Cornell University Press, 1979) p. 346:

> Lacking a coherent system of belief or a credible idea of order, the modern writer, [Eliot] suggested, must either appropriate one from a past writing, as Joyce did in *Ulysses*, or fabricate his own system, as Yeats had in *A Vision*. In either case the appropriated or fabricated system would serve as an *a priori* source of images, a privileged point of reference. This timeless fiction (that of a circle totalizing its images, themes, and so on) not only lends authority to the signs or images appropriated from it, but signifies the general form of mastery or totalization. Thus allusion, quotation, reference, and the like re-enact the gathering of the many into the One.

22. See in this regard, John T. Irwin, *American Hieroglyphics: The Symbol of the Egyptian Hieroglyphics in the American Renaissance* (Baltimore, Md.: Johns Hopkins University Press, 1980).

23. The first section of *Turtle Island*, 'Manzanita' (originally published independently by Four Seasons Foundation, Bolinas, Cal., 1972), is named for a plant local to Snyder's home, a kind of brush plant which is in the process of reclaiming mined land in Snyder's locality. Snyder's house is itself named for another local plant, kitkitdizze, a nomination which suggests the organic relation between the ground and the process of inhabitation. The poetic references to these plants suggests that naming itself constitutes a vital dimension of the restructured relation to the ground – a notion developed by my book's conclusion.

24. Jacques Lacan, *The Seminar of Jacques Lacan, Book I: Freud's Papers on Technique, 1953–1954*, ed. Jacques-Alain Miller, trs. John Forrester (Cambridge: Cambridge University Press, 1988) p. 241.

25. Faas, *Towards a New American Poetics*, pp. 139–40.

26. Claude Lévi-Strauss, 'The Effectiveness of Symbols', in his *Structural Anthropology*, trs. Claire Jacobson and Brooke Grundfest Schoepf (New York: Basic Books, 1963) p. 204. Subsequent references give pagination in main text.

27. Lévi-Strauss draws similar conclusions in his immediately subsequent essay in *Structural Anthropology*, 'The Structural Study of Myth', pp. 206–31.

28. Compare this fragment from 'Hitch Haiku' (in *The Back Country*, p. 29):

> A truck went by
> three hours ago:
> Smoke Creek desert

in which the mundane fact of a passing truck is rendered highly significant – although not symbolic – by the juxtapositional addition of the temporal and spatial dimensions, which thereby figure solitude in the starkest terms.

29. See Roland Barthes, *Mythologies*, trs. Annette Lavers (London: Granada, 1973) pp. 125–35.

30. By a revision of the dominant interpretive categories by which poetic tradition is understood I am referring both to Bloom and to the legacy of T. S. Eliot – to the problematic, that is, discussed above in note 10. Within this perspective, since *Myths & Texts* can be read as a response to *The Waste Land*, it can therefore also be read as some kind of response to the notion of tradition put forward by that poem's author (both in that poem and elsewhere). (The continuities between Bloom and Eliotic New Criticism have also been noted by Frank Lentricchia in *After the New Criticism* (Chicago, Ill.: University of Chicago Press, 1980) and by Peter de Bolla, *Harold Bloom: Towards Historical Rhetorics* (London: Routledge and Kegan Paul, 1988).)

31. See, for instance, Andrew Ross, *The Failure of Modernism: Symptoms of American Poetry* (New York: Columbia University Press, 1986) p. 63: 'Whatever we know in *The Waste Land*, it is not enough, for it always lacks some consistent point of view.'

32. See Hélène Cixous, 'Sorties', in Hélène Cixous and Catherine Clément, *The Newly Born Woman*, trs. Betsy Wing (Minneapolis, Minn.: University of Minnesota Press, 1986) pp. 62–132.

33. The postmodern as a cultural 'condition' has been theorised most famously by: Jean-François Lyotard, *The Postmodern Condition: A Report on Knowledge*, trs. Geoff Bennington and Brian Massumi (Minneapolis, Minn.: University of Minnesota Press, 1984); Federic Jameson, 'Postmodernism, or, The Cultural Logic of Late Capitalism', *New Left Review*, vol. 146 (Summer 1984) pp. 53–92; and Jean Baudrillard, *Selected Writings*, ed. Mark Poster (Stanford, Cal.: Stanford University Press, 1988).

34. See, for instance, Linda Hutcheon, *A Poetics of Postmodernism: History, Theory, Fiction* (London: Routledge and Kegan Paul, 1988); and Alice A. Jardine, *Gynesis: Configurations of Woman and Modernity* (Ithaca, N.Y.: Cornell University Press, 1985).

35. The way in which canonical texts of poetic modernism can be characterised as postmodern according to the dominant accounts of the postmodern suggests a more genealogical and less disjunctive relation between the modern and the postmodern. The question of a postmodern Pound is addressed in my essay 'How Long is the Pound Era?', forthcoming in *Paideuma* (1990).

36. See, for instance, Jacques Derrida, 'Structure, Sign, and Play in the Discourse of the Human Sciences' (1966), in his *Writing and Difference*, trs. Alan Bass (Chicago, Ill.: University of Chicago Press, 1978) pp. 278–93.

37. Jardine, *Gynesis*, p. 24.

38. Compare Grossman, *Against Our Vanishing*, on the postwar condi-

tions under which postmodern poetry emerged:

> Poetry was not helping us learn how to live because the High
> Moderns did, as I have said, set poetry against life. They seemed
> to have established the outcome of poetic enterprise outside of
> life in unreachable transcendentalisms which no longer made
> any sense at all. The immediate response to the High Moderns
> was first to conserve them academically and therefore neutralize
> them, and then to retrench upon the world not of transcendental
> reality but of what, loosely speaking, can be called an immanent
> counter-reality.   (p. 38)

39.	See Kherdian, *Six Poets of the San Francisco Renaissance*; Paul, *In Search of the Primitive*, and Sherman Paul, 'The Genesis of the San Francisco Renaissance', *Literary Review*, vol. 32, no. 1 (Autumn 1988).

40.	Faas, *Towards a New American Poetics*, p. 121.

41.	For contemporary responses to *Howl*, see Lewis Hyde (ed.), *On the Poetry of Allen Ginsberg* (Ann Arbor, Mich.: University of Michigan Press, 1984) pp. 23–84.

42.	I discuss this problem at greater length and in relation to Foucaul-deanism, psychoanalysis, and gay political criticism, in my forth-coming essay, 'Where Does the Resistance Come From?'.

43.	Hutcheon, *A Poetics of Postmodernism*, p. 3.

44.	Altieri, *Enlarging the Temple*, principally pp. 29–52. Beyond the criticisms already noted, we may also indicate the requisite sim-plification of Altieri's Romantic models of symbolism and imman-entism: when Altieri takes Wordsworth as the exemplar of the immanentist paradigm (having to do with the discovery of what already exists in the natural world), we might counterpose the Wordsworth of *The Prelude* who discovers – most strikingly in the 'spots of time' passages – that what already exists in nature is always culture – that the natural is always already culturalised, attributed meaning by the operations of human sign-systems. In this sense (and by the terms of the Romantic models), immanent-ism is thus always already the product of prior symbolist opera-tions.

45.	An alternative way of thinking about Snyder as a postmodern poet – a way which we can only adumbrate here – has to do with his poetic technique as opposed to his poetic content. I am thinking here of the postmodern as that architectural style characterised by the juxtaposition of various historical styles, the 'patchwork' quali-ty of postmodernism, if one may use that distinctly pre-modern metaphor. The postmodern element of Snyder's work in this sense would then consist in his conception of the poet as a Coyote figure, a Trickster (or figure for the unconscious) in Indian culture, and a scavenger, a taker of scraps. Snyder has said (in conversation with me) that he thinks of his poetic technique along these lines – using what he can find, operating as an artist like a thief, a scavenger.

Snyder added that Coyote is a creation deity in many Indian myths, but that, significantly, Coyote never creates a perfect universe in myth (personal conversation, 11 July 1987). On this question, see Gary Snyder, 'The Incredible Survival of Coyote', in *OW*, pp. 67–93; and Paul Radin, *The Trickster: A Study in American Indian Mythology* (New York: Schocken Books, 1956). On the broader question of Snyder's relation to, and use of, Indian mythology, see Michael Castro, *Interpreting the Indian: Twentieth-Century Poets and the Native American* (Albuquerque, N.M.: University of New Mexico Press, 1983); and Peter Easy, 'The Treatment of American Indian Materials in Contemporary American Poetry', *Journal of American Studies*, vol. 12, no. 1 (1978) pp. 81–98.

46. The third section of Snyder's essay, 'Poetry and the Primitive', is entitled 'The Voice as a Girl' (*EHH*, p. 123) and mediates upon the etymological and conceptual links between the feminine and the Muse (as inspiration or breath) which will be figured poetically in *Regarding Wave*.

47. The notion of the sexual as that most intimate and predicative of relations and yet as that whose violence is disruptive of relation is figured somewhat differently, but extremely prominently, in the early lyrics of Hart Crane: see my forthcoming essay, 'Anatomizing the Sexuality of Rhetoric in Hart Crane's *White Buildings*'.

48. Martin Heidegger, *Poetry, Language, Thought*, trs. Albert Hofstadter (New York: Harper and Row, 1975) p. 29.

49. 'The Cool around the Fire', conversation between Gary Snyder and Roberta Berke, BBC Radio 3, Spring 1988.

50. Ibid.

51. On Wordsworth's relation to other people and other consciousnesses, compare: Frances Ferguson, 'Historicism, Deconstruction, and Wordsworth', in *Diacritics: Wordsworth and the Production of Poetry*, ed. Andrzej Warminski and Cynthia Chase, vol. 17, no. 4 (Winter 1987) pp. 32–43, and her 'Malthus, Godwin, Wordsworth, and the Spirit of Solitude', in Scarry (ed.), *Literature and the Body*, pp. 106–24, and her *Solitude and the Sublime: The Aesthetics of Individuation*, forthcoming from Methuen (1990).

52. If one were indulging in Michael Fried-style literary criticism, one might read in Jimmy Jones's initials a substitutive inscription of the first volume of Snyder's poetry – JJ for *RR*. Such interpretation is not necessary to find the links between 'Look Back' and *Riprap*. Regarding the Jones massacre of 1978, see Fitzgerald, *Cities on a Hill*, p. 69.

53. Roland Barthes, *S/Z: An Essay*, trs. Richard Miller (New York: Hill and Wang, 1970) p. xi.

54. See: Thomas Weiskel, *The Romantic Sublime: Studies in the Structure and Psychology of Transcendence* (Baltimore, Md: Johns Hopkins University Press, 1976); Harold Bloom, *Agon: Towards a Theory of Revisionism* (Oxford: Oxford University Press, 1982); Neil Hertz, *The End of the Line: Essays on Psychoanalysis and the Sublime* (New York: Columbia University Press, 1985); *New Literary History* (special

issue: 'The Beautiful and the Sublime: Reconsiderations') vol. 16,
no. 2 (Winter 1985); Mary Arensberg (ed.), *The American Sublime*
(Albany, N.Y.: State University of New York Press, 1986); *Studies in
Romanticism* – *The Sublime: A Forum*, vol. 26, no. 2 (Summer 1987);
Peter de Bolla, *The Discourse of the Sublime: History, Aesthetics and the
Subject* (Oxford: Basil Blackwell, 1989); and Ferguson, *Solitude and
the Sublime*.

55. See Neil Hertz, 'A Reading of Longinus', in his *The End of the Line*,
pp. 1–20.

56. Immanuel Kant, *Critique of Judgement* (New York: Hafner Press,
1951) p. 104.

57. Ibid., pp. 93–4.

58. Neil Hertz, 'The Notion of Blockage in the Literature of the
Sublime', in Geoffrey H. Hartman (ed.), *Psychoanalysis and the
Question of the Text* (Baltimore, Md: Johns Hopkins University
Press, 1978) pp. 62–85 (reprinted in Hertz, *The End of the Line*, pp.
40–60).

59. Bierstadt's *The Sierra Nevada in California* is only one of a series of
versions of what could be seen – and indeed *have* been seen – as the
same painting (as critical and institutional confusion over various
paintings and their titles has demonstrated). The 'scene' to which
Bierstadt insistently returns in his painting of the late 1860s and
early 1870s is not the geographical region of the Sierra Nevada and
Mount Whitney (the painting I reproduce for discussion was, after
all, painted while Bierstadt was in Europe), but rather the 'scene' of
American sublimity which the repeated and reconfigured visual
elements I discuss came to represent. The proximity of sublimity to
that which exceeds representation might suggest that Bierstadt's
repeated return to the scene of sublimity consists of an obsession
with representing – and hence of negotiating for the subject of the
American sublime via those representations – the unrepresentable.
See (besides Plate 6, originally titled *Among the Sierra Nevada
Mountains, California*): *The Yosemite Valley* (1867; Wadsworth
Atheneum, Hartford); *Sierra Nevada Morning* (1870; Thomas Gil-
crease Institute, Tulsa); *Mount Whitney* (1874; The Rockwell Foundation, Corning, New York), all in Gordon Hendricks, *Albert Bierstadt: Painter of the American West* (New York: Harry N. Abrams,
1974) pp. 146, 195, 234–5, respectively. Interestingly, this book
contains no mention of the painting I reproduce as Plate 6 under
any title, even though the book includes a supposedly exhaustive
list of Bierstadt paintings in public collections in the United States,
including those held by the Smithsonian Institution.

60. '"Among the Sierra Nevada Mountains" by Bierstadt', *Boston Post*,
11 October 1869, p. 4; quoted by Trevor J. Fairbrother in Theodore
E. Stebbins; Jr, Carol Troyen and Trevor J. Fairbrother, *A New
World: Masterpieces of American Painting, 1760–1910* (Boston, Mass.:
Museum of Fine Arts, 1983) p. 251.

61. One of the specifically American sources of this identification
between mountains and the Deity – indeed, the precondition for

such an identification of the natural with the metaphysical – must be the Puritan system of typology, which extended a mode of biblical interpretation to a whole cultural ideology – one in which all natural phenomena were to be 'read' and interpreted in spiritual terms. Hence the Puritan divine, Jonathan Edwards, could write in his *Images or Shadows of Divine Things*, 'Hills and mountains are types of heaven', since such earthly phenomena point, both literally and figuratively, heavenward (Jonathan Edwards, *Images or Shadows of Divine Things*, ed. Perry Miller (New Haven, Conn.: Yale University Press, 1948) p. 67).

62. See John Wilmerding (ed.), *American Light: The Luminist Movement, 1850–1875* (Washington, D.C.: National Gallery of Art, 1980).

63. Earl A. Powell, 'Luminism and the American Sublime', in ibid., p. 78.

64. Combining an historicist approach with a commitment to the tenets of Kantian idealism, Frances Ferguson makes the interesting argument that a specifically Romantic consciousness – a consciousness (such as Wordsworth's) concerned with sublime experience – emerges in response to the proliferation of other consciousnesses – or, more properly, in response to the claims of other consciousnesses (see Ferguson, 'Malthus, Godwin, Wordsworth, and the Spirit of Solitude', pp. 106–24). The historical dimension of Ferguson's argument partially concerns the way in which the eighteenth century in England consisted of a period when – after, for instance, Mary Wollstonecraft – women's consciousnesses began to count. The sublime then comes to be cultivated as an experience in which other consciousnesses are prevented from getting in the way of one's own consciousness, and in which the sublime consequently converts an excess of other consciousnesses into one's own subjective aggrandisement. My point here is simply that the deer in Bierstadt's painting may function in a way which Ferguson's argument can illuminate: that is, the deer represent initial and provisional points of subjective identification within the narrative space of the painting without posing the problem that another consciousness – and its claims – might pose (since the consciousness of deer cannot 'count'). An interesting counterargument to Ferguson's historical account of the relation between a proliferation of consciousnesses and the sublime can be found in Joan Copjec, 'The Sartorial Superego', *October*, 50 (Autumn 1989) pp. 57–95, esp. pp. 81–7. Against Ferguson's psychological account of the *individuation* of consciousness, Copjec provides a more persuasive psychoanalytic account of *subjectivisation*.

65. See Bryan Jay Wolf, *Romantic Re-Vision: Culture and Consciousness in Nineteenth-Century American Painting and Literature* (Chicago, Ill.: University of Chicago Press, 1982) pp. 182–3:

When populating his scenes with pioneers or woodsmen, Cole frequently introduces the figure of a lone axman engaged in the felling of a tree. The motif, which will recur to the end of Cole's career, though often only as an abandoned ax wedged in the corner of a stump or log, translates Cole's own mastery over the landscape, altering and shaping it to the demands of the imagination, into substitute narrative terms. . . . The woodsman is an image of power, his mastery and view contingent upon an act of despoliation. As a surrogate for the artist, he expresses at what is presumably a preconscious level the painter's sense of struggle with nature for mastery. Though the woodsman's tools are physical rather than imaginative, they share with the artist's brush the capacity to reverse the power of nature by the ingenuity of their handling.

66.   See Powell, 'Luminism and the American Sublime', p. 72; and Barbara Novak, *American Painting of the Nineteenth Century: Realism, Idealism, and the American Experience* (New York: Praeger, 1969).

67.   See Jan Garden Castro, *The Art and Life of Georgia O'Keeffe* (New York: Crown Publishers, 1985) pp. 80–1. Significantly – for biographical purposes – it was via the society hostess and patron of the arts Mabel Dodge Luhan that O'Keeffe visited and painted New Mexico landscapes at a time when another of Luhan's associates was Ansel Adams. Further significance derives from the fact that it was Mabel Dodge who played a pivotal role in the American assimilation of Freud, disseminating versions of psychoanalysis by way of her salon, and serialising her own analysis with A. A. Brill in the Hearst Press during the 1920s. Psychoanalysis and the sublime can thus be seen to share a common representational history – never separate from the question of the woman, I might add – in the early decades of the twentieth-century in the United States.

68.   See Jonathan Green, *American Photography: A Critical History 1945 to the Present* (New York: Harry N. Abrams, 1984) pp. 27–8.

69.   Weiskel, *The Romantic Sublime*, p. 3.

70.   Emerson, *Selected Essays*, ed. Ziff, p. 275.

71.   The most recent accounts of sublimity, namely de Bolla's and Ferguson's (see note 54), would seem to indicate a shift of emphasis away from psychoanalysis as the best discourse through which the sublime may be thought.

72.   See Jacques Lacan, 'Kant avec Sade', in his *Écrits* (Paris: Seuil, 1966) pp. 765–90; translated as 'Kant with Sade', *October* (1990, forthcoming). Weiskel (*Romantic Sublime*, pp. 150–1) makes passing reference to Lacan in his psychoanalytic study of the sublime, but he confuses the category of the self with that of the subject (the two being vastly distinct in Lacan), and fails to recognise – in his account of the mirror stage – the radical meaning of the concept of the Other (the meaning, that is, of the Other as the register of the Symbolic), which then allows his literalised and personalised 'classical' Freudian account to assimilate the Lacanian concept without any problem. As I suggest below, the recognition of the potential of Lacanian theory in the form of an invocation of the mirror stage represents a recognition in the form of a mis-

recognition which but repeats the conceptual elements of the theory in the form of a symptom.

73. The opening pages of the English translation of Lacan's *Écrits*, 'The Mirror Stage as Formative of the Function of the I', (Jacques Lacan, *Écrits: A Selection*, trs. Alan Sheridan (New York: Norton, 1977) pp. 1–7) contain the favourite Lacanian concepts emphasised by many English-speaking critics 'dabbling' in Lacanian theory. We may outline both reasons for and consequences of this emphasis here. First, to indulge momentarily in a psychology of reading, we might speculate that 'The mirror stage' – as the first, the shortest and perhaps the easiest to grasp of the writings – constitutes that text beyond which many readers fail to pass in this most difficult of books. Secondly, and as an elaboration of the point about its comprehensibility, we should note that the rhetoric of origin ('the mirror stage' as an account of the child's first conception of itself and of the world), combined with the traditional imagery of mother, child and mirror, make of the narrative contained within those seven pages a conceptual arrangement which is both attractive (an account of first causes), non-abstract (the familiar elements of mother, child and mirror) and appealingly literalised, visualisable. In other words, from an 'easy' reading of the text of 'The mirror stage' comes the de-radicalised Lacanian notion of the Other as another person (the mother), or at least another thing (the mirror reflection). Hence the subsequent tendency precisely to misrecognise the concept of the Other, to reduce the category of the subject to the banal notion of the self, and, ultimately, to recognise in Lacanian theory not the irreducible otherness of an absolutely novel and radical account of inter-subjectivity, but rather the familiar face of a domesticated Freud – a comforting *image* of Lacan. We can thus deduce that 'The mirror stage' functions as a fetishised Lacanian fragment in that the critical treatment of the text tends toward mirroring elements of the theory in which the fragmented part is mistaken for the whole.

74. See Jean Laplanche and J.-B. Pontalis, *The Language of Psycho-Analysis*, trs. Donald Nicholson-Smith (New York: Norton, 1973) pp. 232–3. Although it may seem a little late in the proceedings to refer the newcomer to psychoanalysis to this book, it must be adduced that it is the place to begin for understanding those technical terms which, whether or not they form part of the vocabulary of modern everyday life, are not always necessarily familiar or thoroughly understood.

75. See, for an endorsement of this traditional critical understanding of the sublime as characterised by terror – an understanding derived principally from Burke's *Enquiry* – Hugh Honour, *Romanticism* (Harmondsworth, Middx: Penguin, 1979) p. 57.

76. Jacques Lacan, 'The signification of the phallus', in *Écrits: A Selection*, p. 285.

77. Jacqueline Rose, 'Introduction – II', in Juliet Mitchell and Jacqueline Rose (eds), *Feminine Sexuality: Jacques Lacan and the école freudienne*,

trs. Jacqueline Rose (New York: Norton, 1982) p. 29; reprinted as 'Feminine Sexuality: Jacques Lacan and the *école freudienne*', in Jacqueline Rose, *Sexuality in the Field of Vision* (London: Verso, 1986) p. 52.

78.   See Jacqueline Rose, '*The Man Who Mistook His Wife for a Hat* or *A Wife is Like an Umbrella*: Fantasies of the Modern and Postmodern', in Andrew Ross (ed.), *Universal Abandon: The Politics of Postmodernism* (Minneapolis, Minn.: University of Minnesota Press, 1988) pp. 237–50 (first printed in *Identity: The Real Me*, ICA Documents, no. 6 (London: Institute of Contemporary Arts, 1987) pp. 30–4). See also Jacqueline Rose, 'Sexuality and Vision: Some Questions', in Hal Foster (ed.), *Vision and Visuality*, Dia Art Foundation Discussions in Contemporary Culture, no. 2 (Seattle, Wash.: Bay Press, 1988) pp. 115–27. The accounts of postmodernity discussed and critiqued by Rose are principally those of Jameson and Lyotard (see note 33).

79.   Rose, 'Fantasies of the Modern and Postmodern', p. 248.

80.   See, for instance, Leslie A. Fiedler, *Love and Death in the American Novel* (New York: Criterion Books, 1960); and the interview with Frank Lentricchia in Imre Salusinszky, *Criticism in Society* (London: Methuen, 1987) p. 203. See also the recent work of Eve Sedgwick, particularly her *Epistemology of the Closet*, forthcoming.

81.   Nina Baym, 'Melodramas of Beset Manhood: How Theories of American Fiction Exclude Women Authors', *American Quarterly*, vol. 33 (1981) pp. 123–39.

82.   See Sigmund Freud, *Totem and Taboo: Resemblances Between the Psychic Lives of Savages and Neurotics*, trs. A. A. Brill (New York: Random House, 1918); and Luce Irigaray, *Amante Marine: De Friedrich Nietzsche* (Paris: Minuit, 1980).

83.   For the relation of American women to the frontier experience, see the work of Annette Kolodny: *The Lay of the Land: Metaphor as Experience and History in American Life and Letters* (Chapel Hill, N.C.: University of North Carolina Press, 1975), and *The Land Before Her: Fantasy and Experience of the American Frontiers, 1630–1860* (Chapel Hill, N.C.: University of North Carolina Press, 1984). Kolodny's work provides useful historical information about women on the frontier, and her analyses are partially motivated, she comments at the start of *The Lay of the Land*, by a concern with the contemporary treatment of the American environment (which thus links her project to the Snyderian project). Her methodological approach is partially derived from psychoanalysis, and she speaks of 'America's oldest and most cherished fantasy: a daily reality of harmony between man and nature based on an experience of the land as essentially feminine – that is, not simply the land as mother, but the land as woman, the total female principle of gratification – enclosing the individual in an environment of receptivity, repose, and painless and integral satisfaction' (*Lay of the Land*, p. 4). While this designation of the primal cultural fantasy sounds correct to me, Kolodny's analysis is not without its problems – problems which I see as stemming from the relation of her method to a

certain Americanised version of psychoanalysis. With reference to the passage cited above, it is not clear how the relationship between fantasy and 'reality' operates – how, that is, either conditions or affects the other; nor is it clear how either fantasy or reality are related to gender categories, since 'female', 'woman', femininity, and maternity seem to be referred to almost interchangeably. The source of these problems may be located in the source of Kolodny's psychoanalysis – an American Freudianism derived from the Marcuse of *Eros and Civilization*: an American Freudianism which sacrificed the concept of the unconscious to an account of adaptation between the subject and the social (thereby losing that category which most crucially indicates the impossibility of any complete adaptability or harmony between subject and social – the unconscious as the index and effect of that impossibility), and against which Lacan began the 'return to Freud' in the first place.

84. See Murphy, 'Sex-Typing the Planet'. The fundamental difference between my own analysis of this point and Murphy's analysis lies in his implication that Snyder *intends* to subvert patriarchy: since the category of gender is what determines my understanding of the notion of patriarchy (as a feminist notion), and since that is the category persistently repressed from Snyder's understanding of the concept, the implication of my argument is that Snyder instead *reinforces* patriarchy.

85. Quoted by Paul, *In Search of the Primitive*, p. 299. My attention was redrawn to this passage by Murphy's essay cited above.

86. This assertion is supported by my analysis of Turner and of Hollywood Westerns in Part 1, but see also, for an account of postwar American masculinity in its relation to national politics, Barbara Ehrenreich, *The Hearts of Men: American Dreams and the Flight From Commitment* (London: Pluto Press, 1983).

87. The question of whether the present-day American West can be characterised correctly as 'post-frontier' is not only answered in the negative by Frank J. Popper ('The Strange Case of the Contemporary American Frontier', *The Yale Review*, vol. 76, no. 1 (Autumn 1986) pp. 101–21) but also by Snyder himself in '"The Trail Is Not a Trail"', (*LR*, p. 127). It would seem that the frontier is so much more a category of fantasy than anything resembling historical reality (at least so far as its effects are concerned) that its continued existence can be both asserted and disavowed without consciousness of any contradiction.

88. See Ann Douglas, *The Feminization of American Culture* (New York: Alfred A. Knopf, 1977).

89. Frank Lentricchia, *Ariel and the Police: Michel Foucault, William James, Wallace Stevens* (Madison, Wis.: University of Wisconsin Press, 1988) p. 138.

90. For an excellent feminist critique of Lentricchia's 'feminism', see Melita Schaum, '"Ariel, Save Us": Big Stick Polemics in Frank Lentricchia's *Ariel and the Police*', *Genders*, no. 4 (March 1989) pp.

122–9. I include some critical consideration of Lentricchia's attack on American feminism – specifically in the form of Gilbert and Gubar – and his corollary, implied condemnation of Emily Dickinson, in my 'Dickinson in the Field of Vision', forthcoming.

91. Kit Knight and Arthur Knight (eds), *The Beat Vision: A Primary Sourcebook* (New York: Paragon House, 1987) p. 8.

92. On the relation between journalism and the rise of the novel, see Lennard J. Davis, *Factual Fictions: Origins of the English Novel* (New York: Columbia University Press, 1983). The situation in the United States must be qualified as at least a little different than my distinction allows, however, since Whitman (in *Democratic Vistas*, 1871) calls for an American literature which is properly dissociated from its classical and Romantic European past, and Whitman's development of an American poetic is closely linked to his own experience working as a journalist.

93. Michel Foucault, *The Order of Things: An Archaeology of the Human Sciences* (New York: Random House, 1970) p. 35.

94. Viktor Shklovsky, 'Art as Technique' (1917) *Russian Formalist Criticism: Four Essays*, ed. and trs. Lee T. Lemon and Marion J. Reis (Lincoln, Neb.: University of Nebraska Press, 1965) p. 12.

95. For a rather different, un-Lacanian emphasis on the *materiality* of writing in realist representations, see Michael Fried, *Realism, Writing, Disfiguration: On Thomas Eakins and Stephen Crane* (Chicago, Ill.: University of Chicago Press, 1987). Although Fried makes reference to Lacan (p. 185), the *meaning* of language's materiality in Lacan is nowhere assimilated to Fried's argument. Materiality in Fried's account is persistently reduced to the local, the personal and the biographical – Stephen Crane's 'fear of writing', for instance, in which the historical detail of Crane's laborious penmanship comprises the determinative level of critical emphasis. Critical confusion about the materiality of language – about, that is, what accounts such as Lacan's could possibly imply – is evident at note 28 (p. 185), where conceptual terms and theories are invoked which are radically incompatible with avowed – and manifest – critical allegiances. I term this confusion because no explanation for the theoretical incompatibilities is forthcoming.

96. Gary Snyder, *Good Wild Sacred* (Madley, Herefordshire: Five Seasons Press, 1984) p. 11 (available in the United States as: 'Good Wild Sacred', in Wes Jackson, Wendell Berry and Bruce Colman (eds), *Meeting the Expectations of the Land: Essays in Sustainable Agriculture and Stewardship* (San Francisco, Cal.: North Point Press, 1984) pp. 195–207).

97. Compare the information given in the second epigraph of Denis Hollier, 'French Customs, Literary Borders', *October*, 49 (Summer 1989) p. 41:

Datelined 'Yellowknife (Northwest Territories)', a *New York Times* article of October 3, 1987 announced preparations for an upcoming bicentennial in 1989. The Native Americans of the

Great North had persuaded the Canadian government to grant that our current year [1989] would be marked by a return, on all official maps, to native place-names. It had been, in fact, in 1789 that Sir Alexander Mackenzie, in reaching the Arctic Ocean by an inland route, opened the *terrae incognitae boreales* to penetration by the English. But now, after two Anglophone centuries, the Arctic landscape – its rivers, lakes, rocks, forests, bays – will, de-christened, refind their local linguistic beds, their proper, indigenous, endogenous names, their authentic place-names, home-grown like those Proust like to see budding in the French countryside.

98.   In his second seminar on metaphor and metonymy, the seminar of 9 May 1956, Lacan says:

> *D'où résulte par exemple cette formule, que la métonymie est une métaphore pauvre. On pourrait dire que la chose est à prendre dans le sens exactement contraire – la métonymie est au départ, et c'est elle qui rend possible la métaphore.* (Jacques Lacan, *Le Séminaire, Livre III: Les Psychoses, 1955–1956*, ed. Jacques-Alain Miller (Paris: Seuil, 1981) p. 259)

99.   Emerson, 'The Poet', in *Selected Essays*, ed. Ziff, pp. 268–9.
100. The political power of poetic naming has not been missed by feminist writers: compare both the sentiments and imagery in Audre Lorde, 'Poetry Is Not a Luxury' (1977), in Hester Eisenstein and Alice Jardine (eds), *The Future of Difference* (New Brunswick, N.J.: Rutgers University Press, 1985) p. 126:

> For women, then, poetry is not a luxury. It is a vital necessity of our existence. . . . Poetry is the way we help give name to the nameless so it can be thought. The farthest external horizons of our hopes and fears are *cobbled* by our poems, carved from the *rock* experiences of our daily lives. (emphasis mine)

Index